HIGHER EDUCATION:

DEMAND&
response

The Quail Roost Seminar

W. R. Niblett, Editor

Published in Great Britain by
Tavistock Publications Limited

HIGHER EDUCATION:

DEMAND&
response

Jossey-Bass Inc., Publishers
615 Montgomery Street • San Francisco • 1970

HIGHER EDUCATION: DEMAND AND RESPONSE
    W. R. Niblett, Editor

Copyright © 1970 by Jossey-Bass, Inc., Publishers

First published in Great Britain in 1969 by
Tavistock Publications Limited
11 New Fetter Lane, London
Copyrighted in 1969 in Great Britain by W. R. Niblett

Jossey-Bass, Inc., Publishers
615 Montgomery Street
San Francisco, California 94111

Library of Congress Catalog Card Number 71–110637

Standard Book Number SBN 87589–064–4

Manufactured in the United States of America
    Printed by Hamilton Printing Company, Rensselaer, New York
    Bound by Chas. H. Bohn & Co., Inc., New York

JACKET DESIGN BY WILLI BAUM, SAN FRANCISCO

FIRST EDITION

Code 7003

THE JOSSEY-BASS SERIES IN HIGHER EDUCATION

General Editors

JOSEPH AXELROD
San Francisco State College

MERVIN B. FREEDMAN
*San Francisco State College
and Wright Institute, Berkeley*

Preface

The Seminar whose proceedings are recorded in this book was concerned with some of the fundamental, and therefore continuing, problems of higher education. Many conferences on higher education concentrate upon a particular area of practical concern – upon university organization and administration, for example, decision-making, student development, the causes of student drop-out, curriculum design, problems of costing, etc. This one was at bottom philosophical in its interests; concerned with presuppositions often taken for granted in higher education in our time, with why? questions as well as with questions of what? and how? and apt to inquire how relevant some of our present objectives and practices really are.

Participants in the Seminar were drawn from the three major English-speaking countries of the West, and the enterprise was financed from sources in each. Those who came are named in the Appendix, which lists also five people who were not actually there but were supporters of the idea behind the venture and would have been present but for illness or other unavoidable crises. Two of these, indeed, contributed papers.

The chapters of the book reproduce the papers given at Quail Roost, though in a few cases in slightly amended versions. The interchapters contain first the contributions of those who opened the discussions following the papers themselves and then an account of the subsequent discussion. There is an element of interpretation as well as recording here, though the editor believes that the main course of the argument is followed in each case.

The Seminar was welcomed to North Carolina in person both by Douglas Knight, President of Duke University, and by William Friday, President of the Consolidated University of North Carolina. Very efficient arrangements for the accommodation of the Seminar at the Quail Roost Conference Center were made by Everett Hopkins. But for his keen support and the enterprise of Arnold Nash it could not have been held at all. Neither could it have been held without financial backing from the Regional Education Laboratory for the Carolinas and Virginia; the Ontario Institute for Studies in Education; and an English Foundation which has asked to remain anonymous.

Sheila Niblett acted as editorial secretary to the Seminar and to her hard work and good judgement we are greatly indebted. To Robert Colver and Mary Featherston at Quail Roost and to my own skilful and patient secretary in London, Susan Rawlings, we all owe much. We record our grateful thanks to them.

London   W. R. NIBLETT

Address of Welcome

Douglas M. Knight

I envy you the week you have ahead of you, as you explore the ideas that presidents need most to learn about. The real question, I take it, is what the universities need, what they face, and what they are for. I hope that behind everything you do this week is going to be the establishment of some of the lines of force which go to make up the magnetic field of universities today. Some of these lines are strikingly similar to those which have animated universities since even before they were called that. Those of us whose job it is to keep universities together as communities while we help them to change, to become new kinds of communities, need to know more about these lines of force, about this very complex magnetic field and how we can operate more effectively in it.

While we can make rather wry jokes about the dispensability of university presidents, we suspect that there is something equally awry in the conception which society has of the university, and awry in the stresses put upon it both inside and outside. We have to match these things to each other so that the precarious balance which a university really is — and which a civilized society really is — can be maintained and furthered in a way that is living and therefore changing — not in a way that merely echoes the past.

This is the real problem before us in the late twentieth century. On my way to Quail Roost I was listening to Prokofiev's First Symphony, and in one curious way it was a paradigm of the venture you're involved in. As you know, Prokofiev claimed that he was going to write as Mozart would have written if he had been born in the twentieth century and were a twentieth-century musician. Those who have listened to and pondered that symphony since say that what we really have there is Prokofiev committed, as all of us are committed, whether we like it or not, to the mode and manner of our time. He was trying very hard to write as if he were an eighteenth-century musician, which is another exercise of the mind and spirit, the attempt to express a twentieth-century set of mind in an eighteenth-century musical mode.

I suspect that the university world carries on both these exercises, and a hundred others as well. I suspect it needs to know more than it knows now about how to move in the complexities of time, and how to move beyond it, how to move in the complexities of new social structures without being merely an instrument of revolution. I suspect that it needs to know how to move inside the human spirit in new ways without for a moment forgetting that some of our greatest images of the human spirit are 2500 years old, and some of them even older; and that time is one of the most curious dimensions of life, but not a fixed dimension. The university world should be the true extension of our time, in short, but at the moment it is not. I hope that your discussions this week can help us rediscover our best purposes, and I wish that I could be part of them in action as I shall be in spirit.

Contents

The Contributors

Claude Bissell, President, University of Toronto

Asa Briggs, Vice-Chancellor, University of Sussex

John Deutsch, Principal and Vice-Chancellor, Queen's University at Kingston, Ontario

Northrop Frye, University Professor, University of Toronto

Richard Hoggart, Director, Center for Contemporary Cultural Studies, University of Birmingham

James Jarrett, Associate Dean, School of Education, University of California, Berkeley

Dean E. McHenry, Chancellor, University of California, Santa Cruz

Warren Bryan Martin, Project Director, Center for Research and Development in Higher Education, University of California, Berkeley

Paul A. Miller, Department of Education, University of North Carolina at Charlotte

Ben Morris, Department of Education, University of Bristol

Arnold Nash, Carolina Population Center, Chapel Hill

W. R. Niblett, Department of Higher Education, University of London Institute of Education

Marjorie Reeves, Fellow, St. Anne's College, Oxford University

Nevitt Sanford, Director, Wright Institute, Berkeley

Edward Sheffield, Department of Higher Education, University of Toronto

Edward Joseph Shoben, Jr., Executive Vice-President, The Evergreen State College, Olympia, Washington

Martin Trow, Department of Sociology, University of California, Berkeley

F. Champion Ward, Vice-President, The Ford Foundation, New York

Bryan Wilson, Fellow, All Souls College, Oxford University

HIGHER EDUCATION:

DEMAND&
response

The Quail Roost Seminar

CHAPTER 1

Ahead – but in what Direction?

W. R. Niblett

Why hold this seminar now? Because we want to ask more probingly than usual some questions about the nature and the task of higher education at a time when almost everybody agrees upon the need for the rapid and continued growth of universities, polytechnics, and colleges of many sorts, but few are willing with enough resolution to inquire into the presuppositions they work to. Many of the assumptions which inhabit universities they owe to history: that is a good reason for spending a little of our time on looking at the way in which they have developed. But today many of the fundamental problems for higher education are the same in Britain, Canada, and the United States. Any solution to them may well involve the disturbance of assumptions that have long been deeply held.

One of the assets of an international seminar like this is that the varied backgrounds of those present make it a little more likely that presuppositions will be challenged or at least brought further up into consciousness. This in fact is one of the first seminars of its kind ever to be held. There have been European, Commonwealth, and Anglo-American gatherings of university presidents and vice-chancellors concerned with the impact and progress and planning of university education. There have been world-wide conferences of subject specialists (sociologists and psychologists, for example) to help them disagree more lucidly with one another – and of course of specialists of many kinds. But this Anglo-American-Canadian mixture of presidents, administrators, and teachers drawn (within the limit of two dozen or so) from a variety of disciplines and meeting for an intensive week's thought about higher education: this, so far as I am aware, is a pioneer venture.

The timeliness of our meeting is underlined by events on university and college campuses throughout the West. Since the middle of the sixties there have been smoke signals that we are not going to be allowed as easily as in the last thirty years to go our ways unchallenged and unmolested, or even in that state of 'incorruptible indecision' (to use Charles Carter's phrase) natural to academics. The questions fired at us by students about the purposes of the higher education they were receiving, about university and college organiza- tion, courses, methods of teaching, examinations, etc., are not always on target, but the difference their urgent concern has made is marked, even when their accusations may technically be rebutted. We are not able as gracefully as we were even a few years back to take it for granted that a university's most important job should be to function as a service institution, to help, for example, to supply the needs of its country's industry or agriculture.

Many, if not most, academics are of course more or less content to pound along the traditional tracks, occasionally pausing, like bears, to sniff the ground but then continuing to follow the trail. Theirs not to worry too much about possible long-term consequences or objectives when there is such a lot of obviously useful and absorbing work to be done in research, in teaching, in the kind of day-to-day administration which can demand 100 per cent attention for 100 per cent of the time – if you let it. Following the gleam in the research laboratory is without doubt one of the most fascinating occupa- tions of our time, though following a rather different gleam in consultancy work may have its fascination too. What is significant, however, today is how many find research or consultancy work so much more attractive than teaching students, or anybody else. If one is cosily worried about the prob- lem actually in front of one in the laboratory or the computer programming room or the administrator's office, at least one can save oneself from worrying at large about people, or civilization, or the sins of big business, or those of the university or college itself.

It is clear enough that the vast increase in provision which has been made for higher education in the last quarter of a century, and is still continuing, would not have happened unless many men expected far-reaching social benefit to result. No comprehensive study exists, so far as I am aware, of the varieties and strengths of the pressures which have combined to make the movement for more higher education so tremendously powerful. But among them are the hopes that it might give us people with the mental equipment to produce the sophisticated technology and instrumentation, so that more comfort, more health, more prosperity were paid as dividends to all of us – and this prosperity both for home use or (with an expression of smiling beneficence) for export. Inventiveness, one-upmanship, whether in circum- stances of war or peace, political expertise, marketing expertise: these and many others were part of the social payoff it was assumed that higher education would bring. In a measure it has done this. And anyway we had little choice. If we invested little hope and little money in it and our competitors invested a lot, we knew we might find outselves obsequiously dependent upon them and upon the trained brains they could spare us. A developed nation surely was one which cultivated its brains and reaped the harvest.

Yet at no time in any of our countries did the idea of the social benefit to be given by investment in higher education exist unassociated with genuine conviction that a period of university education might bring personal enhancement too. Parents and university professors may have defined such personal benefit in terms that differed; middle-class parents seeing their children off for their first year of residence at Yale or Oxford, Manitoba or St Andrews, Ann Arbor or Swansea, might have hoped most for some expansion of confidence, a rubbing-off of corners, a finding of a socially acceptable mate. Middle-class professors and teachers might speak of the power of a good college or university to discipline the mind, give intellectual integrity and independence, open new awarenesses, in one case historical, in another mathematical, in another scientific. A university is still seen by many – even if fewer than it was yesterday – not only as having a mentally educative function for the individual, bringing him more clarity of thought as well as building sounder bases of judgement within him, but as having a morally educative function too: causing him to be more tolerant, more open to listen to the evidence, more balanced, freer to reason and be reasonable, and at last sounder as well as more informed in his views and convictions.

In sum, it has been very generally hoped that on the one hand social benefits, and on the other personal benefits, would accrue from the wider and wider spread of higher education – whether for an increase of 10 per cent to 25 per cent of the population, as in England, or from 40 per cent to 90 per cent, as in California. Productivity economic and social; productivity in terms of young men and women who would be more developed and civilized – these are among the expectations still widely entertained, though maybe not always so consciously expressed.

Now, as long as a society is steaming rapidly 'ahead', it may not be as obvious a question as in some other conditions to inquire in which direction 'ahead' may be. If a country is making more or less clear demands upon universities or colleges to run business schools, to train teachers, to produce the technologists of the thousand kinds it appears to need as well as want, and if it is prepared to pay for all this to be done, the impulse may not be strong in many to inquire – what is it all for? Where to is 'ahead'? What does development mean – whether social development or personal? What is it all in aid of?

But there are beginning to be signs in our more doubting and permissive society that before long questions of this kind are likely again to be asked – by students, who are not so certain that what universities are giving them is too acceptable anyway; by taxpayers, who are not so sure that the dividends coming through are quite as expected; by teachers and research workers within the tertiary education system, who, looking around, may begin to wonder why they are spending their lives as they are. If society is, whether more consciously or less, making demands of them, what is it anyway that is causing society to ask for these particular things rather than others? When universities are so busy fulfilling society's apparent requirements, who is pulling the strings to which presidents, vice-chancellors, professors, and all appear to have to dance?

As soon as there has been a break of confidence that is wide enough, all sorts of questions begin to flood in. How free are universities really? How free have they ever been except to obey the contemporary commands of their society? And if their society loses faith in or respect for them and the goods they produce can they for long go on having respect for or faith in themselves? Fine talk can continue about the free intellect, obedience to reason, following the truth wherever it may lead. But if it leads to bitter criticism of the very society which sustains and finances the whole higher education system, what then? Is the free intellect all that important? What do we mean by the term anyway? Is the contemporary concept of rationality at all adequate – sufficiently comprehensive or sufficiently in touch with the springs of feeling and action? But where are colleges and universities to get the necessary confidence to change? Where are they to get the confidence to be able to criticize their society, in an age when students, taxpayers, and governments are all dubious about them save as instruments that can be used? They may well be entering upon a period of financial enfeeblement: robust in its challenge to priorities and to central purposes.

And yet, clearly, if even universities cannot at times stand over against their society to comment upon it, if they cannot be places which are powerfully normative and directive in some of their influence, to what other agency can we hopefully look in our time? If this is not part of their job whose job is it? It is on them more than on any other institutions that we depend for the production of enough people to run our sort of civilization – but running it includes not merely adding technical devices to it but supplying a good· quality of motive spirit with which to make it go. It was a Victorian who referred nostalgically to the 'dreaming spires' of Oxford; and a very early twentieth-century Oxford graduate who declared that one of the chief blessings of a university education was that it provided 'the gift of an interval'. Both seem dated notions now, like compulsory dinners on five nights a week, gowns, quadrangles, silence, and other protections against the world. Romanticism has had its day, and can no longer protect us. But what can? Shall neutralities? or the powers of productivity? or the present gifts of foundations, or the hope of greater gifts from them still to come? Some of the smaller suspicions whether universities are quite so much worth investing money in as used to be thought are to be seen perhaps in the relatively greater ease with which money is now to be obtained in a number of states and countries for more colleges of advanced arts and technology instead. They are no doubt greatly needed, but not as substitutes for places where thinking shall be done about what the real social or personal benefits are that higher education can give.

CHAPTER 2

The Contribution of Higher Education to the Life of Society

Nevitt Sanford

I begin with some discussion of the functions of higher education in relation to social change. We must bear in mind that higher education includes all kinds of educational institutions of a very wide range beyond the ordinary school; we are not just talking about Berkeley, Oxford, Harvard, or the University of Western Ontario. There is a connection between the functions of institutions of higher education and the stage of social development in the country that starts them. There are different conceptions at different times and in different places. In the United States, for example, as the country developed and the need for further education became very clear, the Land Grant Colleges were started. In the so-called newly developing countries (in South America, for instance) the accent is now on something like the Land Grant College idea – on the need to produce technologists and engineers quickly. This worries scholars trained in Europe because they think that higher education is accenting these subjects too heavily. Some of the humanities men even complain that all the great subjects are being neglected. But young people see that their future lies in engineering and technology. Great Britain perhaps stopped too long on the traditional subjects and delayed introducing the technological subjects, and some time ago found itself not producing enough technologists and technicians to run the country. Recently, however, at least some British universities have become more like those in the USA.

The two world wars have had an enormous impact on universities. The necessity for the US to go to work to help win the war was the beginning of university collaboration in the development of machines of war, and of the various managerial techniques which go with a nation on a war footing. The industrialized nations of the West have acted as if war were going on all the time, so it was necessary to organize some kind of total effort – which included harnessing the energies and capacities of people in institutions of higher learning.

Riesman says that institutions may start with one avowed purpose but as times change they take new directions. They function as 'enterprises', doing whatever is necessary to win the support of their clientele at particular times. In industrialized and highly differentiated societies today, the various (and sometimes conflicting) demands upon or expectations of institutions of higher education include research, scholarship, the training of scientists and scholars, training for other professions and vocations, giving general education – for more and more people, including adults – offering direct service to society as instrumentality, critic, or innovator.

Today there is a big conflict between the young people and the 'over-thirties'. Young people think that the chief function of universities should be that of innovator and instrumentality of social change; that change in capitalist countries is called for, and that universities should lead the revolution. They regard present universities as rationalizers or apologists for whatever *is*. See for example the challenging article by Lichtman in *Center*,[1] in which he accuses universities of being sold out to the military and industrial complex, providing the ideology which enables society to function as it does. This is what the conflict now (especially in France) is mostly about: the contention that universities should be at least a base for operations for fundamental change in society.

One way of grouping the major functions of a university would be under the three traditional main headings: (a) the development of the individual, (b) the preservation and advancement of culture, and (c) the maintenance and further development of technology. In order to become a person, an individual needs to grow up in a culture, and the richer the culture the more of a person he has a chance of becoming. The central purpose of institutions of higher education is to educate (adults as well as young people); and the aim of education is to develop each individual as fully as possible, to make man more human. The central problem is how to integrate the diverse jobs of the university in a meaningful way. To carry out its central purpose a university or college must be, and exist within, a good society – one that accords primary importance to the individual and conducts its affairs in accordance with values that favour full humanity. First among these values are trust, love, justice, freedom, and truth.

A university or other institution of higher education serves society best by

[1] The magazine of the Center for the Study of Democratic Institutions, Santa Barbara, California.

upholding these values in its corporate actions, in its evaluations of events and processes in the larger society, above all in its efforts to build devotion to them in its members. A university or college can serve by being a model for other subsocieties; within limits set by its requirements of autonomy, it can act to improve the larger society.

But while individual development is the supreme goal of a university or college, it is interrelated with the other two goals. Each depends to some extent on the others. It is possible to arrange things in the university so that all three goals are favoured, so that actions that serve one serve the others as well. Trouble comes when individual development is sacrificed to cultural or technological advancement.

In order to develop and defend this thesis I must attempt:

(a) to set forth the basis of the ethical position taken and deal with some criticisms of it; (b) show something of the interrelations of the three sets of goals and indicate what an institution that gives priority to the humanistic goals would be like; (c) show how individual development is (or can be) promoted in institutions of higher learning, and why the basic values noted above are of crucial importance; (d) describe some of the consequences of the neglect of those values in recent years; and (e) discuss some concrete ways in which a reconstructed system of higher education can in the circumstances of today contribute to the life of society.

The concept of education as individual development is largely a restatement in contemporary terms of the traditional philosophy of humanistic education. We find it expressed in the Ancients; the British university colleges were strong on it and so were the Founding Fathers; this concept is still set down in the catalogues of our liberal arts colleges as their main objective. It is not out of date. The full development of the individual as a person is not only the major aim of institutions of higher learning, but a fundamental aim of the political and social order itself. A good society will come when its members are capable of the highest satisfactions of the mind and spirit.

I am not talking just about excellence in productivity of various kinds, but about a tasteful and fulfilling use of leisure; about a kind of logical rigour which enables people to enjoy taking part in argument; about creative expression for individual fulfilment as well as for the sake of culture or technology. I am talking about the inclination and capacity to contribute something to the community and to social action – about a whole range of interrelated qualities of the person. This is in keeping with the old image of universities as institutions that should enable their students to enjoy life, to participate fully in the life of their society. This is the kind of education often called aristocratic, often associated with British universities which try to do something for a young person besides enabling him to learn a trade. In our affluent post-industrial societies of today there is call for aristocratic education for everybody, or at least for as many as possible.

For solving the kinds of problem confronting us on our campuses today, expecially in Canada and the US, the only thing really workable will be this developmental approach. It is no good for our great metropolitan universities today to stick to the notion of a set curriculum or the idea that higher education is only for those who can benefit from it as it is. More and more people are going to be included in.

This kind of developmental education must be guided by a theory of *what* a person can become and *how* he can be enabled to become this or that. We must accept the fact that a lot of eighteen-year-olds do not know very much and that many will be unlike the students usually admitted to four-year colleges. We shall, however, find in this new breed of student plenty of talent which, though of kinds not previously rewarded, is well worth rewarding and using. In deciding upon an appropriate tertiary education for these young people, we can still learn much from the liberal arts college tradition.

Further in support of the present ethical position, we may take any virtue of the sort liberal educators have listed among their goals – competence, wisdom, compassion, among others. It is easy to start arguments about how high it stands in a hierarchy, but no one will deny that it is *a* virtue. We then think of how it might be developed; for example, educotors might say competence is to be developed in schools, compassion in other institutions. But personality functions as a whole; virtues are interrelated; and actions to promote one will have consequences for others. From the point of view of personality theory what is most to be desired is a state that favours high development in many virtues and a chance for superlative development in some, and that does not lead to serious neglect of any; this state is one of complexity and wholeness in the person.

The contemporary neglect of the concept of the person is a serious matter. Professional practice in education as well as in the health and welfare fields is rarely directed to a person but only to particular capacities or needs, a state of affairs that is related to the declining popularity of personality theory in social science: the person is fragmented by psychologists, merged with collectivities by sociologists. Many university teachers do not see how the liberal arts curriculum, which they care deeply about, can affect personality (though of course it can, in crucially important ways). The university in America today is organized under a whole range of offices each having some particular responsibility directed towards some particular process or function of the person; there is no one around to deal with the student as a whole man. It seems that the only agent left who is concerned with the integration of the whole person is the boy's mother! Integration is essential if, under the pressures of our present fragmented society, the personality is not to disintegrate altogether.

Our first goal must be to reconstruct the idea of the person. Research, scholarship, the development of strong professions, are, in the last analysis, for the benefit of man and society, for the service of distinctively human needs, not merely for keeping people alive and enabling them to kill other people for the state. Students, like other men, should be regarded as ends, not means; it makes no sense to dehumanize students now, while they are in school, in the hope that their processing will somehow enable them to contribute something to mankind later on.

Other functions of universities and colleges – the technological and culture-preserving – may be viewed in this perspective. Just as in the larger world culture and (sometimes) technology can serve man, so in a university research, scholarship, professional training, and direct service to society should be carried out in such a way as to serve educational purposes. If these activities contribute nothing to education they might as well be done elsewhere; if they interfere with education they were better done elsewhere.

Education depends heavily, of course, upon culture. It is mainly through the use of culture – shared symbolic experience – that men find meaning, resolve inner conflicts, develop, sustain, and express their individuality. Education for individual development is therefore inconceivable without a curriculum deeply based in a cultural heritage. But such education is a far cry from mere exposure to that heritage, from the mere learning of facts, and from the sort of academic training that prepares a person to become a specialist in a subject. Education occurs when the student truly assimilates, in his own way, some cultural product; when he becomes capable of using that product in expressing his emotional needs or resolving his inner conflicts through imagination or vicarious living. We know that this is happening when a student becomes involved with, gets excited about, or falls in love with a subject. It is almost impossible to predict what will assure such responses in students, so we make no mistake in offering a wide range of subjects. It does not follow, however, that for purposes of individual development one subject is as good as another. Cultural products – and whole cultures for that matter – have to be evaluated. This is a matter for continuing inquiry, the basis for evaluation being how well these products or cultures serve man's distinctively human needs.

As education depends on culture, so culture depends on education. Cultures need to be improved, and institutions of higher learning are directly involved in this work. The key role here must be played by relatively highly developed individuals – people who can appreciate and people who can create.

Culture, technology, and education can, in theory, be mutually supporting. The trouble is that technology without deliberate control tends to be the most determining of the three. Our world is increasingly filled with manufactured objects, including buildings, with no symbolic or aesthetic value; and institutions originally designed for human welfare more and more follow the model of industry, with specialization of function, rigid definition of roles, no chance for the expression of personality. Graduate students in many institutions suffer as much as undergraduates from the impersonality of their environment. Consider an example. Graduate students who were members of a teachers' union at a great American university decided after much debate and searching of consciences to go on strike and to set up a picket-line. Professors by and large ignored the strike, but in order for some to get to their offices they had to pass within a few feet of those striking students with whom they had been working very closely – whose dissertations they were supervising, for example. In many instances they did this without speaking to these students or permitting themselves to catch their eyes – acting, in short, as if students with whom they had intense discussions yesterday did not exist today. To match this behaviour, we would have to go back to the Hollywood practice of letting a man know he was fired by removing his name-plate from his door, or even the practice in Hitler's Germany of treating an old friend who had been condemned by the Nazis as if he were already dead. It is painful to think of the psychological state of graduate students treated in the way described. Not only must they realize that what they thought was a personal relationship does not in fact exist and probably never did but, unless they wish to sacrifice their whole careers, they have no alternative to going back to their professors and acting as if nothing had happened; they have to face the fact that they are effectively enslaved.

Clearly, we must find some way to humanize and to unify – to humanize through unifying – our institutions of higher education. The scientific and artistic goal of finding unity in diversity has its parallel in the practical task of integrating the activities of the university. The student is the only person who interacts in a human way with all the features of a university; nothing except concern for him could possibly bring together all the people who work in universities. What else could they find to talk about? Students have the largest stake in this undertaking; happily, they realize it with increasing clarity and thus furnish a motive force for change.

We must deliberately go about the task of de-bureaucratizing the universities. We ought to be able to use our intelligence and our science to construct an organization, an institution, that really is devoted to humanistic ends. This is what social scientists should be studying. They could quickly overcome the hiatus between science and practice if they made the institutions in which they live the object of their own inquiry and their own value judgements.

We have been discussing moral issues – what man ought to become, what institutions ought to do in order to favour man's becoming all that he can. In post-industrial society, as the church declines in influence the burden on the university increases. Moral principles that used to be taken for granted in the universities now have to be spelled out and their implications made clear.

No one will deny that truth is among the highest values in an institution devoted to education. Our self-development and our mastery of the environment depend directly upon it. But perceiving truth depends on freedom; and men will not care about freedom unless they have justice and love (care). As Bryan Wilson[1] has pointed out, people today have a lot of freedom *because* nobody cares what they do – but it doesn't make them very happy. Trust is even more basic; without it there can be no stable human relationships.

This hierarchy of values is essential to the educational purposes of an institution. Unless the values are upheld there is little point in even discussing conventional educational procedures. It is much easier to see the consequences of their neglect than to describe their positive effects – just as the consequences of breathing impure air are more noticeable than the consequences of breathing pure air. We are talking about what people need in order to be human.

We have to think of ways in which devotion to these values may be developed in students, and other people. Obviously it is no good simply preaching them. Here, probably more than anywhere, teaching has to be by example. If we had teachers who really embodied integrity, tolerance, independence, fairness, decency, and faith, we would worry much less about students. Show me a colleague that you and I can trust and I will show you one that students trust.

Trustworthiness in administrators and faculty members ought not to be regarded primarily as a character trait which some have and others lack, nor is the behaviour of the American professors toward their striking students to

---

[1] Bryan Wilson, 'The Role of Institutions of Higher Education in Preserving Values in Society' (unpublished manuscript).

be explained on the basis that the university had somehow been invaded by low types. The inconsistent or impersonal behaviour that students observe is due less to personality than to the various and sometimes conflicting requirements of the roles and statuses of faculty and officials. These men, in other words, are caught in a system – one in which virtues like trustworthiness apparently are becoming irrelevant. I venture to say that my story of the professors and the striking students could be told, and told with passion, before an average academic audience and most of those present would feel nothing.

We in the United States have gone pretty far towards dehumanization in our university life and it is very difficult to see how our course is to be reversed. It may help a little, however, if we can understand how we got into our present situation.

Things were not always this way. Universities in the United States before the Second World War were still human communities, and universities in Canada and the United Kingdom are so today, I think. It was after the war that our universities really entered the market-place or, more precisely, when faculty members in great numbers began using government largesse to advance their own specialized professional interests.

At the University of California at Berkeley, for example, we in the Psychology Department eagerly seized upon the available federal funds to expand and upgrade our department. We were out to make Psychology the best faculty at Berkeley, and the Psychology Faculty at Berkeley the best in the world. More than that, we were focused on developing and strengthening psychology as a discipline on the assumption, I suppose, that what is good for psychology is good for the nation. Accordingly, we began appointing and promoting solely on the basis of achievement in reasearch, encouraging all members of the department to apply for research grants, and raising the standards for admission to graduate standing.

It was not until I had left Berkeley and began working at a college that I realized that most other university departments were doing as we had done, that undergraduate education was being seriously neglected in the universities, and that four-year colleges were trying hard to be like universities. It appeared that the parochialism and drive for success in which we had participated had by the middle nineteen-fifties become well-nigh universal. The appearance of the Sputniks served to speed the movement of the universities in the direction they had already taken. Specialization and professionalism could now be further justified on the basis that they were strengthening the nation. Instead of being communities of scholars, universities became constituted of 'gangs of scholars', and within each gang individuals and sub-gangs competed for the best place in the sun. Universities themselves, considered as corporate bodies, entered into the spirit of the thing, going after success in the eyes of the world and, having found that this kind of success is very expensive and having lost their sense of inner direction, increasingly acted as if their public service function were best performed through devotion to the interests of the rich and powerful.

Enormous interests are now vested in this state of affairs. Government and industry have good reason to be happy about the university's contribution – through research and training – to technology. Most parents are happy to have their sons and daughters receive the vocational training that will enable them to go up in the world, and the great majority of students come sooner or later to see the advantages of adapting themselves to the system. Most important of all, from the point of view of the educational reformer, is the fact that most university professors are prepared to resist change in a system within which they have become successful. There is no denying that the kinds of changes now being urged in the United States by Black Student Unions and 'Third World' students – which have been urged for many years by progressive educators – would cost established professors something. (It would cost them something in terms of power, status, and the comforts of habitual ways of doing things; it could liberate them in other ways, particularly from dependence on such sources of satisfaction as these.) This holds for members of education and social science departments as much as for members of other schools and departments; and it has to be taken into account in evaluating the large educational and social scientific literature in which the existing university system, a product of the times and the present condition of society, is treated as if it came fully developed from On High and in which the only thing to be explained is the 'pathology' – social or individual – of student activists.

Not much of what I have said here has been lost upon intelligent students. They – and I – have perhaps exaggerated in order to make a point. The university does not sell its soul every day in order to get money. But we need to understand that it need do so only once in order to disillusion a few thousand students.

One way in which students respond to present conditions in the universities and colleges is by demanding that their education should be 'relevant' – often without saying what it should be relevant to or even what is meant by relevance. One kind of relevance which students desperately want and need has been described for them by John Dodds of Stanford: 'We have too often failed to make the humanities *relevant* to the human and cultural needs of our students. If I have a main point, it is this: that to deal with the full robust range of life which is the essence of the humanities and to render that life sterile is the unforgiveable academic sin ... If, as we pretend, the philosophies and the literatures and the arts distil the wisdom of the centuries, somehow we must make that wisdom *viable* for our students – or at the very least, we must not desiccate it. If we really believe that the humanities feed the needs of the human spirit, we must lead people to see the relevance of the humanities for those needs today.'[1]

Professor Dodds is polite. The desiccation has already gone far. While there are many professors of humanities who see things as he does, most influential departments are dominated by men who want to apply the simple quantitative methods of science in their scholarship – or else have gone in for a kind of compulsive antiquarianism. Students don't need to limit their criticisms of universities to involvement with the Institute for Defense Analyses – they can criticize professors on the basis that, in their concern for their own careers and their professionalism, they have neglected education: it is as simple as that. Note that Dodd says 'we must lead *people*', not just students. What people outside universities are doing today in order to 'feed the needs of the human spirit' often seems to border on desperation, as witness the flowering in the United States of all kinds of wild 'encounter groups'.

By 'relevance' most people mean 'social relevance'. There are rising expectations that the universities will now 'do something' about poverty, race relations, and the deterioration of cities. And the universities are responding in a characteristic way. Now that outside demands are being heard for particular kinds of service, or inquiries into particular areas, the universities speak as if these were the things they had wanted to do all the time. The setting up of Institutes for Urban Studies, however, is not likely to satisfy radical students or those at the bottom of our social heap. No change in the structure of society is involved, nor any change in the relations of the university to society.

It is unfortunate that universities in the United States, because of their practice of trying to meet all demands that are backed by money, have created the impression that they can and will take action to change conditions in ghettos and to improve the lot of the poor, particularly those who are poor and members of racial or ethnic minorities. It is true, as we shall see, that the university can do a great deal to improve society, but what it can do by way of direct action to change conditions in urban or rural slums is severely limited. These conditions will yield only to the right social and economic policies, and whereas university scholars and scientists can serve as con-

[1] 'How Human are the Humanities?' *Stanford To-day*, Summer/Autumn, 1968, p. 25.

sultants in these matters, the university itself, acting through its schools, departments, or institutes, cannot make or implement such policies. To do so would be to lose what is left of its unique status as an institution that is beholden to no particular group of constituents and is thus free to pursue the truth, to generate and entertain all kinds of ideas including radical ones, and to serve as an intellectual critic of society.

It is true that the university is to a considerable extent 'politicized' now in the sense that it serves directly the interests of some segments of society such as agriculture, industry, and the military but not others such as welfare recipients, or unorganized labourers. This, of course, is unfair, but it does not necessarily follow that if the university can serve as a kind of research arm of a grape growers' association it can help workers in the vineyards organize themselves and lend its moral support to their efforts to secure their rights. The two kinds of action are not directly comparable. For one thing, the university function of aiding technological development has a long tradition behind it, is almost universally approved of by the man in the street, and although it surely favours entrenched interests, it has never been recognized as political by those who carry it out or benefit from it. What is clearly needed now by poor people is political power, and this is well enough known to everybody for university actions that did not contribute to such power to be regarded by poor people as trivial, and actions that did so contribute to be regarded by other people – particularly those whose interests were threatened – as purely political and thus a radical departure from the university's traditional way of functioning. What also needs to be understood by poor people and their supporters is that powerful groups that have access to the university's services do not owe their power primarily to the university; they have been able to command these services *because* they are powerful, and the same rule will hold for poor people. In their quest for political power they can form alliances with students and faculty members, they can be sure that increasing members of their young people will have access to the same kind of education the powerful have had. They can easily obtain expert knowledge and consultation from university people, but they cannot expect the university itself, or parts or sections of it, to lead their fight for political power.

As the poor obtain power a balance will begin to be restored with respect to whom the university serves. Meanwhile the answer to selective politicalization is de-politicalization. Instead of trying to make the university review a new set of political interests, and thus threatening it with the loss of such autonomy as it has, students and their allies might well work to bring about its withdrawal from those arrangements that have been entered into merely to serve the powers-that-be or to get money or status.

The university cannot do everything asked of it today. Above all, it cannot be both a centre for free inquiry and an adversary in political struggles – except in defence of values upon which its life depends. A way out may be found in two parallel lines of endeavour: encouraging the development of other institutions and agencies to take pressure off itself and working for internal reform which, coupled with the education of its publics, will enable it better to serve society on its own terms.

There are other institutions such as governmental and quasi-governmental institutes for research and development, industrial research organizations, voluntary agencies, professional societies, and independent institutes that can well perform some of the tasks now expected from the university.

Especially important services to society can be performed by independent institutes for applied social science, or better, for social action-research. Problems centring about race relations, poverty, and welfare are bound to be controversial – and thus not well suited to the university – and to call for a kind of involvement that is not in keeping with the academic style of work. What is needed – in the United States at least – both for the amelioration of problems and for the advancement of social science, is an agency that can define a problem, make inquiries into how to attack it, take action affecting it, and evaluate the effects of that action before deciding what to do next.[1]

There is also need at the present time in the United States for special schools to serve the interests of racial and ethnic minorities. In response to the urgings of students, universities and colleges are now in the process of setting up departments or schools of 'black' or 'ethnic' studies. It may be doubted, however, that many minority-group students will find these innovations satisfying. What they need, and are beginning to ask for, is something like the 'labour schools' which flowered during the several decades before the Second World War, that is, schools which are frankly devoted to the institutionalization of black or minority-group power through building group solidarity, training leaders, offering instruction in political action. Departments or schools of black or ethnic studies in universities or colleges may in fact serve this purpose; they may evolve in the direction of becoming schools-in-the-community; like some of the progressive colleges in the United States of the nineteen-thirties, they might adopt highly flexible standards of admission, accent fieldwork or part-time jobs for the students, make use of teachers with ghetto experience but no academic credentials, and build curricula around the current needs of students. If they do this, however, they will confront directly the issue of racial separatism in a nation in which integration is the law of the land, and they would confront, too, all the

[1] N. Sanford, 'The Activist's Corner', *Journal of Social Issues*, 1968, vol. 24, pp. 165–72.

academic opposition to progressive education which might turn out to be stronger than opposition to separatism. It would certainly seem the better part of wisdom to develop alternatives outside the university at the same time. These would be private rather than public schools, but ways could be found of making some public funds available to them. Meanwhile universities and colleges can do a far better job than at present of serving society directly. For one thing, multidisciplinary problem-oriented institutes should be set up within universities. They could not go as far as independent institutes in advocating and carrying out actions, but they could make hard-hitting analyses of problems and issue policy statements. They could even go so far as to build prototypes of ideal social arrangements; for example, an institute for research and development in education should by all means have its own experimental school.

Resistance to such institutes comes less from external pressures on the university than from interests within it. Academic social scientists tend to have a low opinion of what they call 'applied science', higher status being accorded to pure research, which is almost always highly specialized. It is not commonly recognized that the kind of action-research that can come to grips with social problems is far more demanding intellectually than the usual academic exercises of spinning out theoretical models or carrying out conventional research designs. Again, the organization of the university around departments and professional schools is highly resistant to change. This structure rests heavily upon the intrinsic intellectual appeals of the disciplines, but its rigidity has more to do with its control over the pathways to success, status, and identity. An academic man who thought to make a career through combining two or more disciplines in his work or as a 'generalist' would have to be prepared to live dangerously, and most academic men, after years of socialization in disciplines, find there an important basis for personal identity.

At the same time, however, faults of the present system are widely recognized, many faculty members are unhappy about its restraints upon them, and fresh efforts are being made to counter the fragmentation of the university and to render its social scientific activities more socially relevant. The Institute for the Study of Human Problems at Stanford University, for example, was founded in 1961 with the idea that a generalist approach to inquiry and action on problems would also provide an ideal atmosphere for undergraduate education.[1] Since then new colleges have been started – for example at the State University of New York at Old Westbury and at the

[1] N. Sanford, 'A New Approach to General Education', *Saturday Review*, 18 Jan. 1964, pp. 62–4.

University of California at Santa Cruz, in which it is planned that students will spend a good part of their time at fieldwork in cities while being offered a curriculum that is integrated with their experience. This plan is so fully in accord with what increasing numbers of students are demanding today that we may well ask what will happen to the scholarly disciplines once the generalist approach to education, inquiry, and action has become dominant. The answer is to build institutes for *them*; let there be institutes for advanced study in economics, sociology, political science, psychology, and so forth where scholars can pursue their specialized work in peace, free of the responsibilities for undergraduate education with which they are now burdened – and which burden undergraduate education even more.

When we think of the university or college entering the community, as at Old Westbury or Santa Cruz, we are led to consider a form of service to society that has been sadly neglected, and that is the education of the general public. Adult education has been regarded by university men with much the same contempt that has been accorded applied science; it is widely held that courses for adults have to be watered down; it is even still believed by many that adults cannot learn. But times are changing. It is increasingly well understood that adults must be further educated if they are to provide a climate in which the university can flourish or offer the moral and financial support it needs. Adults also need education, more and more, in order to keep pace with the changing requirements of their work and in order further to develop themselves and to maintain their humanity in an increasingly cold and complex world. There must be programmes that reach adults where they are, that are organized around activities in which they are already engaged, that do not require adults to adapt themselves to the usual academic ways of doing things. As universities and colleges reach out into the community in this way, they will discover that there are many adults without advanced degrees who have much to teach as well as to learn, that they have much to contribute to the kind of socially relevant education that students are now demanding.

The university should bring to its work with adults the same spirit that informs its work with students. It must be guided by its own light. While listening to what people say they want, it must participate in the definition of their needs, not permitting itself to become a mere instrument in the service of their missions and programmes. It can best serve society by being a model society itself, one whose primary concern is with the good of students, and which knows that what is good for students is good for man.

INTERCHAPTER

I

Response to Nevitt Sanford – BRYAN WILSON

I wish to suggest, first, a different balance from that described by Dr Sanford in the purposes of universities; secondly, that there has been an erosion of the old support for the social values which the universities disseminated, and for their own operation; thirdly, that the affective ends described by Dr Sanford cannot be properly arrived at by instrumental means (the instrumental means *corrupt* the values and the ends at which universities aim); and fourthly, that universities have already allowed their traditional ends to be overlaid by others so that there is only a hollow relationship between what they profess and what they actually do.

The education of the whole man is vital, but traditional pastoral concerns are intimately connected with scholarship, which is the only context in which what Dr Sanford calls university education can occur. Universities should be care-institutions, but not *only* care-institutions. They are not merely therapeutic communities: without scholarly pursuits and disciplines, love, trust, truth, and freedom, the central values to which Dr Sanford refers, have nothing to feed on. There is an analogy here with the family, which in our present society is in a parlous state. The family specializes in affectivity, but affection needs soil in which to grow. This is what the family lacks in our contemporary society, in which all its functions have been taken over by other social institutions. So in universities: the communication of trust, love, etc., need the going concern of scholarship, in which these values function in university life. An active orientation towards participatory concern, not merely a general piety, is needed for a relationship of trust.

Is it true that the professors are not interested in education? In Oxford the historical relationship ensures that those who teach students have a sustained, personal relationship with them. Communication of values takes place, largely by example, in the context of shared concerns, and those concerns are the concerns of scholarship.

All socializing agencies necessarily use affective dispositions as the basis for summoning commitment to role performances. It would be folly for universities to dehumanize students, but for many of them the big mass-university is a dehumanizing experience for which the increasingly large schools, and television, have done little to prepare them. But trust and socialization rely on personal relationships – and on this affective relation. Motivation is implanted and responses are induced appropriate to role performance in the impersonal wider society. We have to prepare people for the dehumanized world in which they will live: the tension in all socializing agencies, in the family as in the universities, is that their operation must begin with the communication of trust and love, and yet that they must prepare men for desiccated roles.

The history of human kind is in part a pushing back of the affective sphere of life into the activities of socialization. Our society relies less and less for its operation on *personal dispositions* such as trust, and more and more on machine-like operations. We rely on technical skills and role performances. The same personal trust is used simply to prepare men for a part in the machine-like operation of modern society: the affective is used to socialize men to accept affectively neutral roles.

Personal dispositions are squeezed out in the productive economic level of organization where life is regulated by role involvements. At the consumption economic level where choice is supposed to operate, men are manipulated by publicity and advertising. In the early stages of industrialization we typically relied on the heightened socialization of individuals as the guarantee that men would perform their economic roles. A man's character was the best guarantee of his attitude to work. A man who was 'conscientious, reliable, punctual, frugal, willing', and possessed the rest of the catalogue of Victorian virtues, was necessarily a good worker. But this was a blanket guarantee of his attributes necessary for the economic operation of society. Today in a more developed society work situations can be controlled much more effectively by equipment – the conveyor belt, electronics, data-processing – and so there is no need to socialize the whole man so thoroughly. Increasingly, control is exerted at the point at which a man works, and not over his whole life activities: as long as he is there, he can be specifically controlled by equipment and need not be controlled through socializing processes in early life, and perhaps – as secondary socialization – job preparation.

Because total moral dispositions of individuals are not now required for the work-order of society, the economic underpinning of morality has gone – and the changing moral standards of society and the changing patterns of socialization, from free expression in schools to the permissive morality in the wider society, are associated with the changing character of social control in economic activities. The problem which remains, however, is that although men can be mechanically and electronically controlled at work they cannot be so controlled in their day-to-day lives in the wider society. Order and cover decency are as necessary as ever, but now they lack the economic support which morality enjoyed in the past.

We no longer concern ourselves with providing men with a sense of inner intgerity so that as *good* people they will be concerned with the maintenance of public order. Here I tend to differ in emphasis from Dr Sanford – societies do not, I think, accord primacy to the individual – all societies must concern themselves with the maintenance of a stable pattern of public order and cover decency.

Universities used to function to socialize men and might still aspire to do so, but the social context makes the task increasingly improbable. The balance of affectivity and instrumentality in modern societies shifts – and this occurs even in our disciplines. The shift to science and technology in universities, and the shift to scientific styles of procedure in the humanities, reflect the increased emphasis on instrumental procedures, and the decline of concern with the humanistic affective aspects of discipline. What, however, seems important to me is that universities should maintain scholarship as the context for their enterprise of socialization, and that will require the maintenance of a humanistic orientation in which the values involved in socialization can acquire expression.

I am somewhat disturbed by Dr Sanford's passing endorsement of the motive force that students furnish for change because so much of their pressure is anti-scholarly. What reasons are there to suppose that revolutionary students have any conception of what universities might appropriately do? Much of the pressure for change is towards the abandonment of both scholarship and pastoral care. The pressure of students often reflects disenchantment with universities, but they often espouse 'change' as a value, regardless of its intrinsic quality. I do not doubt that within many a revolutionary student with a banner of protest there is a spirit of desperate searching for personal involvement, the joy of affective relations, and the benefits of sustained contact in serious concerns of mind and character. But people who suffer from serious infectious disease, and who desire a return to health, do not often do the right things about it. Student protest may be important in arresting the drift of contemporary society, but that depends on how that protest is interpreted and handled.

Dr Sanford said in an aside about San Francisco State College that 'there is a lot of life around'. I hope it is not impudent of me to discuss what is an American problem that does not affect Britain – yet. But there may also be a little death around – for universities if not for individuals. What does a 'black studies programme' which is the cause of the trouble at SFSC really imply? Where is the corpus of black philosophy, black history, black literature, and most of all black science? What is black physics? Is this not merely a demand for the inclusion in the university of an elaborately ideological racist programme? Is it not merely a demand – in a particular form in this case, but a representative of many student demands – for a reduction of standards by the inclusion in universities of students who are objectively unqualified? Can such a programme be a basis for the trust and love which Dr Sanford sees as basic to university concern? Is it not the inclusion in universities of something quite inimical both to scholarship and to the values of trust and love?

As a sociologist, I want to return more centrally to the conception of society that Dr Sanford's paper seems to imply. I have already suggested that there is no society – whether primitive, under the control of custom; medieval, with its legally entrenched rank-order; or modern, with its bureaucratic structure – which really gives primacy to the individual.

Trust and love, freedom and truth, are the principal virtues that Dr Sanford emphasizes as those to which the university should build devotion. I wish to discuss trust and love; freedom I leave aside as an abstraction that I do not wholly understand. It seems to me that the broad sweep of human evolution has been to reduce the extent to which human relations and social organization rely on qualities such as trust and love. In societies in which men are but little differentiated in their daily concerns, they do interact with each other as *total* persons. Role and person are not differentiated, and since the society can be known in all its contours, there is no need to distinguish person and role in order to function in that society – even if such a distinction were conceivable. In some parts of Africa still if one asks a tribesman about chieftainship he can tell one nothing – but he knows about *chiefs*. The abstract concept of chieftainship is unnecessary because the life of the society is direct – experience is concrete.

But in advanced societies we rely less and less on personal trust – trust in individuals as such – and more and more on technical competences and role performances. We slough off personal concern because it is demanding: we reduce our obligation to clipped contractual elements. We reduce investment in other persons and invest in equipment and techniques: we even believe that personal investment can be achieved by techniques, by rational instrumental procedures – partly because affect is hard to administer. Given the increased number of relationships, and the impersonality and transience of many of them, we reduce emotional effort and expenditure in the conduct of our lives. Trust is mechanized as our human organizations are increasingly mechanized, but thereby loses its intrinsic human quality. Love is pushed into the unorganized interstices of social involvement – but love and trust cease to be the bases for other operations. They become increasingly difficult styles even for those ideologically committed to them.

In the growing university detached and impersonal relations become the norm. The extent to which this is the case is reflected in the ease with which radical students deny the human-ness of teachers: their assertion is that academics are just ciphers. And they say this even though their own ideology emphasizes humanity and freedom. Not so long ago the student's relation to his university was expressed in personal imagery. Loyalty was to the *alma mater*, an expression in personalized terms of what was an affective bond, a style of commitment that was not expressible in terms of the new mechanized system of role-relationships. The style sounds almost quaint in the late nineteen-sixties. One might see this process as analogous to that occurring in other social institutions where personal affective imagery is being abandoned. In religion we are faced with the death of God as a theological concept: and with the end of God-talk. This, too, is a rejection of the model of personal relationships as the appropriate guide to behaviour and involvement in all public spheres.

Of all social institutions the education system has been the last – of those which are capable of centralization at the societal level – to experience this process of depersonalization, and religion, which I see as basically communal in the locus of its operations, has even begun to experience the same thing, at least as it is represented by theologians.

The modern mass-universities evoke loyalties on the basis of trust and love less and less effectively both from their students and from the society in which they exist. Some of the reasons for this decreasing effectiveness are:

1. The universities encompass too many people who interact too casually and intermittently for sustained commitment to evolve. Faculties become one sub-culture and students another.

2. Teachers also manifest reduced commitment to their institutions: they move on as soon as better jobs are offered. Interest in career lines conflicts with role performances.

3. Universities have – half unwittingly – adopted bureaucratic structures to cope with increase of scale – and this has been associated with the abandonment of their original concerns, except as a hollow ideology offered in the speeches of vice-chancellors and the opening pages of catalogues.

Universities become less like communities, although this is still a model to which reference is made, and more like corporations and government departments. Their viable mode of operation, given their size, their internal diversity, and their reliance on technical skills and equipment, is by adopting segmentary role performances. Affectivity disappears.

It does not seem to me that universities do act as models for other sub-societies, as Dr Sanford suggests. Rather, they themselves imitate the styles of organization and relationships known in the wider society – as individual communities, and as a collective guild with special prerogatives of autonomy.

What this development in society and in the university suggests to me is the central sociological question – How does society hold together? Sociologists have thought of *values* – the type of values mentioned by Dr Sanford – as the elements on which social cohesion rests. I dissent from that view, and believe that society is held together by the continuing operation of economic, political, and social institutions over time. The rules of procedure and the structure of institutions are the cohesive elements in society. This is the character of contemporary societies; but such societies are not made up of automatons, and men demand, even if they do not know how to obtain or sustain, affective relationships. If these values are vital to education, then I believe that they will not be achieved by instrumental and technical means, because these means are intrinsically inimical to the ends that they are supposed to realize. If the communication of these values is central to the university and if it persists in the use of these means, then I think *it* rather than *society* will be transformed in the operation. The university will become pre-occupied with its own organizational maintenance. That could be a massive deflection of goals, with organizational goals and instrumental procedures displacing substantive values. It seems to me that trust and love belong to *communally* organized societies, and that the search in Dr Sanford's paper is for community, sustained face-to-face relations, without which the fragility of man and the fragility of the transmission of culture might break down. To that community I do not know whether we know the way back.

II

In the discussion that followed it was urged that both Sanford and Wilson had too little regard to student views and student affectivity. Both, though in different ways, were too paternalistic in their attitude to students, both were also perhaps thinking too exclusively in terms of universities in their references to higher education. It is clear enough that from now on the views – and feelings – of students are going to matter a good deal more in the development of higher education, including universities, than they did earlier in the century. They are astringently critical of the apparent alliance between institutions of higher education and the military/industrial/capitalist ethos; but they are critical too of the standoffish attitude of universities to much of the rest of higher education. In fact, society finds indispensable – and will continue to do so – a whole range of people who have had a tertiary education. Whether they have had it in a university or elsewhere matters less to society than university faculty often believe. The time is past when universities can assume that their relationships with the rest of the tertiary system do not greatly matter.

Young people today want to be recognized as adult at eighteen and to be treated fully as men and women throughout their college years. In a technical age they feel they need to be human beings among other human beings – whether or not the others dress, or talk, or are being trained in the same way as university students. They want to feel that they belong to the human race – and this is additional to and, for some, more important than, learning to be good scientists or scholars or functionaries, or even getting safe jobs later on which will yield them economic benefits.

But can universities or polytechnics, or colleges of any kind, in the next dozen years learn how to deal with students more adequately both as people, and as such on a level of equality with their professors, and as incipient experts in need of being educated and trained so that they can become professionals, research workers, technically well furnished? Or is the real job of the university or the college of technology to attempt only to equip people in these latter ways? Is Bryan Wilson right in his foreboding?

The discussion as it continued tackled two main topics: the apparent contrast between the Sanford position and that of Wilson regarding the place of 'hard' scholarship in higher education; and the separation of learning from living as a factor in student unrest.

Is a university to be a place of objective scholarship or is it to be primarily a teaching institution, sharing its concern both for people and for knowledge? Are the two emphases compatible? What, anyway, is meant by scholarship? Most student activists, it was maintained, are anti-scholastic rather than anti-scholarly: they are not against hard knowledge but against the 'old bureaucratic methods' of conveying it. Free universities are essentially protests against the kind of formalized institution that is not at bottom much concerned with a student's education. Many university departments at present do not agree that either their job or that of the university is primarily an educational one. We were reminded of Lord Morris's remark that 'the yearnings of the English universities are fundamentally academic ... not essentially educational in the sense that they care for advanced education as such'.! Several members were convinced that the motto of too many university teachers now is 'What's good for my subject must be good for the university.[1] In many institutions of higher education there is in these days in fact no academic community, only a number of professionalized groups. In these circumstances one hardly sees them developing rapidly into places which are keenly concerned about general education.

Sanford replied to all this that he agreed with much that had been said about the necessity of scholarship within the university. One must have something to talk about: it was no good trafficking merely in feelings. 'Encounters' bringing affectivity into the forefront soon become boring and phoney. The kind of man by whom a student wishes to be taught or counselled may be a man who loves him but he must be someone who loves his subject even more. What we need to do is to make ourselves more fully aware of ways in which scholarly activity can penetrate the whole person, so that it is not just one form of escapism; we want our students to love their work, as some faculty members do, with real passion. Criticism of a student's work by a tutor who is himself a scholar and is in touch with the student as a man is both more personally educative and less superficial than the more detached system standard in the USA.

James Jarrett's criticism of Sanford's position was from a different viewpoint. Sanford had spoken of what might be learned from the student's challenge to traditional curricula and to the idea that an educated man was one who had mastered certain disciplines and skills. But can we not be challenged too if we maintain that students should acquire a particular hierarchy of predetermined virtues if they are to be well-realized individuals? Students are saying – though not always clearly – 'Don't make up your minds too firmly about the *necessary* virtues. Those hitherto thought the right ones may be insufficient; new ones or a different sequence, engendered in the very process of education itself, may now be required.' People learn existentially from being involved in situations and life itself – only in this way indeed can they learn what really are values and what really are virtues.

Marjorie Reeves agreed that some students recognize only a personal development as valuable. But many are in a dilemma about their contribution to society. On the one hand they feel that institutions of higher education are so committed to the forces of darkness that they do not for a moment want to be identified with such sources of power. Yet on the other hand they

[1] 'The Function of Universities Today', in *The Expanding University* (Ed. W. R. Niblett), 1962, p. 24.

want to be able to help the underdog – and with the help of technical knowledge itself. If the aim of higher education is to be stated merely in personal
terms you are not equipping yourself to help the underdog. It is not, in the
end, from power but from the powers of darkness that students want to fly.
Many wish to educate themselves for service to their fellows, but do not
trust the roles they may in present-day society be asked to play. How can
we unite personal development with capacity to play an acceptable service
role?

Some members of the seminar thought that this line of thinking still gave
too much weight to the desire of students for personal and individual
development. It is communal rather than personal development they seek.
They think of economic prosperity and economic power as irrelevancies and
are simply bored by the obsession of capitalist society with getting more and
more money. Many want power which can be used tactically to secure the
disruption of the present order of things not merely in higher education but
in society generally. Nihilism and violence stem from the desire to break the
accepted hierarchy of values by force. Student revolt is itself often a manifes-
tation of role-determined behaviour – a more or less automatic opposition
to the morality of the contemporary world. But the range of views and
positions even among student activists is so great that to generalize with
safety is all but impossible. Extreme Maoists and gentle hippies have little
in common. The frequent identification of the powers of darkness with
capitalists is politically suspect anyway and itself the pursuit of a political
end.

Sanford, in commentary upon some of the points made, defended a
'predetermined' hierarchy of values on the ground that this is derived from
the fundamental social and psychological needs of human beings. To talk of
values at all, of course, makes one sound old-fashioned but one can be old-
fashioned without being out of date. Students, however, should certainly
challenge their professors by asking *why* they believe in this value or that,
and should open up an ongoing discussion with them. The fact is that certain
virtues must develop in individuals before others can grow. Trust must exist
in early stages of childhood if one is to avoid schizophrenia. The very basis
of community life is trust. But it may be well not to name the virtues too
definitively if one implies by this that their particular content is fixed. Nor
should one talk too much about freedom, but rather give each person the
greatest possible opportunity of being free. This will involve educating him
so that he attains a number of competences, intellectual and other, and thus is
liberated, at least to some extent, from the bondage of such self-indulgences
as, for example, sentimentality or the inability to take a stand on anything. In

the long run he must decide for himself what fixed values he wants to adhere to. But this is very different from saying that judgement about what are important values and what are not should fall into the hands of a group of adolescents.

We cannot in fact avoid having some conception of what is good for students if we have to run institutions of higher education; if we seek to escape it we are abdicating our responsibility. No young man or woman can become a fully developed individual unless he becomes also a member of society, not narcissistically preoccupied with himself.

In his concluding remarks to this session, Bryan Wilson developed at some length his thesis that what holds a modern society together is its secondary instrumental values. Its tax-structure, economic organization, defence involvement, the lines of authority through which it works, are the binding factors in such a social system, not an equally diffused commitment to a set of particular beliefs and ideals. Modern society is a consumer society, and in consequence many of its operations are dictated by popular demand. Men cannot be expected spontaneously to choose the more cultivated, the more civilized, and the more humane things when they are offered a free choice, and when they have not themselves been socialized to use informed discernment in their social behaviour. In societies that enjoy affluence and emphasize considerable equality in consumer power, the tension between democracy – particularly box-office democracy – and education becomes a patent fact. The correlation of income and cultivated taste, critical sense and educated values, has broken down in advanced societies. What is consumed is chosen by the less-informed and the little-educated sections of the population, and their democratic right to such choice is vigorously defended by those commercially interested in purveying commodities of small merit. We should not be deceived by that defence, however. It is often an ideological cover for eliminating certain choices – particularly those that need the care, sustained commitment, and expensive concern that goes with excellence. The actual choices are often manipulated in supposedly free, democratic consumer societies. The economies of scale, the benefits of oligopoly, and the imperatives of bureaucratic organization drive out as uneconomic, as 'no demand' items, those things in which, in many ways, the best features of human culture are encapsulated. By advertising, consumer choice can be made into a hollow thing. There is one other consequence of this *laissez-faire* orientation, and that is the emphasis on personal gains and personal status as against social good. Shared commitment to a set of social goals has disappeared. The values that men have in common are simply the rules of procedure and the norms of legitimate activity. Beyond this they have shared interests in the maintenance of a set of operations of an increasingly rational, technical, and mechanical kind that constitute the running of the state and its sub-divisions. The sense of society as an entity greater than the sum of its members has been lost; intrinsic concepts of a qualitative kind – of which the cultural inheritance is a large part – have been abandoned for much more naked individual interests. The cry of 'freedom and democracy' has facilitated this development, but it has resulted in extensive exploitation of men by one another, and has promoted widespread cynicism about civic virtue and social allegiances.

The old values that were inherent in the sense of shared involvement in community life have gone, and many young people now appear to feel the want of them in the anonymous, impersonal, and highly mobile world in which they live. They emphasize getting together, but because it has no shared primary concerns the collectivity of the young becomes not a community but a mob, whether as a student riot or as football hooligans; their activity is restless, sometimes aimless and wanton, sometimes focused towards vague goals formulated in unspecific terms by ideologues. The university is used as a context, but is often little more than a talk-shop, because it, too, has suffered the erosion of its values. The only structure that it enjoys, found in the discipline of learning and research, is often uncongenial to young people who believe savagely in togetherness as a value starkly in contrast with the isolation and individualism of the wider society. But since they, too, unreflectingly accept the *laissez-faire* morality of the wider society, their togetherness remains hollow, without the positive content of community. Their grievances do not stem from economic wants, but from the deprivation they feel in terms of values, shared concerns, enduring participation, and the stable contexts in which such things can arise.

The response of the young to the over-bureaucratized society with its box-office democracy is at once understandable and lamentable. We have put our young people into a situation where no effective guidance is available to them, and this is as true of the university situation as of any other. It is far from clear what people seek in universities – what the whole enterprise is really for. Diverse motivations and vague ideals conflict – and the university, like the society of which it is a part, is sustained not by value-consensus about goals, but by the ongoing procedures of its bureaucratic operations, by the interests of people with jobs, the complexities of administration, so intricate that no one has an overview of what the ultimate business of the organization really is. In such a context, how can we expect loyalty to study, let alone loyalty to an institution, which is more and more an impersonal mass of concrete, offices, and administrative procedures? Where persons interact not as persons but merely as role-players, trust – which is a personal quality – diminishes and loyalty atrophies. For young people, whose live experiences have been highly personal in the modern nuclear family situation, the university comes as a shock, and as an experience that rapidly disenchants, overturning in its bureaucratic operation so much of what has been laid down in earlier socialization processes. In the university, the youngster gets his real taste of the contradictions, falsehoods, manipulative devices, and the rampant cynicism that are increasingly the moral style of modern societies. Only energetic goal-directed activity promising speedy results is capable of engaging them, and so the millennialist enthusiasm is awakened, and intense political commitment (sometimes 'religious commitment' would be not an inappropriate description) elicited. Its real function is to give a sense of momentary purpose, a sense of certainty, and the chance to do something dramatic and important in a world otherwise routinized and trivial.

'Is what I am saying a warning or am I indeed giving up the ghost and accepting the inevitability of decline?' asked Wilson. 'I am not sure. The one hope of modern society might be the university, but the university is increasingly in captivity to the wider society that it should help to preserve from the new values that are increasingly espoused. Increasingly the politicians demand that universities should prove themselves to be useful in the direct ways that they – with the vision limited by the short years between elections – understand. What the universities might do towards educating men for a socially responsible part in a society with firm civic values might so readily be regarded by the wider public as so much talk, and highly expendable talk, since no concrete immediate results are to be seen from it. It is this that informs my pessimism.'

III

And so the way was opened, provocatively enough, for further thought about the personal position of the student in the university today. If many appear to feel the lack of a definitive set of values in a society itself full of uncertainties, it is to be expected that they will be inwardly uncertain of themselves and struggling for an identity. In a modern society, the older aristocratic attitude with its implicit assumption that adults know and younger people do not is obviously open to question – and attack.

For an increasing number of students the break between themselves and those 'in possession', between themselves and the over-thirties, seems absolute. It is necessary, some argue, to make a fresh start, almost at any cost.

The human links joining them with those in authority are either too tenuous to be recognized or ought, it seems to them, deliberately to be cut in the interests of life itself and their own development. The only possible line to take, in their view, may be one of anarchism, a destruction of meaningless continuities with the past and a proclamation of escape and new entry.

CHAPTER 3

The University and Personal Life
Student Anarchism and the Educational Contract
Northrop Frye

The first half of the twentieth century saw two world wars, each of which was started by a reactionary military autocracy operating mainly in Germany and ended in a major Communist revolution, first in Russia, then in China. The second half of the century is seeing the beginning of a new revolutionary development that seems to have more in common with anarchism than with Communism. The anarchist nature of the 'New Left' is often recognized, but usually without much sense of the traditions or context of anarchism.

In my own student days, during the Depression of the thirties, anarchism was a negligible force, at least on North American campuses, and the most influential radical movements were close to Marxism as interpreted by Stalin. The pro-Stalinist radical thought of himself as a 'worker' – that is, he had no quarrel with the work ethic of capitalism as an ethic, only with its economic setting. The metaphors of 'left wing' and 'right wing' were essential to him, because he thought in terms of an eventual separation and struggle for power between proletarian and bourgeois camps. His outlook was intensely international, and his tactics conformed to an internationally directed and organized strategy. His attitude to social issues was rational, every injustice and cruelty under capitalism being only what one would expect of that system. His attitude to the arts was deeply conservative, based mainly on the content of what was said or painted, or, at most, on allegorical reference. I remember a Canadian Communist magazine that condemned practically all twentieth-century Canadian painting as bourgeois formalism, and reproduced Victorian anecdotal pictures, depicting foreclosures of mortgages and the like, as examples of the genuine cultural tradition. The Stalinist's personal ethics, when consistent with his political outlook, tended to be rigorous:

self-indulgence or muddling one's mind with liquor and drugs was for him only the kind of thing that capitalism encouraged.

Hardly any of these characteristics are true of the present New Left. Like the nineteenth-century anarchists, contemporary radicals favour direct action, or 'confrontation', and favour also the kind of spontaneous uprising with no context in past or future, which is without precedence and without direction. The word 'existential' is often used approvingly to describe a political action which has no particular point. Unlike the Stalinist with his sacred texts of Marx and Lenin and his libraries of commentary on them, many who call themselves anarchists today have never heard of Kropotkin or Bakunin, or would take the slightest interest in them if they had. The nineteenth-century anarchists lost out to the more disciplined Communists in the struggle for control of the working class, partly because they tended to the extremes of either passivity or violence. There was the Arcadian anarchism of Morris's *News from Nowhere* and the terroristic anarchism of Conrad's *Secret Agent*. Similarly, radicals of today range from 'flower children' to assassins, though their main centre of gravity is of course in an intermediate activism. Their most effective revolutionary tactics are closer to Gandhi than to Lenin, and their great heroes are romantics like Che Guevara, who commands much the same kind of appeal, and for many of the same reasons, that Garibaldi commanded among British liberals a century ago. Even the Mao Tse-Tung of radical folklore seems more the guerrilla leader of thirty years ago than the present ruler of China.

The contemporary anarchist, like his nineteenth-century forebears, tends to localize his protests: he is well aware of the global context of contemporary unrest, but his own movement is likely to be confined to an immediate area of interest. Hence small separatist movements, like those in Quebec or Belgium, are also a part of contemporary radicalism. The conception of 'participatory democracy', which demands a thoroughgoing decentralization, is also anarchist in context. In some respects this fact presents a political picture almost the reverse of that of the previous generation. For today's radical the chief objects of loyalty during the thirties, trade unions and the revolutionary directives of Moscow, have become reactionary social forces, whereas some radical movements like the Black Panthers, which appear to have committed themselves both to violence and to racism, seem to descend from fascism, which also had anarchist affinities. Similarly, anarchism does not seek to create a 'working class': much of its dynamic comes from a bourgeois disillusionment with an over-productive society, and some types of radical protest, like those of the hippies, are essentially protests against the work ethic itself.

Both political movements show many analogies to the religious movements which preceded them. The attitude of the old-line Stalinist to the Soviet Union was very like that of a Roman Catholic to his Church, at least before the Second Vatican Council. There was a tremendous international institution which was the definitive interpreter of the Marxist revelation, and one could work effectively for the world-wide triumph of that revelation only from within the institution. Contemporary anarchists, at least those who can read, are more like the Puritans in the way that they seek a primitive gospel in the early work of Marx, before social and institutional Marxism began to corrupt it. Perhaps the similarity, however, is less with Puritanism than with the Anabaptists (who in the sixteenth century were also anarchists tending to the same polarity of pacifism and terrorism) and the more fervid evangelicals. Among religious bodies, those who are most dramatically increasing their membership today are the most uncritical and fundamentalist sects, and I doubt whether this is simply coincidence. There are some curious parallels between the present and the nineteenth-century American scene, between contemporary turn-on sessions and nineteenth-century ecstatic revivalism, between beatnik and hippy communes and some of the nineteenth-century Utopian projects. Stalinist Marxism had practically nothing in the American tradition to attach itself to, but anarchism is one of the central elements in American culture. Jefferson's states-rights and local autonomy thinking, Thoreau's civil disobedience, Lincoln's view of the Civil War as a revolution against the inner spirit of slavery, many cultural phenomena as diverse as *Huckleberry Finn*, the Chaplin films, and the *Cantos* of Ezra Pound, all show a radical dynamic that has affinities with anarchism. So did the populist movements at the turn of the century, which showed the same revolutionary ambivalence, tending equally to the left or to the right, that I have just noted in the contemporary scene. As for terroristic anarchism, one hardly needs to document that in so violent a country as America. The spirit of the late Joseph McCarthy is still around, but it is much more difficult for it to regard the current type of radical protest as un-American.

Anarchism has another advantage over Communism in its relation to the creative arts. The primary revolutionary categories of today tend to be psychological rather than economic, closer in many respects to Freud than to Marx, as we see in many of the writers who have tried to articulate the present radical mood, such as Herbert Marcuse. When the contemporary radical denounces intervention in Vietnam or Negro segregation, he does not think of these things as merely by-products of the contradictions of capitalism: he sees the emotional and imaginative factors in these situations as primary, and as the main elements to be opposed or supported. This primary place assigned to emotion and imagination means among other things that the anarchist is not hampered, as the orthodox Marxist was (and still is) hampered, by the canons of 'social realism' which judge mainly by content. A ferment in the arts, including a revival of oral poetry, is an integral part of today's radicalism, as, despite a great many spasmodic efforts, it never became in the radicalism of thirty years ago. The drug cults are another aspect of the same psychologically based activity. They are not intended merely to take one's mind off one's troubles: they are part of an attempt to recharge the batteries of the mind after they have been drained by disillusionment: that is, by the withdrawal of libido from consumer goods, or what advertising is still presenting as the good things of life.

The metaphors of left and right wing are still employed, but they have much less relevance to anarchism than to Communism. The Marxist saw a steadily widening split between two parts of society, an eventual struggle for power, and the final victory of the working class. The contemporary radical seems to think rather in terms of a single society, with localized cells and nuclei of radicalism agitating and transforming it from within. Communism was intensely teleological in spirit: every Communist-directed strike or demonstration was one step in the great campaign of class struggle and revolutionary triumph. The anarchism of today seems almost as indifferent to the future as to the past: one protest will be followed by another, because even if one issue is resolved society will still be 'sick', but there appears to be no clear programme of taking control or assuming permanent responsibility in society.

If I am right, then anarchism is committed by the logic of its position to becoming increasingly non-violent. Violence appears to be an inescapable stage in sobering up an unwilling conservatism and in impressing it with the sense that it is not dealing with children. An ascendant class tends to make an indulgent comic strip out of any group from which unrest seems likely: thus we had the Paddy-and-his-pig Irishman in nineteenth-century England, the Rastus-and-Jemima comic or lovable Negro in white America, and so on. But once the pattern of opposition is established, the effectiveness of violence diminishes. Naturally this does not happen easily, violence being the opiate of the revolutionary: even university students are strongly affected by the 'let's do something and not just talk about it' syndrome. But where there is no really serious conception of a climactic struggle for power in which the victor achieves permanent authority, 'talk' is the final mode of radical action, and the form that its ultimate confrontation has to take. I spoke of the affinity between some contemporary anarchism and fascism, with its belief in violence as being in a sense its own end. In Nazi Germany this took the form of a melancholy *Götterdämmerung* nihilism, whose goal appeared to be not so much its professed one of world-rule as annihilation in some heroic last stand, a second Roncesvalles or Thermopylae. This mood is, I think, intelligible to today's anarchist, who has inherited all the heroic gloom of existentialism, as it was utterly unintelligible to the Stalinist radical. I remember when Yeats's *Last Poems* appeared in 1939, and how brusquely their sardonic bleakness was dismissed as 'morbid' by the radicals of that day. But they speak with a peculiar and haunting eloquence now, even to the most self-righteous of student radicals.

I spoke a moment ago of the anarchist strain in American culture: another example of it is the work of Edgar Allan Poe, whose significance as a portent of many aspects of contemporary literature it is hard to do full justice to. Poe wrote an essay called 'The Poetic Principle' in which he asserted that a long poem was a contradiction in terms, that all existing long poems of genuine quality consisted of moments of intense poetic experience stuck together with connective tissues of narrative or argument which were really versified prose. The fact that this doctrine was preposterous so far as it was applied to Homer or Milton did not prevent it from having a tremendous influence on future poetry, including the French *symbolistes* and Pound and Eliot in England. What happens in literature is very likely to happen in life as a whole a century or so later. In Poe's day, and in fact up to about 1945, one of the most solidly rooted assumptions in middle-class Western culture was the sense of continuity in time. That is, life was thought of teleologically, as something that contained a developing purpose and direction. Some gave this feeling a religious reference: for many Christians the essence of Christianity was in the renewed meaning which the Incarnation had given to human history. In Marxist thought the 'historical process', which is an irresistible force on the side of those who accept it, played a similar role. The artist, if faced with hostility or misunderstanding, assumed, with Max Beerbohm's Enoch Soames, that he would be vindicated by posterity, for whom he was really writing. Others, like Spengler in *The Decline of the West*, saw the teleology in history from the opposite point of view, as an organic process that first matured and then declined. For a great number of bourgeois intellectuals, the doctrine of evolution afforded a scientific proof of teleology in human life, and the doctrine of progress in history, though of course much older than Darwin, became increasingly a mythical analogy of evolution. H. G. Wells in his *Outline of History* (1920) concludes a chapter on 'Early Thought' with a picture of human sacrifice at Stonehenge and an appended comment: 'And amidst the throng march the appointed human victims, submissive, helpless, staring towards the distant smoking altar at which they are to die – that the harvests may be good and the tribe increase . . . To that had life progressed 3,000 or 4,000 years ago from its starting-place in the slime of the tidal beaches.' The death-wish in human life, so dramatically emergent in the First World War, could hardly be ignored by anyone writing in 1920: but although the final remark is intended ironically, it echoes with the complacency of the 'long view'.

One of the most striking cultural facts of our time is the disappearance of this teleological sense. We tend now to think of our lives as being, like the long poem as described by Poe, a discontinuous sequence of immediate experiences. What holds them together, besides mere survival, can only be some kind of voluntary and enforced ideology. Thus the artist may keep his life continuous by a belief in creativity, the businessman by a belief in productivity, the religious man by a belief in God, the politician by a belief in policy. But the more intense the immediate experience, the more obviously its context in past and future time drops away from it. The word 'absurd' refers primarily to the disappearance of the sense of continuity in our day. It is not so much that the world around us no longer suggests any meaning or purpose concealed in its design: that in itself, as Robbe-Grillet says, means not that the world is absurd, but merely that it is there. The sense of absurdity comes from time, not space; from the feeling that life is not a continuous absorption of experiences into a steadily growing individuality, but a discontinuous series of encounters between moods and situations which keep bringing us back to the same point.

In this situation there is one positive feature of great importance: the sharpening of moral sensitivity. I spoke of the complacency inherent in the progressive 'long view', and belief in progress can easily become the most morally callous of all beliefs. The thing about Russian Marxism that most sickened its bourgeois supporters was the readiness with which it could (and still can, evidently) embark on a massacre, an invasion of a small independent country, or a deliberately induced famine, for the sake of the greater good that such procedures would bring, from its own point of view, to posterity. In a now neglected book, *Ends and Means*, Aldous Huxley pointed out how means can never lead to ends, because they condition and eventually replace those ends. George Orwell's *1984*, one of the most important books recording the transition in mood from the last to the present generation, shows more vividly how the donkey's carrot of progress can become an indefinite prolonging of misery. It seems to me admirable that contemporary radicals should be concerned with the rights of those who are alive now, and should be protesting against the Vietnam war because it is killing innocent people at this moment, refusing to listen to any long-term rationalizations about the crusade against Communism or the white man's burden.

A less attractive side of the same situation is the general panic, even hysteria, that the loss of reference to temporal context has left us with. The most obvious form of this panic is the flight from the past: the anxiety to be up to date, to be rid of unfashionable ideas and techniques, to condemn everything unsatisfactory with the same formula, that it is too cumbersome and obsolete for the unimpeded movement assumed to be necessary today. A society with a revolutionary basis, like American society, is often inclined to be impatient of history and tradition. 'History is bunk,' said Henry Ford, at one end of the social scale: 'I don't take no stock in dead people,' said Huckleberry Finn, at the other. The future, in such a view, cannot be the outcome of the past: it is a brand new future, which may be implicit in the present but is to be built out of the materials of the present by an act of will, which cannot operate until it has been released from the past. The strongly negative mood in today's radicalism, the tendency to be against rather than for, is consistent with this: whatever is defined is hampering, and only the undefined is free.

The resulting crisis of spirit is a far-reaching one. That it has caused a political crisis goes without saying. But there is also a crisis in the arts and in the intellect. The creative artist cannot appeal to posterity, as he no longer assumes that the future will be continuous with the present, and, more important, the impetus to produce the 'great' work of art has itself been considerably weakened. For, traditionally, the great work of art became a classic, that is, a work connecting the present with the past. One sometimes wonders if the age of *great* writers or painters or composers is over, and if what is in front of us culturally is not rather a diffused creative energy, much or most of it taking fairly ephemeral forms, a general rather than a specialized social product. Again, there is a crisis in the intellect, for the assumption that science and scholarship are progressively developing, in a semi-autonomous way, is in many quarters questioned or denied. But above all, the crisis is a religious one. The problems connected with the discontinuous and the absurd are problems affecting the way man lives his life, affecting his conceptions of his nature and destiny, affecting his sense of identity. They are, in short, existential problems, and existentialism has been formulated mainly either in the explicitly religious context of Kierkegaard and Unamuno, or in the context of Heidegger and Sartre, which is no less religious for being atheistic. I feel that contemporary radicalism is deeply, even desperately, religious both in its anxieties and in its assertions: that it cannot, for the most part, accept the answers given its questions by the existing religious bodies, and that a great deal of student unrest is based on a feeling that the university ought to be trying to answer such questions, but cannot do so until it has been shaken loose from the 'establishment'. That this is a misunderstanding of what the university is and can do is undoubtedly true. But the questions remain, as urgent as ever, and some people in the universities ought to try to deal with them sympathetically, as questions, before they freeze into immature dogmas.

There are two social conceptions so deeply rooted in our experience that they can be presented only as myths. One is the social contract, the myth which attempts to explain the nature of the conditioning we accept by getting born. The other is the Utopia, the myth of an ideal social contract. Both these myths have religious affiliations: the contract is connected with the alienation myth of the Fall of Man, and the Utopia with the transcendence myth of the City of God. The overtones of the social contract myth are ironic, sometimes tragic. Before we were born, we were predestined to join a social continuum at a certain historical point: we belonged to the twentieth century and the middle class even as embryos in the womb. We belong to something before we are anything, and the first datum of our lives is the set of social conditions and assumptions that we are already committed to. The conservative temperament is strongly attracted by the positive aspects of this contract. He feels that his own development is a matter of growing organically out of the roots of his social context. What is presented to him at birth, he feels, is a set of loyalties given to him before he is capable of choosing them. To try to reject what one is already committed to can only lead to confusion and chaos, both in one's own life and in society. Further, we discover in the permanence and continuity of social institutions, such as Church and State, something that not only civilizes man, but adds a dimension of significance to his otherwise brief and insignificant life.

Such, it seems to me, is the conservative view of the social contract, expounded so lucidly by Burke and still being proclaimed, over a century later, by T. S. Eliot. The radical view of it focuses on the uncritical element in our inherited loyalties, as expressed in such maxims as 'my country right or wrong'. Maturity and development, the radical feels, are a matter of becoming aware of our conditioning, and, in so becoming aware, of making a choice between presented and discovered loyalties. This attitude, developing through Rousseau and Marx, reached a further stage with the existentialism that followed the Second World War. Traditionally, the difference between sanity and hysteria, between reality and hallucination, had always been that sanity and reality lasted longer, and were continuous in a way that their opposites could not be. The rise of Nazi Germany suggested the possibility of a social hysteria indefinitely prolonged by the control of communications.

But perhaps what we have been calling sanity and reality is an unconsciously induced hysteria, and the way to deliverance is through and beyond the loyalty of uncritical acceptance. The only real loyalty, then, is the voluntary or self-chosen loyalty.

This is the state of mind which dominates the radical of today: an intensely Utopian state of mind which feels that it owes loyalty only to a social ideal not yet in existence. The Viet Nam issue, particularly, raises the question of what was called, in the title of an indifferent book of twenty years ago, the meaning of treason. In Dante's *Inferno*, in Shakespeare's tragedies, the traitor, the man who breaks the social contract assigned him at birth, is the lowest of criminals. In our day the word 'treason', almost without our realizing it, has joined the word 'heresy' as a word that could once intimidate, but is now only a Hallowe'en mask.

We notice that the prose romances called Utopias, from Campanella to Edward Bellamy, have been rather compulsive and anxiety-ridden stories. In literature, at any rate, they have made far less imaginative impact than the Utopian satires, such as *Gulliver's Travels*, which ought perhaps to be thought of rather as satires on the social contract. Some of the nineteenth-century Utopias, like Bellamy's *Looking Backward*, might have looked attractive at the time in contrast to the misery and anarchy of unrestricted *laissez-faire*. But reading them now, we simply cannot believe the authors' assertions that the citizens of their ideal states are perfectly happy: if they are, we can only feel, as we feel with all victims of brainwashing, that there is something subhuman about them. The reason for this feeling is not hard to see. The conservative who accepts the loyalties presented to him by his society is, to use two stock words of our time, committed and engaged. Commitment and engagement, in themselves, as just said, contain an uncritical element, and tend also to be somewhat humourless, because, confronted with a genuine absurdity in society, their instinct is to rationalize the absurdity instead of recognizing it. The Utopian attitude begins in detachment, but at that point conceives of an alternative institution and transfers its loyalties to that. This alternative institution will of course also demand commitment, and of a more intense kind: it will tolerate much less dissent and criticism, much less sense of the absurd or ironic, than the conservative outlook, unless frightened by crisis, permits.

It seems to me that the Marxist revolutionary movement is the definitive form of what I have called the Utopian attitude of mind, the transfer of loyalty from one's native society to another society still to be constructed. When Engels contrasted Utopian with 'scientific' socialism he was really completing the Utopian argument. In a world like ours a limited Utopia, confined to one definite place, is an empty fantasy: it must be a world-wide transformation of the whole social order or it is nothing. But for it to be this it must be conceived, not as an *a priori* rational construct, but as the *telos* of history, the end to which history points. The 'scientific' element in Marxist socialism, then, is a religious belief in the teleology of history.

Marxism envisages a social cleavage in which the possibility of argument, discussion, or what is now called 'dialogue' disappears. One does not need to answer an argument: one needs only to identify it as coming from our side or theirs. It is not talk but a planned sequence of actions leading to an ultimate confrontation or showdown that is important. I suggested earlier that the contemporary anarchist radical, though he adopts much of this attitude, is really a post-Marxist revolutionary, forced by the logic of his situation from action into 'dialogue'. He has no real sense of a proletarian society, and his protest is, primarily and essentially, protest, not a mere prelude to taking power himself. Does this mean, then, that the end of contemporary anarchism is compromise with conservatism? To some extent this may be true: I think democracy is in the initial stages of working out a two-party opposition far less cumbersome and hypocritical, and representing a more genuine division of attitudes, than the one now represented in our parliaments and congresses. But it seems to me that the real end at which anarchism is aiming is very different. (We may note in passing that even anarchism cannot avoid all teleology.)

The conservative preference is for commitment and engagement: the Utopian, Marxist, or existential radical begins in detachment, but annuls this detachment in favour of a new commitment. The end of commitment and engagement is the community: the end of detachment, then, is clearly the individual. This is not however an antithesis: nobody ought to be a mere creature of a community, like an insect; nobody can be a pure individual detached from his society. I spoke earlier of the vogue for certain words which seem for a time to have a magical significance. Twenty years ago one such word was 'maturity', now out of fashion for obvious reasons. It does seem to me to have some meaning, if not a magical one. The child, and the adolescent in a different way, oscillates between loyalty to the community of his contemporaries and moods of rebelliousness and introversion. As one matures, one's social mask becomes more difficult to remove, and one becomes resigned to a continuous social role. But that very process of adjusting to society is what makes the genuine individual possible. The barriers designed to protect the individual from encroachment from without have to dissolve before he can realize that he is not a real individual until his energy flows freely into his social relations. What is true of personal life is true of society. Primitive societies are rigidly ritualized ones; only the mature society permits the genuine individual to emerge. By doing so it does not fall apart: it merely transfers more of its order from external compulsion to internal discipline, from reflex response to the habit of learning. The artist, too, often begins as a member of a school, issuing manifestoes and the like, but tends to draw away from such affiliations as he finds his own style. Yet his growing individuality is also a measure of his social acceptance.

If we take a second look at our greatest Utopians, Plato and More, we notice that Socrates in the *Republic* is not concerned about setting up his ideal state anywhere: what he is concerned about is the analogy between his ideal state and the structure of the wise man's mind, with its reason, will, and desire corresponding to the philosopher-king, soldiers, and artisans of the political myth. The ideal state exists, so far as we know, only in such minds, which will obey its laws whatever society they are actually living in. Similarly, More calls his ideal state Utopia, meaning nowhere. Hythloday (the 'babbler'), who has been to Nowhere, has returned a revolutionary communist, convinced that nothing can be done with Europe until it has been destroyed and a replica of the Utopia set up in its place. But More himself, to whom the story is being told, suggests using the knowledge of Utopia rather as a means of bringing about an improvement in European society from within. Plato and More realize that while the wise man's mind is rigidly disciplined, and while the mature state is ordered, we cannot take the analogy between the disciplined mind and the disciplined state too literally. For Plato certainly, and for More probably, the wise man's mind is a ruthless dictatorship of reason over appetite, achieved by control of the will. When we translate this into its social equivalents of a philosopher-king ruling workers by storm troopers (not 'guardians', as in Jowett, but 'guards'), we get the most frightful tyranny. But the real Utopia is an individual goal, of which the disciplined society is an allegory. The reason for the allegory is that the Utopian ideal points beyond the individual to a condition in which, as in Kant's kingdom of ends, society and individual are no longer in conflict, but have become different aspects of the same human body.

Not only does contemporary radicalism include separatist movements, but it is itself intensely separatist in feeling, and hence the question of where one stops separating becomes central. One feels that the more extreme radicals of our time are simply individualists. The more strident the anarchist slogan (e.g.: 'Let's have a revolution first and find out why later'), the more clearly the individualistic basis of its attitude appears, and the more obviously the Utopian attitude is a projection of it. In the Utopianism of Plato and More the traditional authoritarian structure of society was treated as an allegory of the dictatorship of reason in the wise man's mind. We do not now think of the wise man's mind as a dictatorship of reason: in fact we do not think about the wise man's mind at all. We think rather, in Freudian terms, of a mind in which a principle of normality and balance is fighting for its life against a thundering herd of chaotic impulses, which cannot be simply suppressed but must be frequently indulged and humoured, always allowed to have their say however silly or infantile it may be. In short, we think of the mind as a participating democracy: necessary to live with, yet cumbersome, exasperating, and not an ideal but a process. In such an analogy there is no place for the inner-directed person who resists society until death, like Socrates, or More himself: society is divided and the 'individual', despite the etymology of the word, self-divided.

In this process the refusal of all loyalty and authority, the attempt of the individual to assert himself against his whole social context, is one such infantile impulse, to be listened to and ignored. The mature individual, who has come to some working arrangement with his society, is looking rather for a loyalty which is coherent and objective enough to create a community, but commands an authority that fulfils and does not diminish the individual. Such a conception of authority is the kind of authority that education embodies: the authority of logic and reason, of demonstrable and repeatable experiment, of established fact, of compelling imagination. Formerly, the sources of loyalty and authority were the social institutions which formed the civilized context of individual life; but these institutions have really been projected from the total body of reason and imagination represented by the arts and sciences. In our age the mortality of social institutions is what impresses us, and when they can no longer command genuine loyalty or authority, we can only return to their source. Further, when we take a third look at the greatest writers on the social contract and the Utopia, Plato, More, Locke, Rousseau, we begin to suspect that they are not really writing about contracts or Utopias at all, but about the theory of education. Perhaps the social contract and the ideal state are also projections, into the past and the future respectively, of a source of social authority that sits in the middle of our society, and which I shall call the educational contract.

By the educational contract I mean the process by which the arts and sciences, and their methods of logic, experiment, amassing of evidence, and imaginative presentation, actually operate as a source of authority in society. The authority of the social contract is a *de facto* authority: it exists and it may be rationalized, but it lacks a genuinely ideal dimension, and thereby keeps social ideals in an empty world of wish or hope. Conservatives cluster around *de facto* authority and radicals around ideals, but as long as they are kept apart, the revolutionary argument, that the Utopian spirit can only gather force on its side and destroy the existing contract, seems unanswerable. The educational contract makes it possible for both sides to submit their social attitudes to a tribunal that not only respects but includes them both. What is needed is a free authority, something coherent enough to create a community, but not an authority in the sense of applying external compulsion.

This conception of an educational contract was the main contribution made by the great development of educational theory in nineteenth-century England. It is the area of free thought and discussion which is at the centre of John Stuart Mill's view of liberty, and which is thought of as a kind of intellectual counterpart of Parliament. It differs from Parliament, for Mill, in that the liberals can never have a majority, which is why democracy has to function as an illogical but deeply humane combination of majority rule and minority right. In Matthew Arnold the educational contract is called culture, and Arnold is explicit about its being the source of genuine authority in society and at the same time operating in a Utopian direction, breaking down the barriers of class conflict and heading in the direction of a classless society. Newman's distinction between useful and liberal knowledge is parallel, when we realize that it is a distinction between two aspects of education, not two kinds of education. All forms of education are at once useful and liberal: they help us to locate ourselves in existing society and they help to develop us as individuals, detached but not withdrawn from that society. Of course Mill's area of discussion, Arnold's culture, and Newman's liberal knowledge are conceptions far wider than the university, but the university is obviously their engine-room, and their power can last only so long as the university keeps operating. The university, then, is the source of free authority in society, not as an institution, but as the place where the appeal to reason, experiment, evidence, and imagination is continuously going on.

It is on this basis, perhaps, that we can deal with the demand of student activists for relevance in relation to personal as distinct from social life. Using Newman's distinction, there are two aspects to this demand: a utilitarian aspect and a liberal one. The utilitarian one is for subjects of education to conform to what the student thinks to be his present relation to society, so that, for instance, twentieth-century literature would be more relevant than medieval literature. This is, of course, an immature demand, and should be met with massive and uncompromising resistance. In literature, which is what I know best, every major writer may be studied in his relation to his own time, or in his relation to the communicative power that makes him relevant to us. To concentrate solely on the latter distorts him by translating him entirely into our own modes of thought. When we study him in relation to his own time we are led into a different kind of culture, with unfamiliar assumptions, beliefs, and values. But contact with these is what expands our own view of human possibilities, and it is what is irrelevant, in the narrow sense, about what we study that is the liberalizing element in it. The same principle enabled the classical training of humanism, from the sixteenth to the nineteenth centuries, to be a far more genuinely liberal education than it is often given credit for being. The study of an essentially alien civilization, even one which was at the historical roots of our own, was probably a much better preparation a century ago for civil service in India than cost accounting or personnel management.

The other conception of relevance needs to be more seriously considered. It rests, in the first place, on a division between two types of academic discipline, often identified with the humanities and the sciences, though not quite coterminous with them. The word 'scientific' implies among other things a desire to escape from controversy, to rest one's case on evidence, logical and mathematical demonstration or open experiment, which are, as far as possible, beyond the reach of the kind of argument that attacks the validity of its postulates. The assumption is that while what is true today may be insufficiently true tomorrow, still anything that has ever been true – really true, not just believed – will always be continuous with whatever is going to be true. But there are other subjects which deal, not with the world around man (the sciences), but with the world that man is trying to create. These subjects can never escape from controversy or radical questioning, because existential values are built into them. I should call them the mythological subjects: they include large areas of history, political theory, religion, philosophy, psychology, anthropology, and sociology, and the key to them is literature, the laboratory of myths. It is these subjects with which student activism today is largely concerned. The sciences are to a degree impersonal, but the mythological subjects have to be more personally taught. There is always something of Mark Hopkins and the log about them, whereas the sciences can never dispense with complicated apparatus, and are quite right in refusing to have anything to do with any logs that do not roll.

We have to start again with the decline of the sense of continuity and teleology, already mentioned. Knowledge is, of course, and always must be, continuous and structured. A generation ago, this feature of knowledge was taken for granted, and the continuity of the university was accepted, even by the most radical, as a part of the general continuity of human existence. Much student unrest today springs from what is actually a very ancient conception, though never expressed now, so far as I know, in its traditional terms: the superiority of wisdom to knowledge. Knowledge is knowledge *of* something: wisdom is a sense of the potential rather than the actual, a practical knowledge ready to meet whatever eventualities may occur, rather than a specific knowledge of this or that subject. Formerly, wisdom was associated with seniority, it being assumed that experience carried with it a residual continuity which gave older people a fuller perspective. Or, as Yeats says, carrying the same principle one logical step further: 'Wisdom is the property of the dead.' The loss of belief in any form of continuity has led to a feeling of the necessity of breaking through the habits of knowledge. What many students today want is some guidance in how to deal with their own sense of the discontinuity in experience. Knowledge for them is propaedeutic: one needs only the minimum of knowledge that will introduce one to the great existential issues. After the three R's, the three A's: anxiety, alienation, absurdity. Instead of entering into a structure of knowledge, one seeks the higher wisdom through 'unstructured' means, chiefly informal discussion. In this quest the word 'dialogue' has acquired a portentous verbal magic, like the ninety-nine names of God in Kabbalism.

This movement began with the impatience of students with instructors who regarded their teaching as a second-rate activity and an obstacle to research. As research is largely a matter of specialization, this meant that the instructor who was bored by his teaching was really attaching social status to his ignorance rather than to his knowledge. The feeling that the quest for the esoteric needs to be pulled down periodically into the ordinary area of communication was undoubtedly normal and healthy, and throws a very different light on what Sir Charles Snow, in his account of the two cultures, stigmatized as the 'Luddite' attitude of the humanities. Humanists always have to be Luddites to some extent, but what they are breaking are not machines but the cells of specialization that are walled in from the human community.

But as the student protest has gone on, it has sometimes tended to take an anti-intellectual form, to become, in its most extreme versions, a repudiation of the educational contract itself, a refusal to appeal to reason or experience or history or anything except emotional reflex. In its anti-intellectual form it joins on, naturally, to the anti-intellectualism of the past. Fifty years ago we had Stephen Leacock and his recipe for starting a university with informal discussions among students, going out to 'hire a few professors' when he got around to it. This in turn reflected the old Oxbridge mystique of the commonroom, the myth of the Sitting Bull, the rationalization of the fact that for an ascendant class, as such, the point of a university education was in its social contacts rather than in its intellectual training. Its reappearance in our day is part of the general confusion among students about whether they want to be a privileged class or an intellectual proletariat.

What seems not to have been noticed is the fact that there is really no such thing as 'dialogue'. Just as some children try to behave like the heroes and heroines in the stories they read, so 'dialogue' is a literary convention taken to be a fact of life. The literary convention comes from Plato, and we notice how clearly aware Plato is of the fact that unstructured discussion is a collection of solipsistic monologues. The etymology of the word symposium points to the fact that the presence of liquor is necessary to make the members of such a group believe in their own wit. Nothing *happens* in Plato until one person, generally Socrates, assumes control of the argument and the contributions of the others are largely reduced to punctuation. This means, not that dialogue has turned into monologue or democracy into dictatorship, but that Socrates had discovered a dialectic, and has committed himself to following it wherever it may lead. From there on, Socrates and his listeners are united in a common vision of something which is supreme over both.

Education can take place only where there is communication, which means the conveying of information from A to B, or a discussion united by the presence of a specific subject. Such discussion is educational in proportion as it is structured. This takes us back to the principle that everything connected with the university, with education, and with knowledge, must be structured and continuous. Until this is grasped, there can be no question of 'learning to think for oneself'. In education one cannot think at random. However imaginative we may be, and however hard we try to remove our censors and inhibitions, thinking is an acquired habit founded on practice, like playing the piano. How well we do it depends on how much of it we have done, and it is never autonomous. We do not start to think about a subject: we enter into a body of thought and try to add to it. It is only out of a long discipline in continuous and structured thinking, whether in the university, in a profession, or in the experience of life, that any genuine wisdom can emerge. The fox in Aesop was wiser than he knew: grapes prematurely snatched from the highest branches really are sour.

What is it, then, that the more restless and impatient students of our time are trying to break through their university training to get? I suggested earlier that they are seeking guidance to the existential questions which have largely overwhelmed what confidence they ever had in the discipline of thought. In other words, their quest is a religious one, and they are looking for answers to religious questions that the university, *qua* university, cannot answer. I do not mean by this that such students should be sent to the churches: the number of people there who can deal with their questions is no greater than it is in the universities, and they start from postulates that relatively few students accept. The scholar can only deal with these questions as a person, not as a scholar, but no one who would turn away a serious student on the ground that these questions were out of his field deserves the title of teacher. The professor in our day is in the same position as the modern doctor who has to try to cure *Weltschmerz* as well as bellyaches. The doctor may long for the simple old days when hysteria and hypochondria were specific disturbances of the womb or the abdomen, but he is not living in those days, and must struggle as best he can with the intangible.

Nothing seems less likely today than a return to the introspection of the Eisenhower decade, yet I cannot help feeling that such a return is just around the corner. Student unrest is not a genuinely social movement: it has no roots in a specific social injustice, as Negro unrest has. Like the beatniks, who have gone, the hippies, who are on the skids, and the LSD cults, which are breaking up, student unrest is not so much social as an aggregate of individual bewilderments, frustrations, disillusionments, and egotisms. It takes patience to grant students everything that can be granted in the way of representation on decision-making bodies which are restructuring the curriculum, and to look with a friendly eye on the founding of 'free' universities, which, as just said, are really religious organizations. The reward of the patience is that students soon come to realize that these things are not what they want, and that, after every possible effort to climb over the walls has failed, there is no avenue of real escape except the open door in front of them.

INTERCHAPTER

I

Response to Northrop Frye – JAMES JARRETT

Student radicals are a diverse lot. Indeed I find it particularly uncooperative of students not to present a greater degree of uniformity for those of us who would study them. Their differences are not only from each other, but also from the past. If many of them are Marxists, theirs is a new kind of deviation. Even Marcuse, who sees students as the replacement of the television-opiated workers in the revolutionary forefront, is not safe from their barbs. And if they are anarchists it is anarchism with a difference – indeed with such differences that it becomes exceedingly risky to speak, as Professor Frye occasionally does, of what the logic of anarchism implies, where anarchism is taken as a position already historically defined. And yet such terms are unavoidable. We are almost desperate for a vocabulary with which to describe essentially new phenomena, and 'anarchism' surely must still mean a hatred of authority, regularity, repression, bureaucracy, bigness, and an affection for spontaneity, new freedom, individuality – or at least radical localism of groups.

Educationally, it seems to me, this is chiefly being manifested in opposition to formal examinations, grading, stabilized curricula, lecturing, academically selective admissions procedures, and, perhaps above all, to requirements with respect to what courses one must take, what bodies of knowledge one must become competent in for a degree.

I expect the single greatest change in American universities and colleges in the next decade to be in the disruption of the courses of studies, with a virtual abolition of general education requirements as they have been known, and an unbelievably greater emphasis upon student-initiated and in many cases student-conducted courses. For the moment anyway, I give this as a value-neutral statement, a kind of prophecy, but it occurs to me that a great many of the things that can be said about student dissenters today almost require of us a polarity in our discourse. Ideally, this should amount to a dialectical argument, but I will have to be content with suggesting how a number of statements about today's students can be put either positively or negatively, either in a way to make us cheer, or in a way to make us groan with despair. These can be taken either as differences among students or as differences in the way of perceiving what students are up to.

Thus:

Students are now inclined towards activism, to real involvement in political and educational matters. For years we have been criticizing them for apathy and passivity. Now they say: if the established powers do not respond to our pleas, we will force them to respond by demonstrations, by disobedience, by strikes. Students today believe in participatory democracy – that is, not just formal and empty democratic rhetoric and machinery, but full involvement of people – i.e. students – in the governance of institutions that directly affect their lives – such as universities.

Students are now strongly bent toward violence. Observe how the various non-violent strategies of the civil rightists have been abandoned for the action which will invite, very nearly require, 'police brutality'. Students today are anti-democratic. They really don't believe in hearing the opposition out. They are impatient of discussion. They believe that if a speaker is saying unpleasant things he ought to be booed off the stage, the meeting disrupted. Free discussion of issues is a bourgeois prejudice.

Students today are showing us a new kind of free, uninhibited behaviour, one that betrays the Puritanism latent in the mores of even the most liberal of us aged ones. They are showing us the superficiality of the affluence we tried so hard to achieve, the madness of a world presided over by the bitch goddess success, the apotheosis of the entertainer, the madness of war.

That is, they are hedonists. As someone recently remarked, here is the first set of revolutionaries in history who are self-indulgent. Some of us in Berkeley used to make a careful distinction between the New Left and the Pot Left, but the distinction has got blurred: the dependence upon drugs, the use of bizarre clothing, the turning away from the world of work, are now also characteristics of many of the political revolutionaries.

The students of today, as Dr Frye has told us, are oriented in the present. They show us the dangers of talking only of the safely past, and insist upon rubbing our noses in the ugliness of the world we inhabit. I am reminded of a scene, from a film shown shortly after the Berkeley Free Speech Movement crisis, in which a father talking to his son said, 'Why can't you realize at least this much: that your generation didn't invent radicalism? – that I myself was a radical. I myself participated in the uprisings at UCLA in 1932. I was out there on the campus demonstrating and making speeches. Why can't you understand this?' The boy paused; then very gently and with proper respect, said: 'Dad, we're not much interested in the *history* of radicalism.'

That is, they are anti-historical. They act as if the world only just began. Their anti-historicism quickly degenerates into a more sweeping anti-intellectualism, as the intellectual tradition becomes for them identified with all the repressive, or at least complacent, forces of society.

They are egalitarian. They push us beyond the safely liberal rhetoric of slow evolutionary progress toward greater freedoms and better-distributed wealth, and insist that now, not later, the downtrodden in society must at last be given their due, or indeed rather more than their seeming due, as slight compensation for a long history of abuses.

That is, the students throw out all sorts of standards. They talk about admitting people to universities regardless of their capacity for scholarship, simply because the tests have been biased and discriminatory. They pretend that there is no real difference in intelligence or other human qualities, and go far towards depriving us of intellectual and cultural leaders.

The students are, far more than their elders, inclined towards a *principled* ethic, rather than a merely conformist ethic. There have even been some studies by social psychologists that show this, and Keniston's[1] studies do too. Students today, as Dr Frye suggests, are existentialist, many of them, and concerned about what he called religious questions.

In their contempt for bourgeois values, however, some are capable of the most wanton violence and destructiveness, not excluding murderous attacks and arson – all in the name of a better world and apparently oblivious of the right-wing repressiveness they are almost certain to invoke, as in the case, say, of Greece.

I do not intend these pairings as irresoluble logical antinomies nor yet as an exercise in valuational relativism. I do hope that they suggest some justification for the ambivalence many of us feel toward the dissident students' position.

I will conclude with a remark about the literary aspects of Dr Frye's paper. Even more than he, I would stress the point that this is, in the current phrase, a 'Now'-generation. This makes it very difficult for professors of literature (and others) who say 'But I have Yeats and Eliot and Wallace Stevens on my reading-list – what do you mean by saying I'm not up to date?' But these are writers who are approximately as dead and gone as Browning, as irrelevant as Tennyson. And the fact that these professors themselves are not ashamed that they do not believe in or know about the

[1] *The Uncommitted*, New York, 1960.

literary heroes of their students is perhaps some confirmation of the students' point. The students themselves are talking not about *1984* but about *A Clockwork Orange*, not about Eliot or even Dylan Thomas, but about Robert Creeley and Gary Snyder, and so forth.

This is not just a matter of being up to date. There is a distrust of – sometimes a contempt for – the great works of literature and our great men of the past: a tendency to say about poems that they are, and probably should be, ephemeral productions, to be written and put up some place to be taken down tomorrow – or not even written down at all, but oral. Along with this different conception of what a poem or an artefact is or how it functions, there is a tendency to disregard and hold in contempt traditional art and scholarship, especially if it shows corresponding contempt for the present, or if it enshrines the genteel tradition, aestheticism, and political non-activism.

We of the professoriate are not ready to own up to the fact that these attitudes are in part a rejection of us as models. Willy-nilly, we teach not just what we know but also what we are, and we do appear to a great many students as pussyfooting, unadventurous, unwilling to make sacrifices on behalf even of our strongly professed ideals such as peace, freedom for all, equality of opportunity, the abolition of poverty. To their cry for compensatory education for the ethnic minorities they say we have only countered with Rigour and Standards. We are, more than we can know, for many of them the Up-Tight generation. Are we beyond their help or they beyond ours?

II

Most of the discussion following Frye's paper and Jarrett's response to it dealt with two main issues: the effect upon the scope and content of higher education of accepting that for modern man the sense of stability has largely disappeared: life comes to many, and especially younger people, as 'a discontinuous sequence of immediate experiences'; and the preservation of lines of communication with students.

Roy Niblett discussed the kinds of approach to knowledge that were likely to be meaningful to students in the times ahead. 'Start where they are' is a familiar enough maxim, generally approved. But in days like these how, doing that, are you to take them somewhere else? Is logical, sequential thinking the only sure way to wisdom? It is undeniable that a preoccupation with the technical is one way of escaping from meaninglessness into certainty – the techniques of controlling machinery or fiscal arrangements or consumer demand can be learned, and year by year with increasing efficiency. But such certainty is limited in range and often without sufficient relevance to human need, especially individual and interior need. Much student discontent and some student anarchism is existentialist in tradition, emphasizing the importance of the student's feeling involved and committed (even if not necessarily to the same things two days running). It is difficult for a philosopher following the English tradition, which is by and large antipathetic to existentialism, to sympathize with such an emphasis.

But is the only way, or even the most promising way, of getting contemporary students to use their minds to give them a choice between technical accomplishment and proceeding by means of rational and rather abstract argument? *Of course* they should acquire expertise of many kinds; *of course* they must be disciplined to face facts and follow logical arguments where they lead. But in addition are there not other parts of rationality that are of particular significance and appeal? If one is really caught up by a performance of, say, *King Lear* or *Othello*, is one not disciplined in mind and made more rational, at any rate for the time being, by the very experience? Thinking in the ordinary sense may not be involved, but existential sharing and illumination certainly can bring reason, as well perhaps as humility, to birth. One is moving from knowledge to acknowledgement, but that is neither irrational nor inhumane. It is significant that young people throng to concerts of classical music and show an immense, if intermittent, devotion to worthwhile causes. Ought not higher education, among other things, to be recognizing the educative value of the arts much more than it habitually has done? Ought it not to value more than is at all usual the kind of teaching of any subject that involves the teacher as an experiencing man or woman as well as a scholar or research worker of parts?

Warren Martin did not want structured thinking itself to be regarded as dependent upon cognitive knowledge only. Contributions to thought are not always cognitive in origin: some draw upon insight and immediate experience. Mary Bunting defended the sciences as educative, in part just because they bring people to work together in laboratories or in teams and to argue with one another, intuiting ideas each from each, 'not sitting alone in a corner of the library reading' as the arts students often seem to do. There is an experiential element not to be underestimated within both the teaching and learning of science.

The concept that life is a sequence of immediate experiences, whether true or not and though upsetting to conventional ways of regarding the world, has vitalizing power. The belief of many of our forefathers that progress is inevitable and continuing, likely to go on and on – that there is an automatic element about it – is an invitation to thoughtless and unimaginative cooperation with the *status quo*, and a cooperation without involvement.

Several members of the seminar stressed the especial importance, at a time when students see themselves as living in a discontinuous world, of appealing directly to their senses and experiencing power. But how is this to be done? Perhaps by putting ourselves further into our teaching: the point of contact is the experiences we have had ourselves and are able to pass on in a vital way. But these include our understanding of traditions and of the past, which have themselves to be assimilated and communicated as living things to the next generation.

To this part of the discussion Frye replied drily that you can only teach what is teachable. There are some things that cannot be taught at all unless you are a person. When students say 'Why does *King Lear* mean so much to you?' you have to become involved as a person as well as a scholar. But teachers must also be devoted to their subject in order to stand the test: he did not believe in subtracting the intellect from the rest of the mind. Students could sense if the teacher was totally committed, but could you possibly show this in the classroom to *begin* with? One must establish a point of contact with students so that they 'see', but this may have to be planned for. Blake's work was full of very explosive material; you should not start with the explosion, but plant the dynamite carefully so as to start the operation going in the student's own mind. There should be direct contact between teacher and taught in such teaching, not simply a reference to books on the subject that are in the library. What is important, however, 'is not you or I, but what we are both involved in'.

Referring back to the contemporary outlook of the young, several speakers allowed that there are contrasts and divergencies as between countries and types of institution of higher education. Is there any common denominator? One thought that this denominator is a common rejection of the idea that there was any body of knowledge or experience that has to be accepted as true simply on the authority of adults. People in higher education can learn much from the practices of the best English primary schools, where there is almost no attempt to transfer or teach 'pre-digested knowledge'. The tone or essential quality of the relationship between teacher and taught does not change with age. The language and content of what is taught to 5-year-olds and 21-year-olds will differ, but the nature of the relationship will be the same. The heritage of the past can only be passed on if the modern student feels in need of it. Is science a body of knowledge or one set of principles about knowing and how we should know? It is of little use to teach history without letting the students see how history was created and particular events came to be. Becoming human is not a matter of taking over what is there, but of learning what one can do and what one really feels and thinks. We tend to be in too much of a hurry; rigour and discipline can be introduced too early and too often as ends in themselves, so making Frye's open door 'lead into a museum instead of real life'.

Joseph Shoben thought that the value commitments of most academics were in fact essentially those of cognitive rationality. But the strategies of scholarship are by no means necessarily the same as those of education. The aim of many universities is 'to hook the brightest kids' and to make as many of them as possible into scholars and research workers. This means that the faculty tends to trade chiefly in attitudes that are cool, dispassionate, removed. But students' attitudes tend on the contrary to be warm, *engagé*, full of anxiety about issues in the contemporary world. This conflict must be resolved, and the onus is on the faculty to resolve it. Attitudes and ideas have consequences; and students sometimes realize what these really are more rapidly than most of their teachers. We used to have genteel rules in dealing with contentious issues and the play was slow, as in a cricket match. But students today want their contentions dealt with quickly. Frye suggested that one could only teach what is teachable. But is learning really always the outcome of teaching? Is the amount learned related at all closely to the amount even that has been well taught? There are many levels at which things can be learned.

There is little doubt that the older generation and the younger are often in these days far apart. The discontent is not individualized, and the frustrations felt by the young can lead to a deep-seated hostility that will reinforce inclinations to violence. In all this, 'the greatest deficiency is the lack of a legitimating ideology' capable of enlarging the sphere of generosity and friendliness in the older generation, including members of faculty themselves.

Richard Hoggart believed that when one was teaching literature 'for every proper way of letting relevance emerge, there are dozens of improper ways'. The teacher needs to attend with fidelity, discipline, and humility to the thing that is there: its genuine relevance will not emerge until it is looked at 'as itself'. The temptation on the part of the teacher might be to be an actor, or emotional procurer, or just detached – for example, to introduce his students to the subversive ideas of Blake while himself being quite happily sure of his own secure place in the society and the world.

Frye, concluding the session, spoke of the attractiveness of literature as compared with science to many students today. Science has its methodology: the idea of clean, lucid exposition. In the last generation Marxists were drawn to science but much more now to more humane studies. In the literature class particularly, faculty and students are trying to unite on a level of equality in an attempt 'to escape from the intolerable burden of being teachers and taught'. But it is easy in this atmosphere for the teacher to become a substitute for what he is teaching. The good teacher must be translucent not opaque: the subject he is teaching remains.

III

No one supposes that institutions of higher education in our time function in a world of their own choosing. What indeed would the world of their own choosing be like? But in fact society around has become more demanding, and with increasing urgency, though it may be far more conscious of some of its needs than others. Of some of its real needs, however, it remains perhaps unaware. It is easy to become preoccupied with the more superficial, violent, or dramatic aspects of student revolt. Who knows what may happen in the next few years that may catch the headlines and public attention? But the questions about academic values, purpose, and policy remain and about what is or is not relevant in higher education today.

It was a sense that the basic questions are not only contemporary questions – though they may have special forms in the last third of the twentieth century – which caused the Seminar to want to look back at the path along which universities had come, both from medieval times and in the much more recent past. Were universities in earlier centuries or earlier in our own century faced with any of the same problems? In a situation where governments themselves more and more pay the piper for the tunes which their system of higher education plays, is there guidance to be got from previous history? How prevent the particular needs that are clearly seen by politicians and business men from being the only ones met, to the exclusion of those, both personal and social, which, though less obvious, it is every bit as important to meet? The history of the development of higher education, and of the way in which, especially in Britain, the State has in this century increasingly been its chief benefactor, might be able to throw light on the questions that concerned us – or so at least we anticipated. It might be illuminating to consider matters of fact, to attend to questions of how and what, even though questions of why and wherefore would never be far underneath.

CHAPTER 4

The European University from Medieval Times
with special reference to Oxford and Cambridge
Marjorie Reeves

In Western civilization, institutions of higher studies have been throughout their history direct products of social needs and pressures. There is, of course, a general sense in which all human activity is moulded by its social setting, a sense so broad as to deprive my statement of any significant meaning. But what I have in mind is a much more specific sense, a sense in which Western impulses towards higher learning appear to stand in contrast to certain distinctive Eastern trends.

Whatever alternative models of higher education can be found elsewhere, it seems clear that in Western culture the learned man practically always stood within a social context and, if he were a teacher, was charged with a responsibility for training young men to play a responsible part in some social organization. This was as true of monastic education as of later medieval civic universities. Perhaps the one partial exception was the education which went on within the hermit or contemplative tradition which was the Western equivalent of Buddhist training. Leaving this aside, we find that within the framework of accepted social obligation there was always a tension between two impulses – one, the drive towards a search for 'pure' knowledge, and the other, the acquisition of knowledge and skills for specific social ends. The point I wish to maintain in this paper is that *both* were always related to the life of society and were recognized as such by most of the great thinkers of the time. They struggled to assimilate new learning to old, to systematize it, and to communicate it. The activities of systematization and communication are of as much social significance as training the next generation of professionals. In this context the conventional antithesis between non-vocational and vocational learning has little real meaning.

There has, however, always been this oscillation between emphasis on intellectual inquiry and on practical training. One sees this in the ambivalence of Greek attitudes towards higher education. In Athens, for instance, the only direct official concern was with the practical training of the *ephebos*, the young adult as he reached the stage of his soldier–citizen education. But the free, unorganized speculative inquiry that went on in the so-called academies was never regarded as socially irrelevant. The condemnation of Socrates bears witness to this fact. In its later, fully developed, form Athenian education combined firmly moulding moral and practical education with free-ranging intellectual inquiry. The institutions in which the *epheboi* were trained were State-controlled; their rector was elected by the citizens and responsible to them; great stress was laid on character-training. 'Whereas the People always has a hearty interest in the training and discipline of the *Epheboi*, hoping that the rising generation may grow up to be men able to take good care of their fatherland . . .'[1], thus begins a decree praising a retiring rector. On the other hand, the *epheboi* were required to attend the schools of philosophers who fought very hard – and in the main successfully – to maintain their freedom from state control. Classical Roman education had a more definite bias in its higher stages towards the requirements of public life. Its emphasis on eloquence and style in speaking and writing shows the high premium placed on the arts of communication in society. When in its last stages the system of the Trivium and Quadrivium (grammar, rhetoric, logic; music, astronomy, geometry, arithmetic) was evolved, these represented the forms of skills and knowledge held to be most relevant to the society of the period.[2] This classical legacy provided the framework for the medieval arts course.

Medieval higher education was equally the product of social need as conceived at the time. Looked at from today's perspective it might well be concluded that what early medieval society most needed was advance in technological education. In contrast, what the leading thinkers of the so-called Dark Ages saw as their most urgent task was to sharpen and refine the weapons of learning in order to fight the devil. This brings out the point that 'need' is always a concept in somebody's mind and therefore relative to a particular age. In any age social need in relation to education is defined by some kind of an elite, by which I mean those who guide, shape, and articulate the aspirations of a society. They may be a few jumps ahead, but to become really anachronistic is to become irrelevant. In the early Middle Ages this elite was religious and monastic. Monasteries were the power-

[1] W. Capes, *University Life in Ancient Athens*, London, 1877, p. 23.
[2] The term 'Trivium' does not appear to be older than the age of Charlemagne; 'Quadruvium' (corrupted to Quadrivium) was used by Boëthius.

houses of a society fragmented and incoherent, relying on faint transmissions from classical civilization until it could, as it were, get rewired. It was the very uncertainty of the age which threw up the concept of Western monasticism, that is, of a colony of heaven, a model society juxtaposed to the chaos of prevalent social conditions. It certainly expressed an ideal of withdrawal, but it was not only the product of contemporary society, it was also one of its most powerful re-shapers. In particular, it provided the first mould for a revived education, in which – somewhat paradoxically – it preserved the curricular shape of the classical education which, as we saw, had been designed for use in the midst of society.

The needs of a growing society could not for long be met through the agencies of monks and monasteries. The elite had to be pressed into a closer engagement with the rest of the social order. The pressures came from bishops and clergy, kings and lords, all demanding the development of skills to be used in the world. This pressure produced a shift of emphasis, first from the education of regular clergy (i.e. monks) to that of secular clergy (cathedral and parish priests), and ultimately from clerical to lay education. Here the derivation of higher education from existing social institutions becomes increasingly clear. By the eleventh and twelfth centuries the cathedral was an important administrative as well as religious centre. It was one of the key-points at which secular and religious organization met and therefore a natural centre for the education of a new type of religious elite which was increasingly giving leadership in secular affairs. Cathedral schools were well established in many places by the mid-twelfth century. They taught the Seven Arts and musical skills appropriate to the needs of the cathedral. But in addition we have evidence of the beginnings, on the one hand, of the highly practical study of law and, on the other, of a more speculative theology. About 1140 Master Vacarius was teaching the developing science of canon law at Canterbury, where Thomas Becket was getting the education which helped to make him such a formidable power, first in the State and then in the Church. In the same period, in the cathedral schools of Chartres and Paris, men like William of Conches, William of Champeaux, and Peter Abelard were widening and deepening the range of intellectual inquiry.

When we move a stage further to the rise of the independent universities, we find a new institution struggling out of its social matrix like a butterfly from a chrysalis, yet still taking its own forms of organization from the society around it. The divergences in the development of the universities of Paris and Oxford arise in large measure from the fact that the cathedral institutions pressed so much more closely on the first than on the second. Both were profoundly affected by their relations, closer or more distant, with the ecclesiastical authority in the first place, and the Crown in the second place. From one point of view it is clear that the university could only grow into the powerful arbiter of thought and conduct which it became by a process of isolating itself, of putting a firm ring round its autonomy. Yet, if its development is looked at from another angle, the medieval university derived so much from the society around it. Most notable of these borrowings was the guild form of organization. It is a commonplace, but a significant one, that when the masters in Paris and Oxford[1] were looking for a form of corporate identity they found their model in the concept of the craft-guild, with its three stages of membership: apprenticeship, journeymanship, mastership. It is difficult to exaggerate the importance of this development right down to the present age. Today there is much talk in terms of other models drawn from contemporary society, such as the producer-consumer one, or the industrial plant concept of a university. This is not surprising – the astonishing thing is that the medieval-guild model has served the Western universities so long and has shaped so powerfully the thinking of so many academic generations. It was, of course, an idea which never fully worked in actuality, but, in its Paris–Oxford form, it gave the medieval university four basic assumptions about itself: first, that beginners were members of the same organism as masters, because engaged in learning the same craft; secondly, that there are progressive stages in learning and that theoretically all are open to all; thirdly, that those at the halfway stage can teach beginners; fourthly, that because the craft of learning is a mystery the masters must keep a monopoly of it and demonstrate their solidarity in defence of its standards. From this last consideration arose the insistence on a licence to practise the craft which is the origin of the examination system. Above all, one must think of the implications of the craft idea as applied to the pursuit of learning, the acquisition of skills and knowledge which led to some form of craft practice.

The feature of the medieval curriculum which astonishes one most is the continuity in the conception of what constituted the basis of learning in a civilized society. The old Trivium and Quadrivium, derived from a pagan classical society, were still there as the framework of the arts course which all must take before moving on to more specialized courses. They represented certain forms of knowledge which it was still thought all educated people ought to have, together with basic skills necessary to the arts of communication. They had, it is true, been Christianized: the seven liberal arts were commonly compared to the seven gifts of the Holy Spirit, while the purpose

[1] For the purposes of this paper I have ignored the alternative form of organization at Bologna.

of the Trivium was described thus: 'The sword of God is forged by grammar, sharpened by logic, and burnished by rhetoric, but only theology can use it.'[1] Moreover, though theoretically the framework remained the same, in fact the emphasis was already shifting in the twelfth century to meet new approaches to knowledge and new demands in the higher degrees. By the thirteenth century, in Paris and Oxford, dialectic and philosophy had taken the place of grammar and logic, while rhetoric had been geared to the needs of law. But the Quadrivium continued to be used and the basic conception remained the same: the men destined for position in Church and State must share a common heritage of knowledge and have some proficiency in those skills of communication which were the foundation of social living. This course could last for anything from six to eight years, and specialized expertise could not be added until it had been completed. The three higher courses of Theology, Medicine, and Law represented the three chief forms of higher technical learning required by a medieval society. Law developed naturally out of the preoccupations of a society which based all its claims on 'rights' and was prepared to litigate endlessly about these. The course in medicine was designed chiefly to counter the influence of charlatans and preserve the classical Greek learning in this field. Theology was as much a vocational course as the other two: its purpose was to train those who must mediate the truth of God to the peoples. Any field of higher learning which might excite the human curiosity must be brought into relationship to the purposes of God. Roger Bacon, for example, justified his interest in optics by the rationalization that the 'miracle' performed by a burning-glass would impress the heathen.

Thus the main stress was always on practical uses. Learning was never divorced from society but pursued in a living relationship to it. But, equally, learning was important to society: there was no question of doing without it. This emerges clearly in the traditionalist approach to knowledge. Medieval society did not start again from scratch. As we have seen, it consciously built itself on the foundations of classical learning. Knowledge was not something to be found out *de novo*: it was an inherited *corpus* to be handed on. Unless it was fully and faithfully passed on, society would be in danger of reverting to barbarism. Of course problems arose in synthesizing classical thought and Christian truth. The essential approach, however, is clear, namely, that learning was the understanding of an inheritance. As Gordon Leff has put it: 'the search for truth was seen as the comprehension of texts'. Thus research in the modern sense happened only by accident. The 'modern

[1] Quoted G. Leff, *Paris and Oxford Universities in the Thirteenth and Fourteenth Centuries*, New York, 1968, p. 118.

assumption that investigation of the natural and human world can lead to fundamental insights into nature and human nature'[1] was almost wholly lacking as a conscious motive. It was there, none the less, since human curiosity will not be denied its answers. The great thirteenth-century scholar, Robert Grosseteste, for instance, added significantly to the sum of knowledge through following his own intellectual drives. Belief that investigation could lead to discoveries which might have a technical application was, I think, wholly lacking. Technological advances were made by people who used their hands to construct things, while learning was divorced from manual arts. This is clearly illustrated by the distinction between medicine, which was a traditional university subject, and surgery, which was a pretty clumsy craft. The effect of this concentration on inherited knowledge was, of course, to send minds turning round and round in a confined space and to focus attention on refinement of methods of thought and expression rather than on increasing the substance of knowledge.

What the internal structure of a medieval university such as Paris and Oxford did was to professionalize learning. This stems from the guild model. Universities dealt in an international commodity increasingly desired by princes in Church and State alike. The object of the masters' organization was to create and safeguard a monopoly in learning, a commodity believed to be of a more or less known, fixed quantity. Those who purveyed it must go through the whole course of training, only trafficking at each stage in the goods permitted. Thus the elaborate structure of the Arts course in the thirteenth century grew out of the need to protect the 'mystery' of the craft. First came a preliminary examination (responsions) for the entry to apprenticeship, the first stage, in which the student simply studied. At the end came the examination by 'determination' (i.e. disputation), which led to the bachelorship. In the second stage, the bachelor was still under instruction but authorized to give certain defined categories of lectures. Finally he had to be examined for his licence – the licence to teach which was everywhere the mark of the master. But the masters guarded their privileges so jealously that at Paris and Oxford, after the licence, they insisted on a special ceremony of inception to admit the candidate to guild membership. When finally established, the monopoly was almost complete: in England practically no higher education existed in the later Middle Ages outside Oxford and Cambridge with the exception of the Inns of Court, to which we must turn later. The universities controlled the content, methods, and standards of all professional education and safeguarded the status of the fully qualified.

Was there, then, no place for the eccentric or the maverick? Certainly not,

[1] Leff, op. cit., p. 5.

but for the powerful thinker who struggled to work within the set bounds there was a tremendous role. However traditionalist the assumptions, knowledge in fact increased, new problems were posed, and sturdy minds pushed the limits of inquiry further. The role of the leading thinkers was to assimilate the new to the old. It was essentially a teaching role: a great master did not wrestle with problems purely for the satisfaction of his own mind, but also because he had a duty to the generation that must be taught. The field of lectures and disputations gradually widened, drawing in matters of public interest in society as well as religion. The type of lecture known as a *Quodlibeta* was developed to enable the lecturer to propound and discuss questions of all kinds. Thus the university classroom could become a sounding-board for contemporary issues. Stephen Langton, lecturing in Paris at the beginning of the thirteenth century, discussed the theoretical justifications for opposing tyrants several years before he confronted King John in his capacity of Archbishop. Here was the academic bringing under critical scrutiny a key contemporary question, subjecting it to a clear appraisal in the light of general principles, and later finding himself committed to action on those principles in all the ambiguity of contemporary politics. Medieval academics did indeed bring under scrutiny many aspects of social behaviour.

But further than this, the medieval university of the thirteenth century achieved a reorientation of knowledge which was of vast import for the future. Three factors in combination produced this creative act: the inrush of new knowledge through developing political and economic contacts with the East; the professional concern of guilds of masters to capture the monopoly of and to render harmless this explosive new commodity which could not be just left lying around; the existence of great synthesizing minds to undertake the task of removing time-fuses and bringing this great new body of material into peaceful use. When, through contacts in the Mediterranean, trade, and the crusades, ways to the eastern world were opened up, Western Europe suffered a cultural impact of high consequence. The complex of new material which we may call 'Aristotelianism' burst in full force on the universities in the thirteenth century. This set off an intellectual conflict which could only issue either in the revolutionizing of learning or in its death. In essence, 'Aristotelianism' was a metaphysical system indispensable at that time for the advancement of learning, but threatening to Christian doctrine. To the existing leaders of thought Aristotle was 'at once both necessary and abhorrent'.[1] There could hardly be in history a clearer example of a cultural revolution, set off by social and political developments, and fought out exclusively in the official centres of higher education which

[1] Leff, op. cit., p. 190.

were the guardians of thought. Except among a few heretical groups there were no other social institutions through which the new thought might percolate, thus attacking the seats of academic authority from the outside. The battle was inside the universities or nowhere. It lasted roughly for a century, beginning with prohibitions of the study of Aristotle's natural and metaphysical works and ending with the *Summa* of Thomas Aquinas. The climax came in the 1270s when Aquinas, in his endeavour to Christianize Aristotelianism, clashed in Paris with the heterodox views of Siger of Brabant and both were under attack from the theological faculty. In the end it was the work of one or two master-minds, alive to the vital significance of the new philosophy, to assimilate it to Christian doctrine and make it safely available for generations of disputation in the Schools. Albert the Great and Thomas Aquinas, in particular, brought into being a synthesis of Aristotelianism and Christian theology which gave the Western medieval world a new *Weltanschauung*. It was a great achievement. Here was higher learning demonstrating its power, not only to transmit a heritage and educate the professions, but also to revolutionize a whole mode of thought and by adaptation to create a new framework of ideas. If it needed outstanding individual minds to do this, it was the institutionalizing of the new thought in the practice of Paris and Oxford which made it dominant. Never again, perhaps, has there been a time when universities could be seen quite so clearly as the intellectual foci of their society. 'New concepts, new problems, new alignments, new modes of thought were the outcome' (Leff, p. 131).

The interaction of the medieval university and society emerges clearly in the history of resistance to outside pressures. Paris University had a long and arduous struggle against those cathedral authorities under which she grew up. Oxford found an easier road to virtual independence because of geographical distance from her episcopal authority at Lincoln. Both were able to free themselves in the course of a century from immediate local control, and the reasons for this are instructive. First, against civic tyrannies or intimidation the two universities were able to appeal both to the highest national authority, the Crown, and to the highest international authority, the Papacy. The history of both Paris and Oxford shows that, with a few exceptions, Crown and Papacy backed the masters and contributed greatly to university independence. Secondly, the international character of these universities and of the learning they purveyed gave them a separate identity and professional cohesion which raised them above local feuds and enabled them to resist local pressures with a united front. Thirdly, they possessed a final weapon which depended on strength of corporate feeling and poverty of endowments, namely, migration, or the threat of it. Lack of possessions paradoxically gave the universities their greatest power, for it meant their complete freedom of movement. Physically, scholars were often in danger of their lives from local violence; intellectually, their freedom was that of an international fellowship, though bounded, of course, by the limits of orthodoxy; politically, they could often escape by migration. It must be emphasized, however, that the high degree of autonomy achieved by medieval universities depended on a fruitful interaction with society, and not on isolation from it. It was because universities were part and parcel of their civilization that they were on the whole successful in establishing their separate identities. Of course, the· infrequency of a head-on clash with authority in Church and State was partly due to the common acceptance of the bounds of orthodoxy as reasonable limits within which academic specu- lation should stay. The trial of strength between Wycliffites and authority, both ecclesiastical and royal, in fourteenth-century Oxford was bound to end in the defeat of the new movement, for 'freedom of thought' in a modern sense was unknown.

Cambridge is a classical example of a university founded through migra- tion. A violent clash with the town in 1209 led to the cessation of lectures in Oxford and the migration of all its scholars to Reading, Paris, and Cam- bridge. When, in 1214, masters and scholars returned to Oxford with a charter of protection against the burgesses, some remained in Cambridge. The future of Oxford was at times in the thirteenth century so uncertain that Walter of Merton bought a house in Cambridge as well as Oxford when he was planning what eventually became the first college in Oxford. In the event, both centres survived the early tensions of relationships. The medieval history of Cambridge follows closely the same lines of development as that of Oxford.

The growing fragmentation of Western Europe in the fourteenth century, however, began to erode the internationalism of universities. Nation-states were forming more distinctly; dialects were developing into national languages; national pride was beginning to demand its own universities. Paris and Oxford were already by the end of the century taking on some of the characteristics of French and English culture. The Great Schism (1378– 1417) crystallized divisions already present, breaking the interchange of scholars and raising barriers between institutions. Local self-interest de- manded its own higher education. 'Local' here did not necessarily mean national: it could also mean civic. The proliferation of universities in Western Europe in the fourteenth and fifteenth centuries was mainly the result of local pride and local interest in the professions. Learning was parochialized.

An outstanding example of a university designed to boost national pride and self-identification is to be found in Charles IV's foundation of Prague University in 1347. Acting as King of Bohemia rather than as Emperor, he consciously used the idea of higher education as a focus for patriotism. He was astonishingly successful: the rate of expansion was such that by 1400 the number of students at Prague was not far short of 4,000. The rise of Prague had two important consequences: the intellectual growth of the Germanic peoples and the opening-up of professional careers to many more in the lower ranks of society. But the process of fragmentation continued. The rising national pride of the Czechs led in the early fifteenth century to bitter disputes between German and Czech in the university, to the assertion of dominance for the Czech language, to the ousting of Germans from the academic seats of power, and finally to their departure to found a new university at Leipzig. Prague University became a more localized, but therefore all the more powerful, instrument of that intense politico-religious movement of Hussitism which gave the Czechs a period of fiery self-identification as a nation before becoming once more engulfed in the Austrian Empire. Two other Germanic universities may be briefly mentioned here as examples, in their foundation, of the motive of princely self-glorification: Vienna (1365) and Heidelberg (1385). In Scotland, St Andrews University (1411) arose to meet national needs at a time when enmity with England and the effects of the Great Schism in Paris made it impossible or dangerous for Scottish students to go to either Oxford or Paris.

Equally significant in the proliferation of universities was the motive of civic self-consciousness. When the spirit of Charles Martel asks Dante in the *Paradiso* whether a man can live without being a citizen, Dante's negative is clear and emphatic. To an Italian a man was hardly complete without membership of a civic society and for a city to be fully itself – to be civilized – by the end of the Middle Ages it must have a university. So we meet many examples of the free enterprise of citizens in creating their own university. This usually began with embryonic professional schools – a 'master in the art of medicine' or a 'doctor of law' teaching privately – which were taken over by a municipality desiring to control and develop professional education. Citizens were also keen to attract crowds of migrating students because of the trade they brought. Siena was probably the first Italian city to try to erect a *studium generale* by a legislative act of the commune. Here and elsewhere the masters, especially the lawyers, were expected to place their expertise at the service of the commune; thus the city contrived to kill two birds with one stone.

Something almost approaching a 'colonial' motive can be discerned when weaker Italian cities were falling under the hegemony of stronger. In

Florence, strangely enough, the university never really flourished and it was dissolved when, after they had conquered Pisa, the Florentines in 1472 deliberately restored the older university there. Academic glory was substituted for political independence and commercial wealth, and Pisa became one of the leading universities of Italy. In the same way Venice used the ancient university of Padua, keeping up the population of its subject-town in a harmless way. Milan's relations with the university of Pavia were perhaps of a similar nature. In Germany the first of the civic universities was that of Erfurt (1379), built on the foundation of four flourishing schools already existing in the thirteenth century. Again, other German towns followed suit in the fifteenth century. In all these we see the university as an instrument of political or social policies and a symbol of civic pride. The international aspect has not disappeared, for cities are both eager to attract migrant scholars and aware that to achieve the success of their educational enterprise they must obtain recognition from one or both of the two international authorities, Pope and Emperor. But universities of the fifteenth century, whether old or new, are much more closely under local and national pressures than were those of the thirteenth. They now have endowments; in some cases colleges have been founded. Security and patronage have reduced independence.

Do educational institutions go out of date through some kind of general law of inertia or for particular reasons? In the case of the medieval university there seems to be a specific answer. Its concept of knowledge limited its intellectual growth, like a pot-bound plant. The concentration of resources within the 'pot' had been essential in the first stages and a plant of great strength had been grown. Its chief fruit was a sharp, precise mind, trained in logical distinctions and methods of verification. As a system of education, however, it did not foster curiosity or experiment nor produce qualities of imagination or perception, though these, of course, were not lacking in individuals. Concentration on methodology finally tended to make it barren.

At a time when cities were still founding and fostering their own universities with a touching faith in the benefits to accrue, the fate of the barren fig-tree was threatening the universities intellectually. Societies in Western Europe were, in fact, making new demands on higher education. Although governments had long used men trained in the universities, and civil servants had by no means always been ecclesiastics, there is a perceptible development from about the mid-fourteenth century, first in demand for more relevant professional training, and secondly in the laicization of the professions. In England the development of the law schools in London illustrates clearly both these points against a background of the failure of Oxford and Cambridge to meet the new needs. The classical–ecclesiastical matrix of the medieval university meant that only Roman law – canon and civil – was officially taught within its precincts, while the study of common law was forbidden. The growing demand for common lawyers is evident, not only in the needs of government, but in the increasing litigiousness of a period when property was changing hands more quickly, trade was posing new legal problems, and old sanctions and forms of medieval life were dissolving. It was in 1340 that Edward III appointed the first lay chancellor, and it was only a few years later that the Temple was leased to professors and students of law who migrated from one of the already established inns in Holborn. Within the next ten years the four great Inns of Court and their cluster of contributory hostels had formed what was in essence the first lay institution of higher education in England. It was more aristocratic than the universities because the fees were high. It attracted upper- and middle-class families because it provided them with the one professional skill (outside fighting) which they most needed.

A somewhat parallel development was taking place in medicine, where surgery – the 'manual skill' excluded from academic study – was emerging with a new importance. John Arderne, who has been called the first great English surgeon, gained his experience on fourteenth-century battlefields and in private practice. Thus his works, though they attained a wide circulation, owed nothing to an academic background. The new consciousness of their importance led the master-surgeons to form a guild in 1368, but they never sought a university context. About 1421, allied momentarily with the physicians, they petitioned the king for professional recognition and the right to have a teaching centre in London. In the end it was with the barbers that the surgeons finally united in the Company of Barber-Surgeons, set up in 1540 with a monopoly of practice and of teaching. As with law, we see here a striking example of a profession brought to a new status and a new level of competence by the independent initiative of its members. Practitioners could be more responsive to the needs of society than academic institutions.

Thus the first respect in which the medieval university failed to meet the new needs of the fifteenth and sixteenth centuries was in providing up-to-date training for professions whose usefulness was being extended and transformed because of social change. A second aspect of failure concerns demand for a new type of higher education: the education of a gentleman-ruler. This Renaissance concept has various roots, in the ideal of the well-rounded individual, in a new awareness of the arts involved in government, in the creation of an elegant society. It was an aristocratic and princely idea of education. One must not, of course, over-emphasize the personality-cult of the Renaissance. The universities continued to educate large numbers and gradually modified their conservative ways, but there is striking evidence of their failure to meet the needs of the new elite in the private educational establishments of humanists and the cultural circles fostered by princes and leading men. The University of Florence, we recall, was dissolved just when the fame of the Medici circle was at its height. The prince and his companions, it was held, must be educated as many-sided men, able to use all their gifts of pen and tongue, their accomplishments of body, indeed all the resources of their personality, to achieve the ambitions of their career. At their service they must have knowledge of history, classical literature and languages, the natural world, military sciences. The instruments of their purpose might equally be the sword, the subtleties of diplomacy, the eloquent speech or letter, the poem, or the musical instrument; they must be able to handle each effectively. This was the philosophy of education behind the school for princes and their companions conducted, for instance, by Vittorino da Feltre for the Gonzagas of Mantua. Other examples could be cited. This education lay outside the scope of the ordinary professions. The gifted individual might – and did – climb from a humble to a high position and for such an enterprise he needed more than the skills of one profession. Equally, the boy born in the purple needed to be educated for all conditions and slave to none. Often the young man who was ambitious but poor got his basic letters in a university and then his real education in the train of some great man. Such was Aeneas Silvius Piccolomini, the fifteenth-century humanist who ended as Pope Pius II. The picture at Siena of the eager young secretary riding out of the city in the train of Cardinal Capranica symbolizes 'matriculation' into the school of world affairs which led ultimately to highest office. Equally characteristic is that famous discussion on the qualities and education of a courtier which lasted through the night until dawn flooded into the elegant palace at Urbino. In recording it, Castiglione caught exactly the mixture of serious moral purpose and secular worldliness which marks Renaissance ideas on education. But however strong the moral tone, the essence of this education lay in the individual's ability to stand alone without a framework and to turn his hand to anything.

Italian models of this type were quickly followed north of the Alps. Perhaps the closest English parallel to Castiglione was Sir Thomas Elyot whose real 'university', it has been said, was Sir Thomas More's house at Chelsea. Thus when he came to write his *Boke called the Governour*, he did not think at all in terms of the medieval university model. His young aristocrat (or governor) must at fourteen begin studying classical and contemporary authors, geometry, astronomy, and the use of maps. At seventeen he must turn to philosophy; at twenty-one he should study the laws of his country, not in order to become a professional lawyer, but as part of a liberal education for one whose life was to be spent in public service. At the same time he must develop elegant bodily skills through swimming, wrestling, hunting, hawking, and archery.

Perhaps the most serious failure of the medieval university was that of denying scope for investigation on the boundaries of knowledge. Nothing illustrates more clearly their different theories of knowledge than the contrast between the modern belief in research as the life-blood of an intellectual community and the medieval neglect of its possibilities. Human curiosity was, of course, always active, but in the field of learning it searched long for an institutional home. Thus the beginnings of scientific research are mainly found outside the universities in the sixteenth and seventeenth centuries. The College of Physicians, housed from 1560 at Amen Corner, London, established a lecturership on Baron Lumley's foundation, and it was as holder of this that Harvey first publicly stated his theory of the circulation of the blood, although he had graduated from Cambridge and Padua fourteen years earlier. John Gerard, whose *Herball* (published 1547) was one of the landmarks in the development of botany, was a Barber-Surgeon. In the reign of Elizabeth the first glimmerings of the idea that research could be useful to the State begin to appear in a plan for a special academy to be quite outside the university framework. This was drafted by Sir Humphrey Gilbert and put before the Queen in 1570.[1] The most original part of the scheme was the plan for research. The Natural Philosopher and Physician shall:

continually practize together . . . to try owt the secreates of nature, as many waies as they possibly may. And shalbe sworne once every yeare to deliver into the Tresorer his office faire and plaine written in Parchment, withoute Equivocacion or Enigmaticall phrases, under their handes, all those their proufes and trialles made within the forepassed yeare.

(quoted Armytage, op. cit., p. 78)

The thirty professors and teachers were to include specialists in Spanish, Italian, French, and High Dutch, a librarian of a copyright library, and a lawyer who should 'teache exquisitely the office of a justice of the peace and sheriff'. The educational function was summed up thus:

by erecting this Achademie there shalbe hereafter, in effecte, no gentleman within this Realme but good for some what. Whereas now the most parte of them are good for nothing.

(ibid., p. 79)

[1] H. Armytage, *Civic Universities*, London, 1955, p. 78.

The clarion call to extend man's empire over nature by research and so to benefit all humanity was sounded by Francis Bacon in the early seventeeth century:

Now among all the benefits that could be conferred upon mankind I found none so great as the discovery of new arts, endowments and commodities for the bettering of man's life. . . . But above all, if a man could succeed, not in striking out some particular invention, however useful, but in kindling a light in nature – a light which should in its very rising touch and illuminate all the border-regions that confine upon the circles of our present knowledge, and so spreading further and further should presently disclose and bring into sight all that is most hidden and secret in the world – that man (I thought) would be the benefactor indeed of the human race, the champion of liberty, the conqueror and subduer of necessities.

(On the Interpretation of Nature)

Here indeed was a modern view of man's relation to knowledge as opposed to the medieval one. Bacon was quite clear that the task he envisaged could not be fulfilled in the existing universities, 'all dedicated to professions and none left free to arts and sciences at large'. The finality of knowledge accepted by university professors made a prison-house from which, if anyone sought to break out, 'he was straightway arraigned as a turbulent person or innovator'. So Bacon propounded in the *New Atlantis* his plan for a new institution, consisting of laboratories for every conceivable subject of experiment. He hoped to gain the patronage of James I for his enterprise, but – not surprisingly – the King could not see so far ahead, preferring to support the plan for a polemical college at Chelsea, to be 'a spiritual garrison, with a magazine of all books . . . in maintenance of all controversies against the Papists'.

To what extent were English universities really relegated to a backwater? Some new literary and theological influences certainly penetrated to Oxford, and more particularly to Cambridge, when Renaissance scholars such as Colet and Erasmus resided there. Visitations banished some of the old scholastic texts and provided for the teaching of more up-to-date subjects. 'We have set Dunce in Bocardo and have utterly banished him from Oxford for ever, with all his blind glosses', wrote an Elizabethan commissioner, 'and the second time we came to New College . . . we found all the great quadrant court full of the leaves of Dunce, the wind blowing them into every corner. And there we found one Mr Greenfield, a gentleman of Bucks, gathering up part of the same book leaves, as he said, to make him savells . . . to keep the deer within his wood, thereby to have the better cry with his hounds.' It has often been argued that not so very many leaves of ancient textbooks fluttered off to the chase and much has been made of the fact that the Laudian statutes of Oxford in the seventeenth century insisted on the teaching of

Aristotle 'whose authority is paramount'. Yet recent studies have shown that to some degree in the late sixteenth and early seventeenth century new scientific studies were grafted on to old curricula in both Oxford and Cambridge.[1] Hakluyt found in Oxford a group of men already interested in the new mathematics, astronomy, navigation, map-making, etc. In Cambridge at the turn of the century a galaxy of mathematicians is found, centred mainly in Gonville and Caius, St John's, Trinity, Kings, and Emmanuel colleges. The point has been made, however, that much of this new learning was pursued in extra-statutory channels. The formal structure of the curriculum was only slowly modified. But the generations of young men coming up to Oxford and Cambridge in Elizabethan and early Stuart times got a basic training through rigorous, if old-fashioned, intellectual drills and with it contact with minds that were ranging far beyond the limits of the curriculum. 'The most direct contribution of the universities to the dynamics of intellectual change was therefore their role in training the geniuses of the seventeenth century. . . . The formal training of the universities prepared men to recognize a significant new fact and to understand how it affected old ideas.'[2] Thus the combination of a conservative curriculum and authoritarian statutes with a new creative and questioning approach to learning in those who operated the system seemed to provide the right conditions for the rapid advancement of knowledge.

Yet it could not be contained within the universities. The leading thinkers may have first tasted the new wine in the old places, but they wanted to create new wine-skins for it. The Elizabethan Richard Mulcaster wanted State reform of the universities on the plan of three colleges of general study (languages, mathematics, and philosophy) to be followed by four professional colleges (medicine, law, divinity, and education). Observe here both the likenesses to and the differences from the medieval shape of the curriculum. Thomas Gresham's foundation of Gresham College sought a new environment for higher education by its association with the City of London merchants. The education of the new elite was the object of Sir Francis Kynaston's *Musaeum Minervae* set up in London in 1635 and furnished with books, musical and mathematical instruments, paintings, and statues. He planned a seven-year course and established professorships in medicine, music, astronomy, geometry, languages, and fencing.

A second stream of educational thinking, running concurrently, placed the emphasis on 'mechanical arts', on mineralogy and other new techniques such

---

[1] See especially M. Curtis, *Oxford and Cambridge in Transition 1558–1642*, Oxford, 1959.
[2] ibid., pp. 247, 249.

as glass-blowing, in short, on a technological education for all. Thus in 1647 Samuel Hartlib wanted to replace the professorships at Gresham College in Divinity, Civil Law, and Rhetoric by others in technology. During the Commonwealth the left-wing Puritan, Gerrard Winstanley, continued this groping after a popular technical education in a scheme which linked the dissemination of knowledge with the propagation of religion by elected divines. He wanted everyone to be educated 'in every Trade, Art and Science, whereby they may finde out the Secrets of the Creation, and that they might know how to govern the Earth in right order'. The knowledge he desired sprang, so he conceived, from five fountains: husbandry, mineral employment, the right ordering of cattle, the right ordering of woods and timber trees, and the exercise of reason upon the secrets of Nature to observe the Sun, Moon, Tides, and Seas. He urged two great principles: freedom of research, 'so that the Spirit of knowledge may have his full growth in man, to find out the secret in every Art', and freedom of discourse for everyone 'able to speak of any Art or Language, or of the Nature of the Heaven above or of the Earth beneath', provided he spoke 'nothing by imagination but what he hath found out by his own industry and observation in trial'. Throughout runs a contempt for traditional learning 'which leads to an idle life' and Winstanley urges that 'no young wit be crushed in his invention' but encouraged by the Overseer in all his experiments. Yet another proposal by Abraham Cowley after the Restoration shows the same dissatisfaction with the teaching of the ancient universities, where academics ignored the application of knowledge to practical living and held 'that idle and pernicious opinion that all things to be searched in nature had been already found and discovered by the ancients'. He proposed an establishment of twenty professors, sixteen fellows, and two hundred scholars, engaged in research, teaching, and travelling abroad to report on all things pertaining to natural and experimental philosophy. All work was to be based on first-hand knowledge, for 'no man can hope to make himself as rich by stealing out of others' trunks as he might by opening and digging new mines'.

Thus the traditional book-learning of the universities was set over against the new conception of education through observation and experiment, through manual activities and contact with things. This new conception looked towards the dominion of man over nature – towards the technological revolution. It was a movement closely linked with social trends – with an expanding City of London, a progressive and wealthy merchant class, a Puritan clergy of energetic mind, an economy ripe for technological progress. It is impossible to conceive of such schemes being thrown up by a medieval society. Yet in terms of political power these schemes lay on the fringes. The ancient seats of learning – whatever the education they gave – were still close to the centres of power in Court and Church and State. The first two Stuart kings endeavoured to bind them closely to the Court, and their political importance is seen in the attacks and changes they suffered from the Civil War period down to 1689. Their monopoly was so much envied that there were various movements of local patriotism to secure such an advantage. A campaign for a northern university started up in the 1590s and about 1640 took shape in a petition for a university at Manchester, followed by a similar one on behalf of York. The argument of the petitioners was that the older universities were unable to provide adequately for the country's needs. During the Commonwealth a similar move was made by Durham and for a time a Durham college did exist, but the experiment was broken at the Restoration, and another for Shrewsbury likewise came to naught. Against all these plans the opposition of Oxford and Cambridge was strong, although they held within them men such as William Dell, Master of Caius College, Cambridge, who attacked their entrenched positions:

Why universities and colleges should only be in Oxford and Cambridge, I know no reason. . . . It would be more advantageous to the good of all the people to have universities and colleges, one at least at every great town in the nation, as in London, York, Essex, Bristol, Exeter, Norwich and the like and for the State to allow to these colleges competent maintenance for some godly and learned men to teach.

(Quoted Armytage, op. cit., p. 110)

Oxford and Cambridge saw to it that their monopoly was not broken. But by the mid-seventeenth century the new scientific interests were penetrating their societies. The group of talented men who first gathered once a week in London to discuss 'Natural or Experimental Philosophy' is found in the 1650s meeting in Oxford, first at the house of William Wilkins, Warden of Wadham, and then with Robert Boyle as host. Boyle established a laboratory in Oxford and introduced the first regular teacher of chemistry. The Restoration saw a setback, for both ancient universities were deprived of many brilliant and forward-looking men, while the Royal Society, incorporated in 1662, was born in London, not in Oxford. Slowly, however, the 'new philosophy' was establishing itself. In Cambridge, Isaac Barrow and his successor, Isaac Newton, developed the new mathematical tradition;[1] at

[1] In Cambridge the Lucasian Chair of Mathematics was established in 1663, the Chair of Chemistry in 1702, and the Plumian Chair of Astronomy and Experimental Philosophy in 1704. The terms of the latter laid down that the professor was to instruct any ingenious scholars or gentlemen who resorted to him in 'Astronomy, the Globes, navigation, naturall Philosophy, dialling and other practical parts of the Mathematicks'. Here are signs of a new emphasis on applied science.

Oxford, chairs of botany and chemistry were established. The Royal Society – at first regarded by conservative academics as a menace – began to stimulate advance. Elias Ashmole, a Londoner and a courtier, endowed a scientific institute in Oxford founded on the ideas of the Royal Society.

Yet neither Oxford nor Cambridge succeeded in recapturing the centre of intellectual vitality or fulfilling at the end of the seventeenth century the role of the medieval university at the end of the thirteenth. Boyle's two famous laboratories were in London from 1668 onwards, and others who had formed the nucleus of scientific teaching in Oxford moved back to London for lack of pupils. Newton's successor in Cambridge, William Whiston, was deprived of his chair and turned to popular lecturing in London and the provinces. An early popular textbook on chemistry was written by Nicholas le Feyre, chemist in charge of the royal laboratory in St James's Palace, while Deraguleir's famous experiments took place after his removal from Oxford to London in 1713. The great strength of the Royal Society was its freedom from tests and therefore its power to admit men of different religions, countries, and professions. 'This they were obliged to do', so it was stated in 1667, 'or else they would come far short of the largeness of their own declarations. For they openly profess not to lay the foundation of an English, Scotch, Irish, Popish or Protestant Philosophy but a Philosophy of Mankind.' By contrast the ancient universities were officially bound by tests throughout the eighteenth century.

This meant that one of the most vigorous intellectual currents of the time was channelled off into the Nonconformist Academies which sprang up in the late seventeenth and eighteenth centuries to meet the educational needs of those shut out of the ancient universities. This was a forward-looking sector of the community, and many of the principles embodied in the curricula of these academies link up with the advance of scientific and technological education. In the academy at Stoke Newington, opened in 1675, Charles Morton followed up ideas born when at Wadham College he had been in touch with the embryonic Royal Society. He built up a collection of mathematical instruments to illustrate his lectures and developed modern studies, including contemporary languages. The aim of the academy, as he saw it, was 'to have knowledge increased and not only confined to the clergy or learned professions but extended or diffused as much as might be to the people in general'. The eighteenth-century academies certainly did fulfil the function of spreading higher education to a middle class of trade and industry below that of the professions. In the north, the Warrington Academy, from 1757 to 1786, was a leading intellectual centre, with Joseph Priestley as its driving force and an emphasis on politics as well as science.

In London, Hackney College took a leading place. There were many more. Strenuous efforts were made in the Schism Act of 1714 to crush them. Significantly, however, those who taught 'any part of mathematics relating to navigation or any mechanical art' were to be permitted. The national need for an applied higher education was thus grudgingly recognized, but this did nothing to shift the foundations in the ancient universities.

The fact was that, in spite of the ferment of ideas about learning and education, general opinion was solidly for the traditional education of a gentleman, as exemplified at Oxford and Cambridge, for this was the cement of society. The function of the ancient universities was to serve the State rather than to create a new intellectual climate. The Preamble to the Elizabethan Act for the Incorporation of both Universities had affirmed 'the great zeal and care that the Lords and Commons of this present Parliament have for the maintenance of good and godly literature and the virtuous education of youth', and such was still the main concern. The universities provided above all the element of stability and continuity in bolstering up an existing order, and for this purpose people still trusted the traditional bookish education more than the new scientific approaches. The ideal of maintaining the fabric of society was impressively rolled forth in the Bidding Prayer at Oxford:

And that there may never be wanting a succession of persons duly qualified to serve God in Church and State, ye shall implore His blessing on all places of religious and useful learning . . . that . . . true religion and sound learning may for ever flourish . . .

The same purpose of a moral and civic service to the community reappears in the first institutions of higher education across the Atlantic. It was expressed by Samuel Johnson, first President of King's College (Columbia University), in 1754:

The chief thing that is aimed at in this college is to teach and engage the children to know God in Jesus Christ . . . and to train them up in all virtuous habits and all such useful knowledge as may render them creditable to their families and friends, ornaments to their country and useful to the public weal in their generations.

In part at least, the first American universities followed this old model. But at the same time the forward-looking champions of a new education hoped to see the developments in America which they could not expect in Britain. In 1666 a certain Dr Beale wrote to Robert Boyle about possibilities in New England: '. . . they may grow as we shrink. . . . They begin for a university and . . . maybe at leisure to be imbued with our suggestions. And it is fit to put new wine into new vessels.' Various scholars crossed the Atlantic with plans for academic reform, including Charles Morton of the Stoke Newington Academy, who became Vice-President of Harvard. Berkeley tried to found a new type of university in Bermuda and, after this failed, exercised influence over various young American universities, leaving his library to Yale. By the mid-eighteenth century the influence was beginning to be the other way round. In 1743 Benjamin Franklin wrote *A Proposal for Promoting Useful Knowledge among the British Plantations* which influenced British thought. Franklin took a large part in the foundation of the secular university of Pennsylvania. At the end of the century a graduate of Harvard, Benjamin Thompson (Count von Rumford), played a part in England in founding the Royal Institution. Certainly North America, though still under the influence of the classical model, was more alive to new trends.

The chief indictments against the ancient universities in England in 1800 must be the absence of critical and creative thought within their walls and the attempt to maintain monopoly. The role of the university as the critic of contemporary society seems to belong to a different world from that of the classrooms where, as Bishop Butler said, lectures were 'lifeless and unintelligent'. Yet criticism might have been thought to be the strong point of a bookish education, with its opportunities for the formulation of general principles and its scrutiny of sources. As for creative ideas and new methods of research, Oxford and Cambridge seemed by this date to have lost the impulses they once had. Above all, their attempt to keep a monopoly of higher education must shock one, since they would not or could not provide for the new educational needs. By the last quarter of the eighteenth century the young American Republic had nine universities (actual or embryonic). Scotland had four. England was stuck with her two ancient foundations.

Intellectual growth had to take other institutional forms. Vitality there certainly was in the England just entering another period of commercial and industrial expansion. It erupted in spontaneous associations of men keenly alive to the new possibilities for extending man's dominion over his environment. Attention was focused on a practical education in the 'mechanical arts'. Malachy Postlethwaite, who compiled a *Universal Dictionary of Trade and Commerce*, wanted to found a Mercantile College. Following Defoe's suggestion, an attempt was made in 1742 to open a university in London 'where all Liberal Arts and Sciences will be most usefully, critically and demonstratively taught'. Nothing came of this, and private enterprise, in the form of public lectures, and private schools and laboratories, continued to fill the gap until, in 1754, the Society for the Encouragement of Arts, Manufactures, and

Commerce in Great Britain was formed.[1] One has only to look at the ground it covered to be aware of the great gap it filled. Public health, agriculture, forestry, colonial affairs, trade, technology, all came on its agenda; it offered prizes for winter foodstuffs for cattle and improvements in corn; it stimulated projects in new agricultural machinery, afforestation, soil analysis; it encouraged the use of drawing in technical education. As the Society of Arts it pushed forward technological developments in every way. In the field of medicine another enormous gap began to be filled with the development of the London teaching hospitals, while in 1745 the Surgeons, having at last parted company from the Barbers, were empowered to examine and license all practitioners in the London area. Another project issued in 1799 in the Royal Institution, 'to teach the application of science to the common purposes of life'. The people who lectured for it – Humphry Davy, Thomas Young, Sidney Smith, Coleridge, Landseer – demonstrate vividly how strongly the intellectual currents were flowing in channels outside the ancient universities. Davy clearly expresses the technological purpose of man: 'by his experiments to interrogate nature with power, not simply as a scholar, passive and seeking only to understand her operations, but rather as a master, active with his own instruments.'

The universities were a product of the particular conditions of medieval society in Western Europe. They took their institutional forms from it; they provided the elite which developed the working of Church and State. Within a given framework they were, for one period in the thirteenth century, the most creative intellectual force in the Western world. The synthesis of new and old achieved then produced a culture, a method of thought, an outlook, which held sway to a greater or lesser degree for several centuries. They could do this because the sum of knowledge was conceived as finite and the authority of the given body of knowledge was absolute. Thus the masters of the universities could formulate and pass on a finalized culture. They were entrusted with this task by Church and State and accorded sufficient autonomy to do it in their own way. The solidarity of corporate feeling among the academics made them powerful to resist interference, though never out of touch with society.

But these medieval universities were essentially a traditionalist force, upholding the existing order. Learning was a force making for the solidarity of society, and its masters became increasingly the agents of stability. By the

---

[1] It is worth noting that in this year Viscount Townshend founded a prize in Cambridge to encourage the study of the theory of trade, in view of the 'infinite advantage to the public if young men acquired knowledge of a science so very important in itself and so intimately connected with the affairs and interests of this kingdom'. So advanced an idea however, never took root, and the prize disappeared after three attempts to set a subject.

end of the fifteenth century they were failing to respond creatively to new needs. Their bookish craft militated against both scientific research and technological advance. In the course of time Oxford and Cambridge adjusted slowly to some of the new needs of the governing and professional classes and the new regime in the Church. Others had to be catered for by professional associations. The statutory courses of the ancient universities did not provide an education for the world, nor could they, as institutions, contribute much to the vast changes in thought patterns, methodology, economic and political theory, etc. taking place from the Renaissance onwards. Again, at the beginning of the technological age the stimulus to inventive thought and experiment had to come from individuals and spontaneous groups. The centres of intellectual vitality must be sought in the circles which gathered round the great minds and, except for brief periods, these were not often located in the old institutions. From the sixteenth to the end of the eighteenth centuries creative thinking was almost always uninstitutionalized. But there is discernible a pattern of unofficial groups with a common enthusiasm who find the need to convert these into permanent purposes and therefore to create new corporations for their new objectives which in turn seek to promote new forms of higher education.

Should we expect long-established teaching institutions to be the growing-points of new intellectual and educational developments? Certainly the whole traditionalist view of knowledge as a heritage to be passed on militated against their assuming such a role. But in any case does not a teaching institution inevitably lay more weight on a corpus of knowledge to be taught than on new discoveries? This brings us straight into the controversy which arises in the nineteenth and twentieth centuries on whether a university is primarily for research or for teaching. In the pre-1800 period it was undoubtedly the latter which was *par excellence* the university's role. It is possible to read student unrest today as disillusionment with the post-1800 university, with its increasing emphasis on research as its prime function. But if today there is a demand to return to the concept of a teaching institution, the old model would not please. We have seen that it contributed stability rather than creativity to the needs of society. Stability is about as far as could be from students' expressed aims today, although the next generation probably does need the transmission of an orderly body of knowledge and values as well as a coherent society in which to learn. Perhaps this is the key task of the university, and possibly to fulfil it properly we have to accept a more modest role. acknowledging what history teaches, namely, that since the sixteenth century intellectual growing-points have more often than not been outside the universities and only inside them by the accident of persons. Any claim to monopoly certainly has bad historical precedents. Should we then relinquish the claim to an intellectual imperium and recognize that a great deal that is of significance in extending the realm of knowledge is going to happen outside the universities? This is not intended to suggest an absolute division between teaching and research. Most of us are convinced of the fertilizing influence of each on the other. At any given moment a particular university laboratory or department may be the creative growing-point for a given subject. The question raised here is whether universities should not deliberately redress their balance somewhat in favour of the teaching model.

If so, we have to take a long look at the teaching role. The historic universities passed on a solid inheritance; when this became irrelevant in a new society, they still passed it on. The upholders of the fabric of society could really get away with almost anything, because stability was valued more than change. The critical role – so often claimed for the university – was hardly ever practised, except by individuals. The nearest approach to it is found in the medieval attempt to lay down general principles on which society ought to operate, but this was always in terms of an ideal, static model. Today, inheritance must be related to change, and the teaching role must be conceived anew in terms of supplying the instruments of that critical scrutiny under which both old and new must be brought. The universities will need much more consciously to relate expertise to broad social principles, and the education of an elite to the education of all. But in my view they should centre themselves upon what was always their historic role: education.

INTERCHAPTER

I

Response to Marjorie Reeves – WARREN BRYAN MARTIN

Dr Reeves emphasized that the medieval university was part and parcel of its civilization; a direct product of social needs and pressures, achieving whatever autonomy it had because of its fruitful interaction with society as well as its acceptance of society's values.

While I do not wish to challenge this emphasis, I would suggest that sufficient attention was not given in the paper to the fact that the university, viewed historically, was actually associated with one element in society – the political, socio-religious, intellectual elite. The great masses of people were poorly represented in the university, had little influence on it, yet were affected by it. While university scholars in the medieval period were concerned for the reconciliation of Aristotelianism with Christianity and with methodological precision or the theoretical nuances of scholasticism, the great precursors of the reformation – Wyclif, Hus, the Brethren of the Common Life – were either scorning the universities or leaving them in order to work for change in other settings. There were, of course, efforts at reform within established institutions, including the universities – the humanists, especially Erasmus, sought to enrich scholarship by reference to Hebrew as well as Greek sources – but these reformers shared a naïve confidence in constituted authority as well as a failure to see that many people would take their call for change so seriously that the reform goal would be nothing less than the complete overthrow of that authority. And Luther provided the necessary leadership. Luther was the revolutionary moment when the surging but submerged reform sentiment became visible. The principal reformers were for the most part university-trained men, but they left that aristocratic setting to go to the people in the market-place and churchyard.

It is important to note that the narrow conception of the nature of the university was ill suited to the rise of technology and scientific freedom in the sixteenth and seventeenth centuries, with the consequence that from that time to this a great deal of creative research has gone on outside the university. Moreover, the identification of the university with the social

85

and political elite, who accept it as a guardian of tradition, established authority, and acknowledged values, has resulted in individuals and movements committed to socio-political transformation either being driven out of the university or voluntarily developing their efforts at change apart from it.

In view of all this history, and present conditions, the question about the university today is not whether it will go too far as a participant in social change but whether it will go far enough. And if it is not relevant as a participant in that way, has it another relevance? Yes, its relevance, that is, its importance, is in the way its conservative character reveals, through its attitudes and actions, the values of the social *status quo*.

I turn now to the matter of governance. It is a misconception that medieval universities operated as autonomous 'republics of scholars' without external controls. The truth is, as Dr Reeves has said, that the universities, particularly Paris and Oxford, achieved some measure of autonomy by playing church authorities off against civil rulers, but they were always accountable to one or the other. In the case of the University of Paris, the Bishop of Paris and the Chancellor of the Cathedral Church of Notre-Dame controlled the university during its early period, and the Papacy later kept it and other universities under continuous though usually magnanimous surveillance by creating the office of procurator for universities. The right of the authorities of the Diocese of Paris to regulate and superintend the affairs of the university, as W. H. Cowley has written, had complete justification in canon law. It rested upon the prerogative which bishops had from patristic times to visit the churches and to supervise them and the church schools of their dioceses. The expansion of papal power during the eleventh and twelfth centuries did not override diocesan power as it related to the lower schools, but it established the Pope's superior right to take the control of institutions of higher education out of the hands of diocesans and to supervise them from the Curia Romana itself.

By the fifteenth century, civil government in both France and England grew strong enough to supervise and restrain the universities through the governmental powers of visitation. An evidence of this came in 1573, when the Parliament of Paris declared the University of Paris to be a secular rather than an ecclesiastical institution. Civil government in Italy had assumed control of the universities even earlier.

It was at Yale that the type of governing board which would become standard American practice – the single absentee body – was inaugurated. Yale raised 'an expedient to the rank of principle' when in 1701 its charter simply made the ten organizing clergymen the corporation. Thus was perpetuated, albeit in an American variation, the tradition of non-resident control of colleges and universities.

Over time many responsibilities were delegated to faculty and to administrators, with the situation today featuring an arrangement whereby the curriculum or academic affairs are delegated to faculty while college trustees retain responsibility for economic policies and usually have influence in the socio-political life of the institution.

But this division of authority is now a factor in campus unrest. What faculty and students do in the academic realm has socio-political and economic ramifications, even as what trustees do in the economic or socio-political realms affects the academic life. Both sides figure in shaping the character of the institution, yet each side feels limited and ineffectual, and communication between them is minimal.

Is there an alternative to the medieval model of control, whereby the institution of higher education was held accountable to some external authority structure to the extent that it had no real autonomy? And is there an alternative to the American variation on that model, whereby aspirations to community are frustrated by having control vested in a non-resident ruling oligarchy which delegates responsibilities in a way that fragments and does not unify?

Finally, I will pick up Marjorie Reeves's closing statement about the central business of the university being education, and will offer an alternative thesis. Certification, not education, has been the main role of colleges and universities. In the best institutions the primacy of the certification task has been qualified by concern for education – training for the professions has been supplemented by knowledge from the liberal arts and by a desire to encourage in the students a capacity for good judgement – but, finally, in almost all schools, education for certification has been and is the end on behalf of which the means operate. This situation has not only prevailed, it has been and is the situation preferred.

Consider the issue from the perspective of several interest groups: parents and the general public demand that students shall be certified as professionally and socially fit for society. Thus the certification requirements, as Jencks and Riesman emphasize, are 'constantly adjusted in order to ensure satisfactory socialization'.[1]

In the medieval period the Church was the guardian of such arrangements. Dr Reeves spoke of the rise of the independent universities, but she documented that, in fact, what always occurred was a shift of dependency, from

---

[1] Christopher Jencks and David Riesman, *The Academic Revolution*, Garden City, New York, 1968, p. 63.

Church to State, or from State to regions, or from Pope to king or prince. In our epoch of secularization the certifying external agency has become what Senator Fulbright and others have called the military-industrial-academic complex. These modern guardians of societal values set the professional and social standards to which institutions of learning 'educate' their students. Just as the so-called independent universities of Paris and Oxford did not extend to the members of their communities the right of heresy, as Dr Reeves has shown, but, rather, demanded orthodoxy precisely because those educational institutions were seen as agents of socialization, so now Berkeley and Columbia, despite their claims to independence, are expected by the society to educate for certification—professional, yes, but also certification in the social and political values of the nation-state.

The majority of students and faculty, it must be added, really do not differ in their definition of education. Most students are in college to accumulate credits or courses leading to diplomas that certify these persons as professionally competent and socially acceptable for high standing in our social stratification system. Students are not much attracted to school work for which they receive no official recognition or reward.

Faculty have their own variation of certification in their preference for what they call 'a professionally oriented faculty'. It is professionalism that provides for faculty a supra-institutional value orientation. But here too, as with the students' emphasis on success measured by the norms of quantification, or with the parental concern for the college diploma, means have been allowed to become ends. The legitimate concern of faculty for quality, and for the standardization of qualitative criteria in institutions for higher education, has now culminated in professionalization being turned in on itself, in standards being inverted and becoming self-serving, in a value orientation that equates schooling with education and makes the credentialling process more important than professional competency. So scholarship becomes a new scholasticism, professionalization becomes professionalism, authority becomes authoritarianism. These are the conditions that stir dismay among reform-minded students and faculty, because in this way the fifty-year academic revolution in America has now become a counter-revolution bent on blocking further change.

In view of the historical realities that Dr Reeves has so brilliantly pointed out, perhaps we should be done with the familiar but erroneous rhetoric about universities being independent and, instead, make clear to all interested parties, but particularly to students, that institutions of higher education have been and are instrumentalities of established values with a mandate to educate for certification.

Does it follow that colleges and universities, as institutions with a preference for stability, are incapable of change? Not at all. Dr Reeves's paper chronicles the fact that in the thirteenth century, when the writings of Aristotle were reintroduced into the West, as in the fifteenth century, with the rise of nationalism, and at other times too, the universities underwent radical changes – but always in response to external developments and their attendant pressures. As society changes, the institution of higher education changes. It does not lead, it follows. But in following the leader, it changes.

Is this one of those critical periods in Western history when changes in the general society are sufficiently major for substantive changes in higher education to be sure to follow? I think it is. But since 'colleges have always been institutions through which the old attempt to impose their values and attitudes on the young',[1] and especially at this time when developments appropriate to the future are coming into being outside the institution of higher education, in part because it is identified with the past and is slow to change, we ought to make clear to those youth who favour radical social reform that they must be very powerful and adroit individuals if they are to stay and work for change within the institution. And we must be fair enough to admit that there is good reason for them to give themselves to movements or agencies out in the larger society, where the action is and where they can be a part of the future rather than to remain within an institution which is a part of the past waiting for the future to find it.

II

In the general discussion that followed, the key questions were seen to be: how far is it the job of higher education to provide for the demands of the society that is contemporary with it, regardless of the price, and how far is it its task to cater for deeper and more permanent levels of human need? What is meant by 'good teaching' in higher education? How is this related to research? In what directions must we go if there is to be more of it?

Everyone granted that Marjorie Reeves was probably right in seeing institutions of higher education as responses to social need. The invention of new kinds of university in more recent times (e.g. the Land Grant College), the development over centuries of particular departments or faculties (e.g. of medicine, and the final alliance of surgery with it), the encouragement of new types of higher education in reaction against the over-domination of

[1] ibid., p. 35.

universities (e.g. the rapid growth of polytechnics and colleges of advanced technology) seem obvious products of social need and social pressure. And if universities today do not provide much of what the world asks for they may well rapidly decline in power and favour: they could be superseded or become a less favoured part of a binary or multiple system of higher education. When, as in medieval times, society was much less complex than it is today and much more unified in the values it believed in, the possible conflict between the act of serving society and that of serving civilization was less likely. But now, as Champion Ward pointed out, there is often an obvious separation between established university principle and what society appears to want to do and where it appears to want to go. This cleavage, indeed, is one of the roots of student criticism. But the fact that universities have embodied traditional principles did not, it seemed to him, necessarily entail the conclusion that Martin had put forward that innovation must come from elsewhere and that the universities as a whole will resist it. If universities would try to bring their ancient principles more fully into the light of day they might well find that there was a fair degree of radicalism already incorporated in them. Even by acting strictly according to their principles, universities could be radical in the impingement they made.

It was acknowledged, however, that this would not be an easy line for institutions of higher education to take. The very scale on which they now have to operate makes it difficult for them to function as unities or to appear to stand for a particular set of values against others. Indeed the plurality of concerns and interests and the vast range of sections of society they serve is often – and perhaps legitimately – a source of satisfaction rather than the opposite. It is one of their great strengths.

Nevertheless, it was urged, the vaunted diversity of universities is largely organizational and structural, not nearly so much at a deep level of values. But the values they stand for are monolithic and conservative in a wrong sense. For example, they give merely token support to black emancipation; they make their acceptance of an occasional maverick or 'sport' into a proof of their enlightenment. But they are in fact rich and stable institutions no longer mobile (universities lost their mobility early, as soon as they got endowments, buildings, and comfortable furnishings); their teaching largely consists in the passing on of a body of knowledge; they produce many graduates whose values are indicated by their wish above all to succeed as business men or in the communications industries – TV, advertising, journalism. Radicals are in a small minority among graduates: conventionalists and conservatives predominate. The symbol is the maypole dance, where the dancers go through the prescribed ritual but bind themselves ever more tightly to the central standard around which, attached by ribbons, they revolve.

Though participants in the Seminar did not deny the shrewdness of some of the points which were ingredients in this view, they believed it to be unduly pessimistic. If institutions are immobile, professors emphatically are not; universities produce both conformists and rebels. Asa Briggs, emphasizing that he was an 'unrepentant pluralist', took the creative conflicts in ideas which so often rage in universities as an indication that they are much less monolithic in their value orientation than had been suggested. Student rebels are often ambivalent themselves – wanting, as it were, certificates for rebellion and the best of both worlds. Ninian Smart suggested that universities do in fact, and not without success, try to instil a questioning and critical attitude into many of their students. It is this which in part is responsible for the challenge that students are now bringing to the whole social scene.

And so to some consideration of teaching and its function and nature in higher education. If teaching is conceived as merely 'the passing on of a body of knowledge to the ignorant young', the institution which is to do this may be thought of by the public as paid to be little but a stabilizing force whose innovative power will be limited and 'safe'. The number of students now receiving a higher education makes, of course, for more and more public debate about what they are doing and ought to do. 'The university belongs to the taxpayers, not to the faculty or the students' is a common and potentially threatening attitude. One of the troubles in parts of America is the very limited concept of the scope of the teaching role in the minds of regents – and even members of faculty. Good teaching involves stimulating the mind of the student and a critical response on his part. It is a shared act of search and inquiry, with the students and professor cooperating in the quest; and the professor able to say what he does not yet know as well as what he knows. It is not an instrument of conservation alone but a questing instrument which may easily seem (and be!) subversive to orthodoxies. But it is to be remembered that the growing habit in institutions of higher education to treat the young as adults has many sanctions from contemporary society.

Sometimes, it was pointed out, members of faculty themselves maintain that the real business of their university or college is research, not teaching; and its proper job to train graduates, not undergraduates. Often such theorists have a very inadequate conception of teaching. We need to introduce students to the world of reason and imagination, and this must involve a far more personal type of teaching than they allow for.

Responding to some of the points made, Marjorie Reeves said that as an institution the university had always been and always would be expected to provide society with the professionally trained and socially adjusted types it wanted, the kind of people 'safe to be let loose in it'. By 'society' today we often mean taxpayers who pay most tax – i.e. chiefly those over the age of forty, who wanted society to go on functioning safely and efficiently. But institutions of higher education can provide society, surreptitiously perhaps, with things it is not conscious of wanting. It has a pluralist role: after all it is the young in any society who have the impetus to create the world anew. Their values are not static, especially today, nor is the body of knowledge they are acquiring. One major task of universities is to discover how teachers and administrators can on the one hand convince their taxpaying masters sufficiently of their own sense of responsibility, of their acknowledgement of tradition, and of their intention to make responsible use of their knowledge, and on the other how to convince students or faculty that we only want the old knowledge in order to create the new. It is imperative to keep the confidence of the public that universities are trustworthy mediators between them and the intelligent young; and yet also to keep the confidence of the young that they are not being betrayed or compromised. At the end of a recent conference in England at which students as well as vice-chancellors and professors were present a young radical student looked across at one of the vice-chancellors and said, 'We've had a wonderful weekend, we've got together in great friendship about all these issues, but can we trust you to behave like this when this discussion is over?' This is just the point.

The crux is in the teaching role rather than in the administration or structure of institutions of higher education. We desperately need new methods and approaches to teaching at the tertiary level. The problem of teaching is fundamentally the same for the 5-year-old as for the 21-year-old; but the 21-year-old has got to be prepared for more long-term discipline. A body of knowledge has to be mastered, which means essentially that the student has to discover it afresh, not just receive it as an inert mass. He has to explore it for himself. The higher up you get the more is demanded from the teacher by way of patience and waiting for results from his students. It is of no use to hand on dead knowledge. Some of us are perhaps beginning to see how sometimes one can combine the passing on of a heritage with the making of a new world.

To illustrate this point Miss Reeves described a teaching situation which was admittedly very favourable – one where there were only seven students with a professor and herself. 'The subject was Dante: on which of course there is a whole mass of traditional material of learning which they ought to read. You set them papers to write, give them a book-list but say it's even more important that they read Dante. I got from them seven papers, all of which were completely non-traditional interpretations. The argument in discussion with the students then turned on the question how far traditional interpretations ought to be re-established. The professor and I struggled a bit to re-establish them. But the point was that the students had been able to make their creative, imaginative approaches direct, without recourse to standard or traditional interpretations. Only after that had they come into contact with works of criticism and so had to modify some of their wild ideas.'

In medieval times society was static, and knowledge could satisfactorily be passed on with far less of the person involved on either side than was now the case. 'It is because medieval society was static that we are stuck with this traditionalist handing-on idea as what teaching consists of.' Teaching now should be far more a matter of joint discovery, of communicating in a creative and personal way knowledge and attitudes and research findings. Only, indeed, if this happens can you overcome the sense of oppression about the mass and weight of the stuff to be read and learned.

At the same time it is well to remember that the staffs of institutions of higher education are not the whole of the elite. Not all the responsibility for renewing and resuscitating thought and values rests with them. 'We should be very modest in claiming anything more than being communicators of our own and other people's exciting ideas. We want to lead students to make discoveries for themselves so that their thought and values and outlook will be reshaped. But much of this will go on outside the universities and after they have left.'

CHAPTER 5

Development in Higher Education in the United Kingdom
Nineteenth and Twentieth Centuries
Asa Briggs

I

It is only during the course of the last few years that it has become possible to talk meaningfully – if, even then, somewhat uncertainly – about a 'system' of higher education in Britain. 'There can be no serious doubt', one writer put it in 1944, 'that there is a great need to rethink and replan our university system, if it may be called a system';[1] and although the first pages of the Robbins Report on *Higher Education* (1963) refer specifically to 'a system of higher education,' the Report states flatly that

even today it would be a misnomer to speak of a system of higher education in this country, if by system is meant a consciously coordinated organization. . . . Higher education has not been planned as a whole or developed within a framework consciously devised to promote harmonious evolution. What system there is has come about as the result of a series of particular initiatives, concerned with particular needs and situations, and there is no way of dealing conveniently with all the problems common to higher education as a whole.[2]

Most changes in British history have to be explained in this way, although attention has recently been paid – rightly – not only to 'particular initiatives', separated in time, but to cumulative and self-generating processes within the history of administration itself. In the history of British universities since the early nineteenth century, it is necessary to separate out four related aspects of history – first, changes within the universities themselves, mainly

[1] J. Macmurray, 'The Functions of a University', *Political Quarterly*, vol. XV, 1944.
[2] Cmnd. 2154 (1963), §14, §18.

though not solely the product of inner forces, some intellectual, some organizational; second, changes within society affecting the demand for university places; third, changes within society affecting attitudes to universities and ideas about universities; and, fourth, changes in the pattern of resources, institutional and governmental, upon which universities can draw.

Each aspect of history can be treated separately, and each aspect has its own complexity. Thus, for example, it is not always easy in examining the internal history of universities to plot the relationship between intellectual changes and organizational changes. The key to understanding, in my view, is to examine the succession and interplay of generations and the modes of intellectual and social transmission as yesterday's students become today's teachers and administrators. Likewise, a study of the demand for university places leads at the same time to a study of other educational institutions – schools in particular – and to a study of professions and graduate occupations. The number of related variables is immense. At the same time, generalization is not easy in Britain because of the diversity within the pattern. Oxford and Cambridge for centuries prided themselves on their differences rather than on their similarities: within each of them different colleges emphasized their own identity. One of them, indeed, Balliol, very different from the rest, made the bold claim on one occasion that 'if we had a little more money we could absorb the University'.[1] The world of 'Redbrick', superficially much the same everywhere, reveals, on a closer examination, at least as much variation, and variation of more than style. British cities in the nineteenth century, out of which Redbrick institutions emerged, were strikingly different from each other in social structure and in cultural drive;[2] and although during the twentieth century there have been many tendencies making for increasing standardization, even the most casual visitor to the universities of Nottingham and Leicester, for instance, is struck with the differences between them.

This paper inevitably simplifies, therefore, and the most that it can hope to do is first to set in perspective some current preoccupations, including those concerned with the sense of a university 'system', and second to show that the study of a selected number of earlier episodes in university history in England may be as illuminating as a study of what is happening here and now. It was Lord Acton who suggested that the study of history not only should ensure that we should understand our own times better, but should deliver us from thraldom to them. The paper is concerned almost exclusively

[1] A remark of Benjamin Jowett, quoted in C. E. Mallett, *A History of the University of Oxford*, vol. III, 1927, p. 456.

[2] See Asa Briggs, *Victorian Cities* (Penguin edition, 1968).

with England, not with Britain, since the Scottish tradition in education, that of what has been called 'the democratic intellect', is different from that of England. Even though persistent efforts were made during the nineteenth century to narrow the differences and to assimilate the Scottish tradition with its European background within the English tradition, it emerged, if not unscathed, at least not destroyed.[1] In its turn the Scottish tradition has influenced, usually obliquely, some features of twentieth-century English university history.

II

Any simple narrative account of the development of English universities during the nineteenth and twentieth centuries – and not only is there no adequate simple narrative account in existence but most general histories of England during this period include few references to them – would probably concentrate on a number of episodes widely separated in time, 'the particular initiatives' mentioned in the Robbins Report. Among them, the first of the landmarks that stand out, is the founding of University College London in 1826, 'the radical, infidel college' which broke the centuries-old duopoly, reinforced by religious tests, of Oxford and Cambridge and provided for the first time in British history the country's capital city with the beginnings, in 1836, of what was to become by British standards a quite exceptionally large and complicated university. Henry Brougham, who was one of the most active of the founders, believed not in one new university, but in several – to make higher education more accessible, or, in his own characteristic words, 'come-at-able by the middle classes of society'.[2] He did not secure that extension of his purpose in 1826. It was not until later in the nineteenth century that the newly-chartered civic universities – the term was coined by R. B. Haldane – came into existence, the origins of which can be traced back to the founding of Owen's College in Manchester in 1851, the year of the Great Exhibition. Leaving in the background Durham, of clerical foundation, each of these ventures was an initiative of private enterprise – and the grants of charters (the Victoria University, Manchester, led the way in 1880) followed sustained local pressure on the Privy Council. The ideal behind the nineteenth-century civic university was unmistakably Victorian, and, like

[1] For a fascinating and controversial study, see G. E. Davie, *The Democratic Intellect: Scotland and her Universities in the Nineteenth Century*, Edinburgh, 1961.
[2] See his *Observations on the Education of the People* (1824). See also C. W. New, *The Life of Henry Brougham* (1961), chs. XIX, XX.

the ideal of the Victorian city itself, it was best expressed by Joseph Chamberlain. 'To place a university in the middle of a great industrial and manufacturing population', he proclaimed at the first meeting of the Court of Mason University College, Birmingham in 1898, 'is to do something to leaven the whole mass with higher aims and higher intellectual ambitions than would otherwise be possible to people engaged entirely in trading and commercial pursuits.'[1] Ideal and reality were thus placed in uneasy relationship to each other.

Nine years before this declaration, however, the government had taken what in retrospect seems to be just as important a step as the local sponsors of new university institutions had taken in Manchester, Birmingham, Liverpool, and Leeds. The Salisbury Government decided in 1889 to distribute £15,000 per annum from Treasury funds to the civic universities and appointed a committee to advise on the disbursement of the grant; Manchester received, incidentally, £1,800 from it. In 1904 the total grant, which then stood at £27,000, was doubled, again by a Conservative government. Once the decision to make such government grants was taken there could be no going back.

In 1919, when the University Grants Committee was formally established, Oxford and Cambridge for the first time accepted grants. The task of the new UGC, which included a majority of academics and was made directly responsible no longer to the Board of Education but to the Treasury, was that of 'enquiring into the financial needs of university education in the United Kingdom and advising the Government as to the application of any grants that may be made by Parliament towards meeting them.' From 1915 onwards, four years before the setting up of the UGC, there were other government grants which extended the range of public provision, for in the heat of the First World War it had been decided – Haldane was involved behind the scenes in the making of this decision also – to set up the Department of Industrial and Scientific Research (DSIR) with an initial grant of £25,000.[2] The same man, Sir William McCormick, was part-time Chairman both of the new UGC and of DSIR: already since 1909 he had been chairman of the committee advising the Board of Education on the distribution of university grants, a committee which on the eve of the First World War was already visiting English universities and meeting, incidentally, with resentment from some of them concerning its modes of inspection.[3]

---

[1] J. Amery, *The Life of Joseph Chamberlain*, vol. IV (1951), pp. 209–21.
[2] For a brief account of the background, see A. Marwick, *The Deluge* (1965), ch. 7. See also a lecture by H. Hetherington, *The British University System, 1914–1954* (1954).
[3] See J. Simmons, *New University* (1958), pp. 41–2, for resentment at Leicester.

The next landmark in the story was 1935, when Sir Walter Moberly, former Vice-Chancellor at Manchester University, became full-time Chairman: he was to stay in the post until 1949, spanning the Second World War. By then Parliament was granting slightly over £2 million each year to the universities, a figure which remained more or less the same throughout the inter-war years and during the Second World War, when there were never more than 50,000 full-time university students in the country. In 1945, after a further burst of pressure for university expansion during the war – as one expression of a greater pressure for post-war social reconstruction[1] – the recurrent grant was greatly increased until it reached £6·9 million in 1946–7. The UGC itself hailed the increase as 'initiating a new era' in the financial relations between the university and the State.[2]

It is interesting to note how, in 1947, the UGC went on to express the relationship between what was happening in the universities and what was happening in society. 'The contributions which the universities were able to make in many fields of war-time activity won for them a new prestige and a place in the national esteem which it will be their ambition to retain in the period of reconstruction which has just now begun. Within the academic sphere itself, the intermingling of institutions of contrasting types brought advantages which went some way to counterbalance the inconveniences of evacuation.'[3] The UGC was encouraged in its plans for expansion not only by the record of the immediate past but by projections of the future, which began to play an increasingly important part in university history, and particularly by the recommendations of the Barlow Committee, which had been appointed in December 1945 to examine problems of scientific manpower and its use. This Committee reported the willingness of the civic universities to increase their numbers by 86 per cent in ten years – it described this figure as 'an appreciable underestimate of what could be done'[4] – and while stating firmly that it was in the national interest to double the output of graduates in science and technology, it also – and this was important – urged an increase in the number of graduates in arts and social studies. The

---

[1] Lord Butler has claimed that the Education Act of 1944, which dealt with schools, had inevitable corollaries for higher education in the future. 'It was I who first recommended Robbins to write his report. And the Robbins Report is a kind of follow-up in higher education to what we did for secondary education in 1944' (*The Times Educational Supplement*, 19 May 1967). The British Association for the Advancement of Science produced a report in 1944 suggesting a doubling of the post-war Treasury grant to universities and an increase in the number of students to 50,000 (*Report of the Committee on Post-War University Education*, 1944).

[2] UGC, *University Development, 1935–47* (1948), p. 11.

[3] ibid., p. 16.

[4] Cnd. 6824 (1946).

UGC referred to the Barlow Report as giving 'authoritative expression . . . to the demand for university expansion'[1] and set a target of 90,000 students in 1948–9. It asked all universities in the light of this recommendation to revise their estimates of possible expansion ignoring financial considerations, and consequently produced a revised total of 88,000. It admitted that 'these recommendations involve changes at the universities which can only be described as revolutionary'.[2]

It should be clear even from this very brief history of landmarks that by 1947 the UGC had already changed its role from a distributor of money to an agent of planning, even though the planning was of the simplest kind, depending on collecting estimates from universities and comparing them with 'targets' set out in official papers. In fact, the doubling of numbers of students in science and technology was reached in two years rather than in the ten years envisaged by the Barlow Committee. The problem of the divergence between projection and accomplishment – the accomplishment being determined by hundreds of 'micro'-decisions in particular universities – was henceforth to become of major importance in university history. The UGC, not surprisingly, had its terms of reference widened in 1946 to read 'to inquire into the financial needs of university education in Britain; to advise the Government as to the application of any grants made by Parliament towards meeting them; to collect, examine and make available information on matters relating to university education at home and abroad; and to assist, in consultation with the universities and other bodies concerned, the preparation and execution of such plans for the development of the universities as may from time to time be required in order to ensure that they are fully adequate to national needs.'[3] Lord Murray of Newhaven, who was to serve as Chairman of the UGC from 1953 to 1963, has described this statement as 'the first open recognition that national needs should be a factor in the development of universities'[4] in Britain.

When the UGC went on in 1947 to make its first non-recurrent grants to universities to meet their capital needs and their needs for scientific equipment – and the power to decide on the distribution of these capital grants clearly increased the influence of the UGC – the Vice-Chancellors' Committee, a body which had first come into existence very informally in 1918, welcomed the new dispensation. 'The universities entirely accept the view that the Government has not only the right, but the duty to satisfy itself that every

---

[1] See H. C. Dent, *Universities in Transition* (1961), pp. 72ff. UGC, *University Development, 1935–47*, p. 26.

[2] ibid., p. 28.

[3] ibid., p. 11.

[4] Quoted in A. Kerr, *Universities of Europe* (1962), p. 206.

field of study which in the national interest ought to be cultivated in Great Britain is in fact being cultivated in the university system and that the resources which are placed at the disposal of the universities are being used with full regard both to efficiency and to economy.'[1]

We seem to be very near to our own times with this statement. Yet it is doubtful whether it would have been subscribed to in 1947 by most academics other than vice-chancellors or even whether most vice-chancellors would have regarded it as more than a concession to expediency at that time. Moreover, the firmness of the statement concealed some doubt as to its exact meaning. Certainly our own times seem so different from those of Moberly that at the recent jubilee dinner of the Vice-Chancellor's Committee, a recently re-modelled body, it was rightly said that the last ten years had seen bigger changes than the previous forty. Moreover, Sir John Wolfenden, the present Chairman of the UGC, remarked recently that 'if Moberly came to Park Crescent [the present HQ of the UGC] tomorrow morning, he would quite simply – for all his great wisdom and experience – not have a clue. The UGC has changed a good deal over the past twenty years and, indeed, over the past ten or five. It has changed, not because there was anything wrong about the way it did its job, but because the job has changed, in size and in complexity if in no other ways.'[2]

In this most recent period statistics have seemed to count more than landmarks. The number of full-time university students increased in Britain from 77,000 in 1947 to over 94,000 in 1957 and to 169,486 in 1965–6. At the same time government expenditure on the recurrent grants to universities rose from £7 million in 1946–7 to £28 million in 1956–7 and £122 million in 1965–6. Non-recurrent grants rose sharply from £28 million in 1961–2 to nearly £80 million in 1965–6. These figures spoke for themselves, or at least appeared to do so to governments: marginal items of expenditure became politically significant items, posing questions both of absolute scale and of priorities within the educational system as it was beginning to be conceived.

At the same time, there have been several landmarks or, at least, what seemed at the time to be landmarks, in the recent history of universities. The first was the setting-up in 1949 of the new University College of North Staffordshire, an institution which deliberately set out to innovate, to look at university education in a new way. The second was the long sequence of decisions, first taken within the Ministry of Education in 1953, which led in 1956 to the designation as Colleges of Advanced Technology (CATS) of

[1] Committee of Vice-Chancellors and Principals, 'A Note on University Policy and Finance' (1947).
[2] Sir John Wolfenden, lecture on 'Universities and the State' (1967), p. 15.

a number of local technical colleges of high standing, financed from 1962 onwards not by local authorities but by direct Ministry of Education grant. They were to be granted charters as full universities from 1964 onwards, thereby broadening the base of the community of universities and widening the scope of the UGC.

The third was the decision taken by the UGC in 1958 to sponsor seven brand-new universities, not upgraded institutions nor institutions subjected, like North Staffordshire, to an initial period of tutelage, but autonomous and free. It is the implications of this decision that have received most public attention. One new university would have been incremental, as North Staffordshire was; seven changed the dynamics of the system, indeed, helped to foster the sense of a system. It was a decision taken in steps without a debate in Parliament five years before the Robbins Report on *Higher Education* – and taken essentially on the same basis, to begin with, as the decision taken to increase university numbers after the Barlow Committee had reported in 1946. The steps were: inquiries to existing universities about the targets they wished to achieve; estimates of national 'shortfall'; determination about new provision. The Barlow Committee, indeed, had recommended the foundation of at least one new university and several university colleges, and it was only after the UGC had found in 1946 and 1947 that existing universities were able more or less to meet the need as defined by Barlow that it had decided then not to pursue this particular recommendation. The language was cautious, moreover, even if its argument was somewhat general. 'It is clear that the situation contemplated by the Barlow Committee does not immediately arise. In these circumstances the establishment of new institutions could no longer be regarded as a necessary means to the policy of expansion, and we have acted on the opinion that, in present circumstances, with shortages of qualified staff and with restrictions on building, greater progress can be made by concentrating the limited men and materials upon the development of existing institutions than by scattering them over a wider field.'[1]

In 1954 and 1955, when the UGC began to consider a shift in its policy, it could go back to the word 'immediately' in the first sentence of the earlier statement and use it in a way familiar to all members of committees, as a link word across time. The argument in 1957–8 for creating new universities looked simple. Existing universities together could not or were not willing to meet the demand for additional university places by 1970, 'irrespective of questions of finance'. It was assumed that they were quite free each separately to determine what their maximum rates of growth and maximum future

[1] UGC, op. cit., p. 42.

targets would be, just as it was also assumed by 1957–8 that it was right that the U G C as a national body should assess future total demand for university places. The national assessment was based on demographic factors – 'Bulge' – and socio-educational factors – 'Trend' – and the demand for action was quickened when it became clear that the government itself was disturbed that unless more university places were provided a sizeable number of those qualified to go to university on current standards would not have a chance of securing a place.[1] Representatives of secondary education on the U G C pressed the same point. Yet from 1954 onwards there was protracted debate inside the U G C (a very English debate) about the quantitative estimates of 'Bulge' and 'Trend', about what lines of action to pursue to speed up expansion, and about how speedy expansion should be. Even as late as 1956, when it was decided to support proposals being made locally in Sussex for a new university to be located in Brighton, there was no commitment to a whole cluster of new universities. It was not until 1960 that York and Norwich were also accepted as new university sites, and the Treasury was informed that three or four more new universities would be necessary.[2] The setting-up of a U G C Sub-Committee on New Universities in April 1959 enabled the U G C to examine and choose between local bids for universities: it attached importance from the start to local enthusiasm and interest.[3] In May 1961 Essex, Kent, and Warwick were approved, and in November Lancaster.

The act of choosing sites took the U G C outside the realm of applied mathematics. So too did a concern for innovation which was already beginning to be expressed in many circles. Yet one other point must be made about the mathematics behind the critical decision, since it has never been made clear to a certain number of commentators in Britain itself. It was assumed that

[1] According to Sir Edward Boyle, the fact that 'the English sense of fairness came into play' was of considerable importance in the making of decisions. See M. Beloff, *The Plateglass Universities* (1968), p. 22. The government agreed to bigger targets on a short-term basis after discussions with the UGC. Thus in 1956 it agreed to 106,000 by the mid-1960s. The UGC stated in the same year that its 'minimum' figure for 1968 was 168,000. In the same year the government announced that authority had been given for capital expenditure to permit a doubling of building starts. 'Large though the increase is, the Government believes that the universities should be encouraged to expand even more. The UGC has advised us that a larger expansion would be desirable if resources can be made available. It would like to invite the universities to consider still further expansion to meet national needs' (quoted in UGC, *University Development 1957–1962* (1964), p. 71). The same process was repeated in 1957–8. It was in discussions about capital between the UGC and the Treasury that the UGC greatly strengthened its role in the planning process.

[2] ibid., p. 100. By then the UGC had settled on a national target of 170,000 for the early 1970s.

[3] For other criteria, see ibid., pp. 96–101.

in the short run there could be only limited growth in the new universities and that the main thrust of immediate expansion should be met in the existing universities, some of which, notably Hull and Leicester, had grown rapidly since 1945 (Hull 800 per cent by 1958, Leicester 1,100 per cent). 'We did not face a choice between expansion of the existing universities and creation of new ones', the UGC reported faithfully in 1964. 'It was clear to us that both were needed.'[1] This was the last bit of mathematics, and qualitative as well as quantitative questions quickly entered into the argument: indeed, they were part of the texture of the argument inside the UGC itself. 'We also had in mind the need for experimentation.'[2] After Southampton, Hull, Exeter, and Leicester had passed from university-college status to full university status between 1952 and 1957, the UGC recognized that an epoch had ended, and that any new universities brought into existence should start freer than North Staffordshire had done. The 'newness' of the institutions and the fact that they were not upgraded institutions with a history was of their very essence. 'New institutions, starting without traditions with which the innovator must come to terms, are more favourably situated for such experimentation than established institutions.'[3] The formula that was devised for the creation of new universities – local initiative; competitive bidding to the UGC; formulation of academic plans by UGC-appointed Academic Planning Committees; granting of charters – encouraged not only innovation but diversity. Each new university appointed its own faculty, devised its own curriculum, its own approach to teaching methods, its own governmental organization, although the Privy Council (via the UGC) had to approve of their charters and the UGC itself could influence their 'mix' of subjects taught and the rate of growth. The diversity was accentuated by the fact that from the start the new universities never worked together as a *bloc* or attempted to bargain together to strengthen their position *vis-à-vis* older universities. Between 1961 and 1968 they moved on separate lines, although they obviously had common problems and sometimes, at least, produced common solutions.

The fourth recent landmark was the Robbins Report on Higher Education, which appeared in 1963. The Robbins Committee had been appointed in February 1961 'to review the pattern of full-time higher education in Great Britain and in the light of national needs and resources to advise Her Majesty's Government on what principles its long-term development should be based. In particular, to advise, in the light of these principles, whether there

[1] ibid.
[2] ibid.
[3] UGC, *University Development, 1952–1957* (1958), p. 5.

should be any changes in that pattern, whether any new types of institution are desirable and whether any modifications should be made in the present arrangements for planning and coordinating the development of various types of institution.'[1] This was the first occasion on which universities had been reviewed along with those other institutions of higher education in Britain that had their own separate histories and their own current group status – colleges for the education and training of teachers, started originally in the nineteenth century by voluntary bodies, mainly religious, but expanded in numbers by local education authorities, which were responsible in 1963 for 98 out of 146 institutions; local, area, and regional technical colleges; Colleges of Advanced Technology; colleges of further education; agricultural colleges; schools of art; and a small number of other institutions. The Report recommended that there should indeed be some changes in pattern, including the conversion of the CATs into new universities, that there should be an augmented Grants Commission dealing with the needs of all 'autonomous institutions of higher education' including non-university institutions, and that, as the basis of statistical projections, there should be sufficient expansion of numbers to permit 'courses of higher education to be available for all those who are qualified by ability and attainment to pursue them and who wish to do so'.[2] This was a new kind of statement in the history of higher education in Britain.

The Report, which reflected and to some extent stimulated greater interest in higher education than had ever been shown before, was clearly concerned more with student demand than with 'national need': perhaps for this reason it produced fewer results than had been anticipated. No new universities were created in its aftermath, nor was a new Grants Committee, although in February 1964 the UGC was transferred from the Treasury to the Department of Education and Science. Teachers' Training Colleges were renamed Colleges of Education, and subsequently B.Ed. degrees were introduced, but the colleges were not transferred directly into the university sector. By 1965 there was as much talk of sectors as there was of systems, and a confused public argument had started (and is still in progress intermittently) concerning a so-called 'binary system' involving the existence side by side of a university sector and a non-university or 'public' sector. The Secretary of State for Education gave a speech on the subject at Woolwich in April 1965 which is in its way something of a landmark: it was followed in May 1966 by the publication of a White Paper (Cmnd. 3006), vague in language and uncertain in intention, proposing the designation of 27 institutions as Poly-

[1] Cmnd. 2154 (1963), p. iii.
[2] ibid., p. 8.

technics, very much *not* to be in the university sector. In April 1967 the 27 became 28, and the green light was flashed: the work in them was to lead to the granting of degrees administered not by particular universities but by a recently founded (September 1964) Council for National Academic Awards (CNAA) and to other national qualifications.

Public debate about the 'binary system' has been confused for three reasons. First, it was never made clear whether the system was considered to be an 'ideal' or an acceptance, largely for economic reasons, of historical fact, involving the 'systematization' of what had hitherto been unsystematic dualism or polycentrism in higher education. Second, the bare economics of the systematization were never clearly set out – relative costs, for example, in universities and polytechnics. Third, the implementation of policy was determined largely by civil servants in discussions with local authorities, and much that was happening was hidden from public view. Although a higher education planning group was set up within the Department of Education to consider the relation between the different parts of the system, its work has been confidential and its statistics have never been published. The Robbins Report had stated that the Committee initiated its own statistical inquiries and surveys because of 'the paucity of information on higher education in general' and that it hoped that 'the information here assembled will serve as the foundation for further observation and analysis'.[1] Yet there seems to have been a retreat since Robbins on this front, not an advance. The Robbins projections are becoming increasingly out of date, and there have been no open moves towards 'ten-year planning' as the Committee recommended.

At this point in time the economic determinants of global expenditure on university expansion and development of other educational institutions have obviously begun to be treated as imperatives. Controls have been tightened, and for economic reasons there has been little preparation for what Robbins anticipated would be a new wave of expansion during the mid 1970s. It was specifically stated in February 1965 that no further universities would be created during the next ten years,[2] and all recent official statements have suggested not increases in but curbs on university expenditure. The gap between aspirations and achievements has widened. The controls have taken different forms – UGC costing exercises, establishment of building and equipment 'norms',[3] limited rationalization of courses; and, in July 1967, the government's decision to give the Comptroller and Auditor-General

[1] ibid., p. 3.
[2] One was created after the seven – Stirling in Scotland.
[3] See Cmnd. 9 (1956); Cmnd. 1235 (1960).

power to inspect university accounts[1] and to report back to the Public Accounts Committee.

The Committee of Vice-Chancellors and Principals has in the meantime been seeking to carry out what internal reforms it can within the 'university system'. It has recognized that while there is now a greater measure of State involvement in university provision than any Victorian, radical or conservative, could ever have contemplated, universities in Britain have retained to the present day a substantial measure of autonomy and that, as the two English universities of 1800 have given way to the 36 of today, universities and government have seldom come into direct confrontation with each other. Between them as a group – and they are a disparate group – and the government there still stands the U G C. They know, of course, as Sir John Wolfenden has stated, that the U G C is a changing U G C and that if the present is cloudy the future is not clear. 'It is not easy', Wolfenden has also stated, 'to combine the proper autonomies of the universities with the proper attention to effective use of scarce national resources. It could well turn out that the degree of success with which the U G C and the universities conduct this (delicate) operation over the next few years will determine their whole future.' The arrangements depend on 'the continued observance of conventions', on 'reciprocal good will', and, not least, in crucial stages on particular personalities.[2] The issues have little, in my view, to do with party politics, which have themselves changed completely during the period since 1800, although they have much to do with opinion. More must be said of that later. Constitutional history and social history cannot be realistically studied in separation from each other, just as social issues cannot be divorced from economic issues, much as we should like to divorce them.

III

A number of points emerge from the bare outline of the story as I have told it so far. First, the history of university development has been one of fits and starts, with much of the *élan* concentrated into short sharp bursts. 'University education', Sir Richard Livingstone remarked in 1948, 'has grown up in the casual English way. It has never been viewed, much less planned, as a whole.

---

[1] For demands for tighter control, see the 'Fifth Report from the Select Committee on Estimates, 1951–52', p. xv; Special Report from the Committee of Public Accounts, 1966–7, 'Parliament and Control of University Expenditure'.

[2] Wolfenden, loc. cit., p. 5, p. 8.

A cynic might give a book on the subject the title of *Drift*.'[1] There has been much more 'planning' – a difficult term to apply to university policy-making – and much more 'system' since 1948, yet, as an educational journalist put it recently, Sir John Wolfenden's successor as chairman of the U G C, who takes up his unenviable post in January 1969, 'confronts a higher education in turmoil. Stop-go economics for the universities, confusion of purposes as Universities, polytechnics and even the Open University expand in directions that only cohere in some sublime pigeon-hole in the Department of Education, and revolting students will buffet him from all sides. Not the least of his problems is the inexorable rise in demand; a rise which, unless some new methods of financing are developed, is going to make higher education one of the Exchequer's biggest headaches in the 1980s.'[2]

Second, the pattern as it has emerged, down to the current question marks, is very similar to other patterns in English history – to that of the social services in general, for example. In other words the outline of university history is not unique within the general web of history. Development has owed much to particular individuals, it has been characterized so far by remarkable continuities more than by sudden reversals, it has depended on delicate conventions and obviated frontal conflict, it has left considerable margins of choice. Each university remains a separate unit, as universities were in the nineteenth century, but the U G C has developed a common system of financial provision and control which affects all universities, including Oxford and Cambridge – although to a limited extent Oxford and Cambridge retain a greater measure of autonomy because of their college endowments and independent finance. The element of competition within the 'system' has been curbed as it has in all other sub-systems of English society since there are more or less common pay scales in all universities and common formulae for dealing with building costs and services. Diversity, therefore, which was such a conspicuous feature of the British solution to the problem of university expansion during the 1960s, is diversity within set limits, and there is always a danger that *micro*-planning within the particular university will be handicapped or frustrated by *macro*-planning or the lack of it in the Department of Education and Science or the U G C.

Third, although the number of university students has increased sharply during the period I have been talking about, the proportion of the age-group attending a university institution in Britain remains small, by both American and European standards. Indeed, as the well-publicized U N E S C O chart of 1957 showed, in the provision of university places per head Britain's

---

[1] Sir R. Livingstone, *Some Thoughts on University Education* (1948), p. 13.
[2] R. Bourne, 'Universities and the Public Purse', *The Guardian*, 11 Nov. 1968.

parsimony was surpassed in Europe only by that of Ireland, Turkey, and Norway.[1] Throughout the nineteenth century and deep into the twentieth century, the assumption that university students constituted some kind of elite – there were differences of opinion about what kind of an elite – was as strongly held, usually without argument, as the assumption that universities were free and autonomous corporations holding property and administering their own affairs. There was a close association (to which we still cling) in the mid-Victorian debate about the university between the theory of the 'clerisy' as advanced by Coleridge – the theory of an endowed class 'comprehended of the learned of all denominations',[2] a theory with a religious pedigree – and the theory of the elite. The theory also had social implications, as strong as the social implications of twentieth-century theories of 'national need'. 'Obligation is a strong word in reference to going to college at any age,' F. D. Maurice wrote in 1837, 'but I do conceive that those who are destined by their property or birth to anything above the middle station in society, and intended to live in England, are bound to show cause why they do not put themselves in the best position for becoming what Coleridge calls the *Clerisy* of the land.'[3]

The main effect of the direct, although strictly limited, intervention of the State into the mid-Victorian affairs of Oxford and Cambridge was to stimulate a movement for internal reform which had gained ground before the State decided to intervene.[4] Colleges revived their community ideal and re-stated it in Victorian language, emphasizing its relevance to moral education and character formation.[5] Universities considered the role of the university as an institution for learning, comparing British with German institutions, and examining the implications of an increase in the number of professors and the encouragement of research.[6] Reformers inside Oxford and Cambridge in this key period were never in complete agreement with each other – nor

---

[1] Beloff, op. cit., p. 23.

[2] See S. T. Coleridge, on *The Constitution of Church and State According to the Idea of Each* (1837 edn), p. 49, for his definition – 'the clerisy of the nation, or national church in its primary acceptation and original intention, comprehended the learned of all denominations, the sages, and professors of law and jurisprudence, of medicine and physiology, of music . . . of the physical sciences . . . in short, all the so-called liberal arts and sciences, the possession of which constitute the civilisation of a country.'

[3] F. Maurice, *Life and Letters of F. D. Maurice* (1885), vol. I, p. 224.

[4] The more Conservative reaction was to claim that inquiry into Oxford and Cambridge constituted 'an unwarranted inquisition' into the affairs of 'venerable bodies'. James II's intervention in the seventeenth century was cited as a precedent.

[5] See S. Rothblatt, *The Revolution of the Dons* (1968), ch. 7.

[6] See J. Sparrow, *Mark Pattison and the Idea of a University* (1965), pp. 91ff., for Pattison's interesting and significant change of views on the relative position of college and university between 1850 and 1877.

were the academic reformers within the new civic universities – but their debate, a far more sophisticated debate than that conducted between radicals and conservatives in Parliament, touched on every relevant issue – the curriculum, which was transformed and extended; modes of teaching and examining; college and university organization; attitudes to the community outside the universities; and university 'extension', which meant in the first instance university expansion. In the often painful process of debate in Victorian England, when the theory of the elite was being given a new form, balances were struck. Colleges strengthened their tutorial system, more university professors were appointed. A new breed of 'dons' emerged, but they were still dons. Many of them, not least Mark Pattison, were disillusioned with the domestic effects of reform, but others were proud of the influence of the universities on public life – both on men of power, public servants as they thought of themselves, and men interested in social protest. Their own influence as dons, indeed, along with their status, was magnified by the influence of their pupils, and by the pull of the university as the minority communications system of the day. We find in the nineteenth century, when we see the debate about the university taking something like its modern form, a whole variety of response. Alongside Pattison's intellectual uneasiness we have to set Jowett's worldliness; we have also to take account of what in the 1880s, when the debates were beginning to shift yet again and a new generation was emerging, was called 'the new Oxford movement', a movement which developed, I think for the first time, an overall though limited view of the relationship between the university and society as a whole. 'The most living interest in Oxford [is] now that in social questions. Yes! Oxford has turned from playing at the Middle Ages in churches, or at a Re-Renaissance in cupboards; and a new faith, with Professor Green as its founder, Arnold Toynbee as its martyr, and various societies for its propaganda is alive among us.'[1]

Throughout the debate, however, university education remained an education for an elite, a social elite living alongside an educational elite. 'Dons did not expect unusual or sudden changes in … social structure; and none occurred, at least none that can support a causal explanation of reform': what statistical evidence there is points to 'a remarkable continuity in the social background of undergraduates'.[2] It was not merely a matter of working-class exclusion: industrial and commercial wealth was not represented signi-

[1] *The Oxford Magazine*, 21 Nov. 1883, quoted in M. Richter, *The Politics of Conscience* (1964), p. 346. The attempt to associate the university or even to identify it with popular forces outside preceded the 1880s, and explains much, for example, of Frederic Harrison's sense of mission.

[2] Rothblatt, op. cit., p. 86.

ficantly either. Even in the industrial cities, where there was access to new wealth, institutions languished for want of recruits. During the late 1860s, when Oxford and Cambridge were in the midst of spontaneous reform, Queen's College, Birmingham was in debt to the extent of £10,000 and its charter was repealed, while Owen's College, Manchester was fighting against what was called 'half-hearted sympathy and openly expressed contempt'.[1] In 1885 James Bryce, who had spent six years as a lecturer at Manchester between 1868 and 1874 before taking his chair in Oxford, pointed out that Germany, with a population of 45 millions, had 24,187 university places, while England, with a population of 26 millions, had only 5,500. 'Nothing', he asserted, 'could so clearly illustrate the failure of the English system to reach and serve all classes.'[2]

Pattison in Oxford and Seeley in Cambridge were only two of the distinguished Oxbridge men who were shocked by this state of affairs, yet essentially it persisted despite the emergence of new institutions in the late nineteenth and early twentieth centuries. It may be said, indeed, that throughout the nineteenth century the universities were influenced relatively little by the economic and social changes which were transforming the country industrially, that many people inside them thought that they stood for a way of life superior to that involved in 'the pursuit of wealth by industrious competition',[3] and that outside opinion, curious or critical, in relation to the universities – leaving aside the opinion of their own graduates, many of whom had figured also as masters in the public schools, with whom they had the closest links – had only an extremely limited influence upon them. While there were some reformers who wanted to introduce more scientists into the elite or to widen the basis of its social recruitment, there was little challenge to the conception of the university as a place where an extended 'clerisy' was not 'trained' but 'educated'. Most Victorians who knew about these things would have settled for something like John Stuart Mill's statement in his inaugural address at a Scottish university – St Andrews – in 1867: 'The proper function of a university in national education is tolerably well understood. At least, there is a tolerably general agreement about what a university

[1] W. H. G. Armytage, *Civic Universities* (1955), p. 220.
[2] Preface to J. Conrad, *The German Universities for the Last Fifty Years* (1885), pp. xiv–xxx.
[3] See G. M. Young, *Victorian England, Portrait of An Age* (1936), p. 95, although Young's conclusion that 'the Universities broke the fall of the aristocracy by civilizing the plutocracy' is not borne out by university statistics. There was a Victorian gap here between aspiration and accomplishment, well brought out in Seeley's dream of 'a great teaching order which shall have its fixed lecture-rooms in every great town' seeking to raise 'the dead-level, insipid, barren, abject, shopkeeping life' of England (*A Midland University: An Address* (1887)).

is not. It is not a place of professional education. Universities are not intended to teach the knowledge required to fit men for some special mode of gaining their livelihood. Their object is not to make skilful lawyers, or physicians, or engineers, but equable and cultivated human beings . . . Men are men before they are lawyers, or physicians, or merchants, or manufacturers; and if you will make them equable and sensible men, they will make themselves capable and sensible lawyers or physicians.'[1] Mill had written earlier that he believed that universities had 'the especial duty . . . to counteract the debilitating influence of the circumstances of the age upon individual character, and to send forth into society a succession of minds, not the creatures of their age, but capable of being its improvers and regenerators'.[2]

This approach to university education – and it was broad enough to encourage research as well as teaching, the discovery of new knowledge as much as the transmission of existing knowledge – permitted or rather stimulated belief in what I would like to call a 'high' conception of the university as a special kind of institution within the constellation of educational institutions. Given the limitations both of undergraduates and of their teachers, given the fact that some at least among the elite might be attending the university for social reasons or, despite what Mill said, for the sake of professional advancement, the nineteenth-century university – the reformed university – should none the less offer the best to the best. The learner should become an explorer as well as a critic. The vision of learning was put most clearly by Mark Pattison when he exclaimed in a college sermon – note again the relationship with the religious background – that the university student should be placed in a position where 'his intelligence is not only the passive recipient of forms from without, a mere mirror in which the increasing crowd of images confuse and threaten to obliterate each other; it becomes active and throws itself out upon phenomena with a native force, combining or analysing them – anyhow altering them, inposing itself upon them . . . The point in time in our mental progress at which this change takes place cannot be precisely marked: it is a result gradually reached, as every form of life is developed by insensible transition out of a lower. As physical life passes into psychical life by a succession of steps in which there is no break, so does psychical life into spiritual. This is the life that the higher education aspires to promote, this is the power which it cherishes and cultivates, this is the faculty to which it appeals.'[3]

[1] Inaugural Address at St Andrews, printed in F. A. Cavenagh (ed.), *James and John Stuart Mill on Education* (1931), pp. 133–4.

[2] Essay on 'Civilization' (1836), printed in G. Himmelfarb (ed.), *Essays on Politics and Culture* (1963), p. 55.

[3] Quoted in Sparrow, op. cit., p. 129.

This statement of a philosophy of higher education is clearly very different from those twentieth-century statements about higher education which are primarily 'organizational' or quantitative in character. Yet it echoes through much twentieth-century writing in Britain and has influenced much English thinking within what may be called, not purely rhetorically, the English tradition. It lies behind the mathematics of the English staff-student ratios, and it has influenced some, at least, of the pioneers of new universities in a quite different phase of twentieth-century educational expansion. It has survived the fragmentation of the clerisy and the loss of the sense of a clerisy – the divisions of the academic community into several sections, each following its own way. For these reasons alone when one is talking about an elite, an excursion into Victorian history is relevant and worthwhile.

It is important to bear in mind, however, that Pattison and many men who thought like him envisaged what they regarded as the central experience of the university student in a broad context. Pattison, in particular, wanted 'the national mind' to work and live as its 'proper organization' in the university.[1] He was concerned deeply about the state of the nation. 'We have no system in anything;' he complained, 'our affairs go on by dint of our practical sense, a stupid precedent implying in all cases the want of method.'[2] He wanted universities to provide something more than a response to the practical needs of the time: to meet a national challenge by going beyond the practical sense, by creating an intelligent, highly-motivated elite, not in his case by underwriting social privileges. He anticipated therefore, in a nineteenth-century setting, the twentieth-century sense of national need.

IV

So long, however, as the social composition of the Oxford and Cambridge colleges remained unchanged and the role of the civic universities remained subordinate, limited, and inferior, the Victorian debate was very different from the twentieth-century debate as we know it. For a quite different view of the universities at the end of the nineteenth century, this time a view from outside, it is useful to turn to George Bernard Shaw's *Socialism for Millionaires* (1901) where he warned millionaires against endowing universities. 'Be careful,' he exclaimed, 'university men are especially ignorant and ill-informed. An intelligent millionaire, unless he is frankly an enemy of the

[1] M. Pattison, 'Oxford Studies', in *Oxford Essays* (1855), p. 259. 'The University must be the intellectual capital of the country, attracting to itself not all the talent, but all the speculative intellect' (ibid., p. 254).

[2] ibid., p. 284.

human race, will do nothing to extend the method of caste initiation practised under the mask of education at Oxford and Cambridge. Experiments in educational method and new subjects of technical education are . . . abhorrent to university dons and are outside the scope of public elementary education, and these are the departments in which the millionaire interested in education can really make his gold fruitful . . . It is the struggles of society to adapt itself to new conditions which every decade of industrial development springs on us that really need help. The old institutions, in the interests of that routine, are but too well supported already.'

This seems to me to be an appropriate text on which to pin much of the experience of the twentieth century, the main landmarks which I have already tried to describe. There were, indeed, more university and college teachers in the United States when Shaw wrote (24,000) than there were university and college students in England, and the American story had already diverged sharply from that of Britain. The Shavian approach – and characteristically it was stated more basically, with less irony and with more crudeness, by H. G. Wells – has become a key factor in twentieth-century English experience for four main reasons – (i) a fundamental change in the provision of school education, elementary and secondary, influencing aspirations, expectations, and the possibility of realizing them; (ii) a growth in the demand for graduates – not surprisingly, the Cambridge Appointments Service was founded in 1899 (it became a Board, with full university provision three years later); (iii) the rise of scale and organization in business, industry, and government, each of which made demands on the universities as science institutions; (iv) an increasing expenditure on scientific and technological research, already on the way before DSIR started with its first small grants during the First World War.

Given these four factors alone, the consequent growth both in student numbers and in university expeditures and the increasing involvement of the State in the process have had about them an air of social inevitability, although in English history, at least, there have always been as many brakes as accelerators. The nineteenth-century echoes seemed to provide as many alarms as inspirations. 'Those who know our universities best', Ernest Barker, then Principal of King's College, London, wrote in 1932 – and he was a university man who spent much of his academic life in Oxford and Cambridge as well as in London – 'are haunted by the fear that a democratic enthusiasm, as genuine as it is ill-informed, may result in an attempt to increase the quantity of education at the expense of its quality.'[1] 'One cannot

[1] E. Barker, 'Universities in Great Britain', in W. M. Kotsching and E. Prys (eds.), *Universities in a Changing World* (1932), p. 118.

but deprecate the attempts that are being made to found universities up and down the country,' another writer on what were then called 'the new universities' – the civic universities – had remarked four years before. 'If matters continue as they are at present we are promised a spate of new universities. They will either lower the standard of education in the universities that are already in being, and widen further the breach which exists between the old and the new, or else they will form a new and surely unnecessary type, perhaps most like the American small town college.'[1] 'Narrow the gates of entry', the Vice-Chancellor of Birmingham warned his colleagues in 1930, telling them that the percentage of really good students was lower than 'indulgent universities' cared to assume.[2]

Although during the 1960s new voices were raised,[3] this line of argument was never broken. 'More means worse' was a familiar cry when the latest batch of new universities was brought into existence during the early 1960s. A few weeks ago a fellow of a Cambridge college generalized boldly that recent student unrest was explicable mainly in terms of quantitative expansion by itself. 'Any community that grew at a rate beyond its normal growth' – whatever that was – 'was in danger of losing its characteristic ethos.'[4]

It would be easy to end the story here were it not for the students themselves and for the changing communications system which not only influences some students across national frontiers in quite different university situations (and the wind blows both across the Atlantic and across the Channel) but also influences public attitudes towards universities – to an exceptional extent perhaps in England – through attitudes towards students. In England, as in other countries, universities have become news largely during the last ten years, and, while public policy is not made by headlines, public attitudes well may be. The anti-student movement is strong, and public reactions, particularly local reactions, to relatively minor forms of student disturbances have been disproportionate, even dramatic, and certainly undiscriminating. Issues have been oversimplified in terms of discipline and authority, and the role of the mass-communications system has been simply

[1] H. G. G. Herklots, *The New University, An External Examination* (1928), pp. 87–8.
[2] Sir Charles Grant Robertson, *The British Universities* (1930), p. 75.
[3] For a trenchant and controversial attack on the attitudes of universities, see an article in *The Economist*, 'Let Dons Delight', 1 March 1958, which attacked elitist views in Oxford and Cambridge, 'imitation' in Redbrick, and 'suave' suggestions that there should be no changes. 'Everything must change,' it went on, 'the varieties of degree, the methods of selection . . . and [the view that] the universities' main task is producing firsts in arts and science for the top jobs.'
[4] Dr T. R. Henn, quoted in *The Times*, 4 Nov. 1968.

to focus on temporary issues, which has made for misunderstandings, rather than what might be called public education about the central issues of the expansion of higher education in the country. If the universities were to be left in these circumstances to the mercy of local pressures – and there are signs that there has been a trend in this direction behind the scenes for some time – then we are in for a very tough fight indeed in the course of the next twenty or thirty years.

Given the limited resources available for British universities and given the relatively generous overall national and local support for students through grants[1] – these are not administered through the U G C but directly by local authorities – any increase in misunderstandings between the public as citizens and taxpayers and the universities as bodies dependent for 80 per cent of their income on the State could jeopardize not only further university expansion but, in Britain, the precarious maintenance both of the 'system' as it exists and of the traditions – particularly the teaching tradition – which survive and, in some cases, have been recently revitalized. A minority, indeed, wishes to see the system go (it does not like systems) and the traditions disappear (it is very uneasy about traditions) without having so far any ideas of how to replace the system or the traditions; and conflict situations – part of the struggle of society, doubtless, to adapt itself to new conditions – have already arisen which do not fit easily into the history of universities in England as I have described it. Such issues could influence the course of discussions not only about university finance but about the still unsettled relationships between universities and other institutions of higher education. The balances on which the English 'system' depend are as delicate as the individual universities themselves are fragile. So much is true also, of course, of all universities at the present time. As Karl Jaspers put it a few years ago, 'complex relationships are not resolved but destroyed by simple solutions, such as separating research from teaching institutes, liberal education from specialized training, the instruction of the best from that of the many'.[2] All this points to the fact that 1968, with its compressed debates, does not provide a very satisfactory vantage point for the historian from which to survey either the future or for that matter the past.

---

[1] Relatively generous overall support that has substantially increased the proportion of students with working-class backgrounds as compared with students in European universities does not mean that there have not been sharp exchanges about the level of individual student's grants. For the effects of recent cheeseparing, see the interesting article by H. Johnson, 'The Economics of Student Protest', in *New Society*, 7 Nov. 1968.

[2] K. Jaspers, *The Idea of a University* (1960).

INTERCHAPTER

I

Response to Asa Briggs – ARNOLD NASH

With Professor Briggs we can endorse Sir Richard Livingstone's contention that the various universities of England are not expressions of any thought-out system. Universities have not been planned as a whole in terms of any conscious scheme of things. That generalization, of course, ceased to be true (for good or ill) over the last decade. The plate-glass universities clearly arose in terms of a substantial measure of centralized Whitehall consideration of and confusion about alleged national needs. Yet I want to argue, too, that although Livingstone is correct at the level of what has occurred in conscious thought, none the less there was *some* pattern underneath higher education in the UK as elsewhere. It's been there, but like good Anglo-Saxons we haven't thought about it. Here, Mark Pattison's strictures, as Professor Briggs reminds us, have been more than justified. Yet, if we are to take seriously Pattison's contention that a university is a place for the 'speculative intellect', is there not something more to be added? Let us then speculate.

You may not know the pattern in accordance with which your heart is beating, but the pattern is there all the time. An electrocardiogram will show both the pattern and the irregularities in that pattern. So, too, in the life of institutions: patterns are there functioning and effective even if we are unaware of them. It is human thought that unmasks, as Karl Mannheim used to say, these patterns for our evaluation by noticing the presuppositions which are entertained and whose presence makes the continued existence of these institutions possible. In this context, of course, the nineteenth century is the focus for our attention, for it was then that the intellectual foundations for Oxford and Cambridge as we know them today, as well as their later rivals, were laid.

There were three main factors moulding the life of the nineteenth century, each of which was antagonistic to careful analysis of the presuppositions which made their existence possible: these three factors were science, capitalism, and religion. The Church of England's attitude towards thought was indicated by the fact that it was prouder of its Prayer Book than of its theology. And the Free Churches were too much the expression of their age

– nineteenth-century liberal industrialist capitalism – to criticize Anglican thought (or lack of it) at the points where criticism was needed. Anglican and Free Churchman alike entertained a basic confusion that clouded religious thought in the nineteenth century, and it mou¹ded alike, before the century was completed, both the ancient institutions and the universities¹ which were founded in the Victorian era. The clashes between the Free Churches and the Anglican Church presupposed at so many points some common understanding of the situation, but this was never looked at. It is typical of controversy in the century as a whole that, being anxious to point out the inadequacies of the other side, neither antagonist looked at what *both* sides came to believe. F. D. Maurice vainly tried to teach his contemporaries better, but everything represented by the Victorian attitude towards progress was against him.

In particular, they identified 'religion' with 'churches' and they identified 'politics' with 'political parties'. And the clarion call as the Redbrick universities were being formed – and in a climate of opinion which finally set the pattern for Oxford and Cambridge, too – was neutrality in religion and in politics. But by this they meant neutrality between the institutionalized forms of these two important aspects of the life of the human spirit.² They did not realize that on the ultimate questions of human destiny the existentialists are correct: neutrality is impossible. Thus 'religious' choices and 'political' decisions are inescapable.

And so we now have a quaint paradox. The universities are now 'established' (their financial resources come more than 90 per cent from the State³) and their precincts have become the battleground for those fundamental collisions of minds and hearts that we can only call 'theological'.

In short, the pattern of thought behind the universities of England from Queen Victoria to Queen Elizabeth has been liberalism and this is the pattern of thought which today is being challenged by students throughout the world. There is a question, therefore, for the members of our generation before we finally have to throw in the towel to the ringmaster, Father Time. It is whether, fully accepting all the weaknesses of the world-view of liberalism, we can nevertheless safeguard those values of freedom of discussion and appeal to reason and fact as we seek to help our students build a world

---

¹ Here I include the 'university colleges' of Liverpool and Sheffield, Leeds and Birmingham, and the like because although they were not chartered as universities in Victorian times their character shaped at every turn the universities proper which sprang from them.

² Karl Marx would have enlightened them on both these points, but they were even less mindful of what he was saying than they were of Maurice's words.

³ Including the grant-aid for student fees coming from State sources.

beyond capitalism, beyond the distinction of 'pure' and 'applied' science, and beyond 'neutrality' in religion and politics. We owe Professor Briggs quite a debt for the skill with which he has described for us where we have been standing during the Victorian age which, beginning in the early nineteenth century, is ending in our lifetime.

II

In the discussion which followed, three main concerns were in the minds of participants: (i) how far is it any longer possible for any national committee – the U G C in Britain, for example – to consider not merely the practical problems of securing a fair distribution as between universities of the large sums of money now involved but the more fundamental question of the means by which the universities of a country can be persuaded to contribute, without robbing them of liberty, to what is thought to be the national good; (ii) as the system of higher education is developing in the U S, Canada, and Britain its overall complexity becomes greater. Can active relationships between the parts be secured so as to prevent the waste of money and waste of spirit there now seems to be? (iii) how organize a new university, or for that matter any new college of advanced education, so that it has, and keeps, essential unity?

With regard to (i) it was obviously easier for questions of first principle to be argued at length when in England the U G C was distributing £25,000,000 a year to 20 or so universities, many of them small, than now, when it was distributing £250,000,000 a year to over 40, many of them relatively large. Even as late as 1949, under Sir Walter Moberly's chairmanship, a good deal of time at quite a number of the monthly meetings was spent in discussing questions of principle with little immediate reference to finance, which was apt to come into the picture later in the day – when some of the principles might or might not be applied. In those days the U G C had no architects of its own to 'vet' the building plans submitted by the various universities or to supply carefully worked-out suggestions about the range of permissible study-bedroom sizes or percentage of circulation space appropriate to buildings of various types. Indeed, the total of backroom boys then employed in the U G C office was small, and universities themselves not accountable to the Committee for quite a number of the initiatives into whose desirability the U G C might now be expected to inquire. They used in fact to be able to take initiatives more freely than they any longer can.

A great deal of consideration was given by the U G C in the later 1950s to the possibility and desirability of setting up a number of new universities; the decisions too regarding where they should be sited were largely policy decisions involving concepts of what the nature and character of universities should be in our time. This thoughtfulness about matters of principle is of course still very typical of the UGC, but the rapid increase of its work and the much closer attention which has to be given to financial control hardly encouraged members to spend more time upon it. It has now a number of advisory sub-committees on a subject basis. However much they merely make recommendations or gave advice, it is clear enough that the more a national committee deputes its work to sub-committees constituted on a subject-area basis, and with a certain loyalty to that subject-area, the less easy it is for it to discuss the shape of university studies or the university curriculum as a whole. Maybe it is for university vice-chancellors or presidents to have nation-wide inter-university discussions on such matters. But why should only vice-chancellors and presidents be involved? And do such discussions in fact take place in a continuing way in any developed country?

The success of the UGC in its heyday – which seems now to be past – was at any rate in part due to the direct contact possible between the chairman of the Committee itself and the top officials at the Treasury who were concerned with university financing. The Chairman and Secretary of the UGC were on close personal and social terms with their 'opposite numbers'. Now the Treasury is no longer the government department with which the UGC deals. The money it distributes comes through the Department of Education, which is also the medium through which the finance comes that nourishes, though without the help of semi-public committees corresponding to the UGC, other parts of the higher education system. It may be significant that the new Chairman of the UGC is an economic historian and economist. Some kind of philosophy of higher education, in the sense of concern about fundamental issues of its purpose and desirable scope, ought to be in the minds of those with power to deploy state or federal or provincial funds to serve it – whether they are members of the British UGC, the Ontario Committee on University Affairs, among the Regents of the University of California, or civil servants in any country whose influence and power behind the scenes may be very great.

(ii) Some of the difficulties of working out a really coherent policy for higher education as a whole in states or provinces or country are obvious. In Britain, despite the rapid expansion of universities in recent years, the fraction of the relevant age-group who are members of them is still small: and in fact if not in theory Britain has decided that 'more means worse'. If she had not thought so she might have allowed expansion on American terms. As it is, she still believes, in 1968 at any rate, in a high staff-student ratio[1] and a good deal more face-to-face contact than is usual at Berkeley.

But the staff-student ratio in other parts of the higher education system in Britain is considerably lower. There is at present far too little contact between the parts and far too little discussion even about the possibility of future contacts. There are areas of secrecy in public life in Britain which do not help the dialogue that is necessary. And the inequality of present provision – for example of library facilities – between the universities, the colleges of technology, and the polytechnics is great.

Some of the recommendations of the Robbins Report, if implemented, would lead to a closer association between parts of the higher education system – more particularly a continuation of the process of closer association between colleges of education and universities that already has begun. But no proper assessment in financial terms of carrying out the Robbins recommendations as a whole has ever been made.

As it is, though, the contact and relationship between established universities and teachers' colleges is probably closer than are relationships between old-established universities and state universities in many states of America which have until recently been teachers' colleges.

(iii) It is interesting to notice how differently and how individually the newest universities in Britain, founded from 1961 onwards, are developing. Each is a unity, but a unity differently secured. Asa Briggs referred to the pattern in his own University of Sussex, by which there are schools of studies, to which students belong instead of to either departments or colleges. This organizational arrangement perhaps brought a greater sense of unity to the university than if departments were competitively powerful. The unity being built up in the University of Lancaster is helped by the careful and complex interlocking of major and minor subjects for study. These can be taken in a great variety of combinations, yet with avoidance of the arbitrariness sometimes attached to the building up of credits. The architecture of some of the new campuses being built in Britain is an active element in fostering unity of atmosphere and even purpose. So is that in a number of the new universities of Canada and the USA.

[1] In 1967–8: about 1:8.

CHAPTER 6

Institutions of Higher Education in the USA
Some Recent Developments
Dean E. McHenry

American higher education is indebted to Britain and Germany for two main patterns. The early colleges – William and Mary, Harvard, King's (later Columbia) – were modelled to some extent on Oxford and Cambridge colleges. The tradition is continued in the undergraduate divisions of the universities and in independent liberal arts colleges that were organized later. The German model greatly influenced the organization of Johns Hopkins in the 1870s and of Chicago and Stanford in the 1890s. Hopkins, founded by Daniel Coit Gilman after his disappointing three years as president of the new University of California, was the first real American university, with a full array of graduate and professional schools and emphasis on research. The older institutions – Harvard, Yale, Columbia, and Cornell – were soon transformed into modern universities. They were joined by Michigan, California, and other state universities.

No one has proposed a widely accepted definition of 'institutions of higher education'. Even if we included all post-secondary units, no agency can tell us for sure how many there are. My estimate is that around 2,500 to 3,000 call themselves colleges and universities and accept students at grades 13[1] and above. Dr Randall Whaley of the American Council on Education has identified more than 1,000 new institutions established since the Second World War.

It is difficult to relate many of these institutions to those in the rest of the English-speaking world. American higher education has bewildering diversity. One needs to know, in judging the value of a degree, something about the institution from which it was earned. Learning the pecking-order requires time, experience, and an elephantine memory!

[1] That is, at a minimum level corresponding roughly to that of the first-year sixth form in an English context.

As most of you know, this situation arises from the fact that the national government, with minor exceptions (such as Federal City College), has little direct role in chartering new institutions. The states have the major role, and they have a considerable variety of laws and regulations on the subject. At the risk of oversimplification, I would say that there are 100 to 150 well-rounded universities that have sufficient graduate and professional work and other attributes to claim the name. To confuse further, these include Dartmouth College and some others bearing the names colleges and institutes that are really universities. These institutions carry most of the graduate and research work of academic America.

Recently the New Jersey Board of Higher Education undertook to define and explain the characteristics of a university. It offers a

. . . wide range of undergraduate and graduate studies in the arts and science, programs in two or more professional fields such as medicine, law, public administration, engineering, or education, and operative programs of instruction leading to the doctorate or comparable terminal degree in at least three disciplines.

The Board also called for accreditation and adequate resources, financial ability, laboratory and library support, and financial base for research.

In addition, there are 100 or more good-to-excellent liberal arts colleges not affiliated with universities and confining themselves largely to bachelor's degree work. And they include many calling themselves universities! Wesleyan University of Middletown, Connecticut, is a good example. These institutions have made their reputations in undergraduate work and most are content to concentrate there. They include such illustrious colleges as Swarthmore, Oberlin, Antioch, Reed, Carlton, Pomona, Amherst, and Williams.

The remaining 1,000-plus institutions include the less prestigious colleges and universities, teacher training colleges, technical institutes, and the two-year community or junior colleges.

California pioneered in attempting to spell out the differentiation of functions among the segments of public higher education. The Master Plan for Higher Education, of which I had the privilege of being a co-author, spelled out the tasks of the three categories:

The junior colleges offer (1) standard collegiate courses for transfer to higher institutions, (2) vocational-technical fields leading to employment and (3) general or liberal arts courses.

The state colleges provide instruction in liberal arts and sciences, in applied fields and in the professions both to undergraduates and to graduates through the master's degrees.

The University provides instruction in liberal arts and sciences and the professions (exclusively in graduate law, medicine, veterinary medicine and architecture) and has special responsibilities in research and doctoral work.

The independent colleges and universities (which include Stanford and Cal. Tech.) were left to define their own functions.

Classification problems plague anyone undertaking description of the institutional framework of American higher education. I have spoken of public and independent segments, yet the difference is often in terms of shades of grey. Stanford and Columbia claim membership in the private sector, yet each received more than $60 million of Federal support in 1966. Pennsylvania and Pittsburgh are considered private, yet receive millions of state funds annually. California is a state university but received around $35 million in voluntary support one recent year. As the years go by the distinction between public and private is being obscured.

Similarly we use an historic term, 'Land Grant College', to misidentify institutions that have little more than vestiges of their agricultural and mechanical beginnings, and are today modern multi-purpose universities. The Massachusetts Institute of Technology, incidentally, was Land Grant. Several great state universities, among them Wisconsin, Minnesota, Illinois, and California, are Land Grant institutions as well.

The name 'state college' is especially confusing to visitors from abroad. The institutions called state colleges range from large and excellent university colleges with professional schools to weak, badly-financed, and small institutions. A shift of importance is the tendency to relinquish 'church-related' status. Many institutions that had religious moorings have moved towards secularization.

Accepting the usual public–private classification, there has been a dramatic shift in workload. In 1920 two out of three students were enrolled in private institutions; today the ratio is reversed – two out of three students are in public colleges or universities. Most of the large campuses are among the public institutions. Of those with 10,000 or more students in 1966, 93 were public and 27 private.

Each decade a higher and higher proportion of the population is in attendance at colleges and universities. More than two decades ago a commission appointed by President Truman reported that at least 49 per cent of young Americans were capable of utilizing 14 years of education. We do not yet have that proportion in post-secondary institutions, but around 50 per cent of high school graduates do go on to college eventually.

The community or junior colleges are likely to bear the greatest quantitive increase. They typically are 'open-door' institutions that require only a high school diploma for admission. They usually offer a wide variety of vocational courses. In California, where we have 88, they provide the first two years of university work to many students, and two years of terminal work for those going directly into employment. Increasingly, apprenticeship in the trades is being supplemented or replaced by instruction in the junior colleges.

INSTITUTIONAL GOVERNANCE

Governing boards – usually called trustees or regents – have changed rather little in form in several decades. They meet as seldom as annually and as often as monthly. They range in activity from near dormancy to over-concern with small details. Private boards are usually self-perpetuating, filling their own vacancies. Public boards often are appointed by an executive authority, such as the governor of a state or the mayor of a city, but a few, including the University of Michigan, have elective members. Both private and public boards may have *ex officio* members, including the chief executive officer of the institution. Pressure is mounting for faculty and even student membership on governing boards, but few institutions have so provided. Recent events in California have led to a considerable effort to take political officers off the regents and trustees.

The president or chancellor is almost invariably chosen by the governing board. He, in turn, is usually given substantial voice in the selection of his vice-presidents or vice-chancellors. The crucial role of the president or chancellor was a main theme for M. R. Ingraham.[1] One reviewer summarized the position as follows:

The typical president of an American university or liberal arts college is a 55 year old man with an earned doctoral degree and substantial experience as a professor. He had held office for 6 years and has another 5 years to go to equal the tenure of his immediate predecessor. He serves as the institution's principal representative to the public, as its internal educational leader, as an officer burdened with too much routine and trivia, and as the member of the academic community most often called on for a variety of kinds of public service. He is the most overworked man on the campus and occupies the most exposed position. Students, faculty, trustees, alumni, friends, and critics are all plural. But he stands alone.[2]

The organized body of the whole faculty, often termed 'senate', has been rising in power and influence in most of the better institutions. Governing boards either delegate directly to the faculty, or to the chief executive. Presidents and chancellors normally are assigned general administrative and business and financial matters. Faculty bodies often are given courses and

[1] *The Mirror of Brass* (Madison: University of Wisconsin Press, 1968).
[2] *Science*, 29 November 1968.

curricula and sometimes admissions. It is common practice to have divided jurisdiction over academic appointments and promotions. Institutions all over America are confronted with new demands for 'student power', but few have worked out a solution that gives a sense of participation without yielding vital controls to apprentices in learning. On campuses with the cluster or collegiate approach, there is substantial delegation of administrative and academic authority to the college level.

STATEWIDE COORDINATION

States with several public institutions quite often develop a need for some machinery of coordination. An older form, recently expanded, is the governing board with responsibilities for multi-campus systems. Examples are the Regents of the University of California, with the President of the University as executive officer, and the Trustees of the State University of New York, with the Chancellor. Smaller states, such as Arizona and Montana, have a common board over several institutions, but without a strong executive officer. These multi-campus boards have some of the allocative functions of university grants committees.

Great change in recent years has come through the establishment of boards to coordinate separate institutions and systems. At least 39 of the states have statutory or voluntary boards; such agencies were virtually unheard of 25 years ago. Coordinating councils and boards not only are more numerous, they are also increasingly endowed with functions and authority. Some are, in fact, superboards. More and more of them have a director or a chancellor as executive officer.

The coordinating bodies are commonly assigned the tasks of programme review, budget review, data collection and reporting, and long-range planning. They are the nearest American equivalent to the university grants committee, yet fall short of the efficiency of the British or Australian versions. I know of no American state in which coordinating board review has replaced fully state legislative and executive review. Instead it adds another layer of control, another wheel to a vehicle that already has four or five. There remains a great opportunity for some state to show what can be done with a coordinating staff so good that its findings would be accepted by governor and legislature without re-examination of details.

Both public and private sectors increasingly are participating in consortia, ranging from bilateral graduate programmes in a single subject to interstate compacts for cooperative relations on broad fronts. The Southern Regional and the Western Interstate Commission on Higher Education are examples of the latter.

THE FINANCIAL PROBLEM

The numbers involved in American higher education are, of course, enormous. In autumn 1968, between 6·5 and 7 million students enrolled. The institutions have current expenditures of about $15 billion this year. About one-third of this money came from the states; lesser amounts derive from national, municipal, and school-district sources. Student fees and voluntary support make up most of the rest. There is almost nothing comparable to British student support. Undergraduate scholarships are awarded on the basis of need determined by review of a parents' confidential statement.

Student fees and tuition have risen steadily since the Second World War. The averages are now at the level of $360 in public (for legal residents) and, I estimate, $1400 in private institutions. Higher education has capital costs of around $3 billion per year, some of which is available from Federal grants and loans. Student housing is financed separately, mainly through loans which are amortized by fees over thirty-year periods. Organized research money comes mainly from Federal grants and contracts. In 1966, 100 institutions received over 70 per cent of all Federal support. From all sides, from every segment, there is abundant evidence of a crisis in finance. Costs are going up faster than sources of income. State spending is levelling off, Federal grants – notably National Science Foundation – are being stretched out, private giving and increased tuition charges are unable to fill the gaps. In the long pull some kind of Federal grants to institutions of higher education may provide the required resources. But there are formidable political and constitutional barriers that must be overcome before block grants can be made to private and especially to church-related colleges and universities.

TRENDS IN LEARNING

I propose now to call attention to several developments in the organization of instruction and its relationship to social factors.

Cluster Colleges. Interest has been high in a revival of the notion of the residential microcollege, associated with other colleges so as to combine the intimacy of small units with the economies of scale possible with larger ones. For many, the models have been Oxford and Cambridge, or Claremont in California. At the University of California, Santa Cruz, we have four colleges in operation and a fifth under construction. Several other institutions have launched house plans that have similar objectives. At Santa Cruz the colleges range in size from 525 to 700 student members, but the next college will accommodate 800. Each college is headed by a provost and fellows, each of whom is half time in the college and half time on campus-wide professorial appointment with what we call the 'board of studies' of his discipline. Many administrative problems are intensified by the devolution involved in setting up semi-autonomous colleges.

Independent Study. It is difficult to get an accurate picture of whether or not independent study is growing. My impression is that expansion is confined mainly to a few rather new centres. One-to-one tutorials are so expensive that few of us who have strict limitations on the number of academic positions can afford many. The group tutorial, which can run to four or five, may be more suitable in some fields and for younger students. In most cases faculty time for close instruction must be 'bought' by having some rather large lectures. Santa Cruz and other institutions are experimenting with some student-taught courses.

Community as Resource. The issue of relevancy can be answered in part through involvement in the community and its use as a learning resource. Our students get a great deal out of serving as elementary school teachers' aides as part of a psychology course. We are now establishing a community studies centre in an underdeveloped neighbourhood of the nearest metropolitan area. One college, Merrill, has fieldwork as a major part of its learning experience. Urban institutions, of course, have abundant opportunities for simultaneous work and study.

The University of California system is embarking on a major effort to meet what President Hitch calls the 'Urban Crisis'. The programme will sponsor projects that approach solutions to unmet needs of underprivileged sectors of the population. Many students and faculty now see themselves as agents of social change. Campuses all over the country are bringing minority students to their institutions in record numbers. The task ahead will not be easy, but it must be done. If it can be done without undermining academic standards and diverting undue amounts of faculty energies from scholarly activities, then both the university and the nation will be the stronger for it.

Study Abroad. Organized programmes for study abroad are now commonplace. They usually offer a chance for students to continue credit work during a period of residence abroad. Some institutions take their students into American enclaves in foreign countries; as a parent of a Stanford student I was pleased with the results obtained under such a plan. Others place their students in foreign universities and encourage them to live with non-American students; the University of California has chosen this more exacting system and is reasonably satisfied. The difference in living costs between the USA and other countries is often great enough to finance much of the necessary travel costs.

Learning Media. Great progress has been made in instructional services Language laboratories and other audio facilities are now widespread. Interest in programmed learning appears to have slowed down; I have noted few advances in teaching machines in the past five years. On the other hand, the expansion of television use and the availability of equipment, thanks often to Federal grants, may soon lead to a quiet revolution in teaching to large numbers. At Santa Cruz we have a new Communications Building with three television studios and with cable ties to all colleges and academic buildings. The hard part may still be ahead: getting the teaching staff to use the facilities.

Year-round Operation. A decade ago the twelve-month academic calendar and year-round utilization of physical plant was thought by some to be capable of bringing a junior millennium. They probably are less sure of realizable economies now. The trimester plan may have been one factor in Pittsburgh's fiscal crisis. Students stay away from summer quarters in droves both at Berkeley and UCLA. Institutions that have retained the two-semester plan and inserted a January intersession may have a more viable alternative. Savings are possible but hard to realize.

CONCLUSION

American higher education, despite its unsolved problems, has made significant contributions. Perhaps the greatest is the provision of wide varieties of post-secondary programmes to fit the diversity of abilities and interests of students. As the door of higher education is opened for more and more of the lower one-half of high school graduates, institutions to serve their needs must be developed and expanded.

Many of us are convinced that the junior or community college is the main instrument through which this can best be achieved. These multi-purpose institutions offer opportunities for study to young people in their home communities; they also bring cultural events to areas virtually untouched by live music and drama for the half century since radio came on the scene.

The USA inevitably has a pluralistic society and it is equally inevitable that the diversity of society should be reflected in higher education. Most of the institutions of higher education should survive in some form. Some private ones will become public, as Buffalo joined the State University of New York, Kansas City University became University of Missouri, Kansas City. Some men's and women's colleges will join together to achieve co-education or develop new consort colleges. A few weak institutions are giving up the struggle and dying. But by and large the academic establishment is reasonably healthy, vigorous, and well supported.

INTERCHAPTER

I

Response to Dean McHenry – EDWARD SHEFFIELD

My role is that of the questioner. The outsider as questioner has one advantage: his questions are not protective; and one disadvantage: his questions may be inappropriate or unjust because they are uninformed. I would like us to consider the marvel of higher education in the USA, fusing British and German models and creating something distinctively American. One of the greatest contributions made to higher education by America is the openness and variety of the institutions it has created. The land grant college has been another of the great American contributions to higher education, responding to the needs of the society and situation in which it found itself. These are great American demonstrations of how relevant to social needs institutions of higher education can be. The liberal arts college was exported from England to the USA and back to England. The Americans thought that they were copying Oxford and Cambridge, but in fact they were developing these colleges in their own American style. Recently, I understand, English colleges have been copying the American. The ultimate in the development of American higher education is the multiversity, which strives to be all things to all men. And the latest innovation is the community college, open to all with the desire for some sort of post-secondary education.

What are the determinants of the course of development of higher education in the USA, as compared with, say, Britain? What were they? What are they now? Are they national? On a governmental level? Or from other sources, for example the Carnegie Commission? Are they state-generated, depending on state financing and policies? Are they institutional responses to felt needs? Are they a multiplicity of demographic and social pressures, responded to on an *ad hoc* basis, but within the context of a clearly felt if not clearly enunciated belief in as much education as possible for as many people as want it and can profit by it?

What do the American people want of their institutions of higher education? Do they want personal benefits such as certification, cultivation, soul-mates? Or social benefits – chemists, doctors, lawyers, teachers, engineers, businessmen, systems analysts, etc.? Do they count on them for discovery or research? Have the universities not provided all this – in social terms and, for *some* (those who attended), in individual terms?

What is the problem? To enable even more to have the experience of accessibility to higher education?

When we talk of relevance or responsiveness, does this mean that institutions of higher education respond to the many winds of demand? Or that they respond mainly to the demands of enterprise capitalism or the military-industrial complex or the funding state, i.e. the sponsoring elements of society? Are universities too responsive?

Look at the composition of governing boards of public universities and of statewide coordinating agencies and legislative budget committees: these often reflect, sometimes too directly, the community at large, even the political community, and too little the academic community.

With respect to involvement and social action, one must ask with Dr McHenry, 'Should institutions of higher education become involved in the community? Should they be agents for change in society? The answer', he says, 'seems to be yes.' In an expansion of a section of his paper which he has permitted me to read to you, Dr McHenry continues:

The University of California is embarking on what it calls an 'Urban Crisis' programme. This programme will support projects in various parts of the state where urban problems will be given the resources of the university to seek solutions to unmet needs.

This involvement in the community has brought about a new set of attitudes within institutions of higher education. Scholars who have traditionally seen themselves as responsible for the acquisition and transmission of knowledge, for sharing this knowledge in expert consultation, and for training the next generation of experts, have begun to identify equally with the institution and with the community in which it is found. Students are frustrated by their political powerlessness both on the campus and in the community. Many students and faculty now see themselves as agents of social change in the society and the former attempts to meet the needs of society are now being revised to exert leadership and to bring about change in the society.

Attempts to bring about change have been evident to all through the host of student demonstrations that have occurred across the country. In many cases only a minority of students and faculty are involved, but there is no doubting that changes have occurred within higher education and within the larger community as a result.

Less radical approaches to involvement in the community can be seen in the development of new institutions that are designed to fit into the existing community and to change it through its presence. The Cleveland State University is being built within the urban setting and will be involved in the lives of all people at all levels through its activities. The training of teachers and leaders, extensive education of many types for adults, and cooperative community action programmes will go along with undergraduate and graduate education.

The new attitude of involvement in the community is also seen at Columbia University, in the wake of its recent troubles, in the decision to expand through the slum area but with the goal of replacing buildings for the poor who will be displaced.

The most subtle involvement in the community includes the programmes which bring minority students or economically deprived students on to the campuses across the country. Yale, Vassar, and UCLA have been inviting high school seniors to their campuses for summer programmes or for work-study opportunities. Other programmes such as EOP (Economic Opportunity Program), which is federally funded, have introduced large numbers of students to higher education. The institutions which participate in the EOP programme have made special admission arrangements and have developed supplementary programmes to assist these students through their adjustment to the new academic demands.

Programmes of this nature have brought about changes both in higher education and in the community. Minority groups have increased their visibility on otherwise homogeneous campuses, and special programmes and courses of study are being demanded. Other young people in the community have become motivated toward higher education through the impact of friends and neighbours who for the first time have been able to get advanced education.

The question is still asked – should institutions of higher education become involved in the community? Should they be agents for change in society? The answer seems to be yes. For many state-supported institutions it is difficult to remain non-partisan, for many private institutions it is difficult to survive as an educational and cultural island. The community is making demands of higher education that it cannot ignore and the choices seem to include: being shaped by the community, shaping the community, or cooperatively sharing the community.

For students, learning should be integral with experience. The search for self-definition occurs through personal experience, and that experience is very much determined by the dominant urban environment of America. The city with its joys and its sorrows is the stage on which individuals must perform. Higher education must be involved with the community if it is to adequately serve the needs of youth and if it is to remain relevant as a leader in society.

Dr Clark Kerr, in a recent Dunning Trust lecture at Queen's University, Ontario, spoke on the report of the Carnegie Commission on the Future of American Higher Education. He said that the Commission would recommend that a foundation should be set up to give massive support to US universities to prepare them to serve the cities and towns. 'It's a little late for universities to preserve their virginity,' he said. 'It's time that the universities were helped to serve all of society in a more equal way.'[1]

What does Dr McHenry mean by his 'community'? Is it local, regional, national, world? How can universities serve *now* and still preserve their detachment sufficiently to prevent the alienation of some members of the academic community, while retaining their capacity to serve *in the future* when forces may be differently aligned?

II

Two main issues were considered in the general discussion which ensued: what are the motivations of people in entering upon a period of higher education – why is there such a demand for it? and do institutions of higher education succeed if they supply a country with people who will be intelligent 'doers' within their society as it is, or is such a test inadequate?

Clearly, one of the forces impelling people in an industrial society towards a period of higher education is the elimination of many of the jobs which used to be filled by people with only a secondary education. In advanced technological societies, e.g. in many of the states of the USA, there is a strong opinion among those already in posts that a period of higher education will help to keep young people out of the labour market – and incidentally off the streets too – for an extra period and thus prevent them from being competitors for jobs. Such opinion is incorporated in the minimum wage laws and laws against the employment of 'boys' which are common in many states. Vocational training pursued to a later age than previously is seen as an answer not only to the demand for skilled people but also to the need for skilled people to be more generally educated and civilized before they enter the labour market.

Once a situation has been created where it is the normal thing not merely for the more wealthy or socially privileged classes to have a period at college or university but for many to do so who have no such special advantages, the status symbols tend to move down. Those lower in the social scale say: 'We'd like to have some too.' This movement, Sanford maintained, is irreversible and one of the chief reasons for the flowering of state colleges all over the USA. Here is 'one of the things that democracy is about'. State colleges in the course of time develop into universities themselves, and an increasing proportion of black students will be a natural expectation. The

[1] *Toronto Globe and Mail*, Dec. 1968.

more education a Negro receives, the more chance he has – even allowing for all the prejudice against him – of getting a better job.

It was pointed out that the system of higher education as it was developing in North America was a powerful instrument for helping people to accommodate themselves to changes in the structure of their society: it gave them training in newer skills; if it was itself sufficiently in touch it would also cater for people who later in life needed training for new jobs because their previous occupation was folding up with the advent of some new technology. Men and women could no longer count on being in the same job for life – but with expansionist pressures so widespread there was no fear at present that there would be too few jobs for those having adequate expertise to tackle what was required.

The comparative contentment up to this point with the diagnoses of what is happening was shattered by accusatory questions from Kenneth Hare and Bryan Wilson. Are students in fact not being fashioned to become useful units in a mechanized and industrialized civilization with the universities (betrayed from within) more and more deprived of the power to prevent this from happening? Are not universities ceasing to be places which cultivate a philosophic sense? They tend to produce a student class not in real communication with other people – out of touch, indeed, save with other students. Are there not far too many students seeking the privileges and advantages of higher education than are really fitted for it, American universities being the victims of many subtle pressures from without to accept them? Does not the enormous demand for people qualified with Ph.D.s lead to a trivialization of research? Is not the situation in fact that many young people are encouraged to aspire much more highly than their abilities warrant?

Universities, it was said, are being deprived of the power to make central decisions or to act from their own centre. And what is happening in the universities of North America is being repeated or about to be repeated in universities in other advanced societies. Presidents and vice-chancellors have lost a good deal of power and authority in recent years; but power which disappears at the top does not necessarily reappear at the bottom. Society expects universities to be able to make rapid and effective decisions; but in the last ten years the whole evolution, especially of the North American university, has led away from this possibility. It is the victim of the demand that it should take in more and more students, exercising a custodial function over them. As R. M. Hutchins once remarked: 'universities are becoming places of accommodation for the otherwise idle young. They must be sanitary and morally effective: nothing else matters much.' In this cynical comment there are seeds of economic truth. The social and economic significance of the vastly increased proportion of the large group which is having a university education we cannot as yet fully see.

Great play is made in Canada about the need for an educated labour force as a step towards the growth of national productivity. Economic growth, it is said, will be retarded unless the labour force is educated well into university level. We are also told that unless we introduce large quantities of research into universities the import of original ideas into industry will be held back.

But what is actually going on in the race for productivity is the selective destruction of jobs. Lots of people are going to be left out or left over. The social consequences in the long term of turning loose people who are now in the higher education system upon an economy insufficiently able to absorb them are horrifying to think about. Should it not be the job of the universities to stress once again, much more powerfully, education for the good life; and liberal, philosophic, and artistic studies? They are neglected in Canada. Yet can the universities really stem the tide, decide to go against the current? For society will not be able adequately to use all those it is training for industrial purposes. It won't need them all. Work is now society's principal agency of social control and universities can only with danger trade out of the system. In the past the custodial function of universities was quite important – as it was in Sunday schools where 'custody rather than sanctity was the first objective' – and custody, lightly imposed, used to be accepted by students. But this reflected a particular concept on both sides of the purpose of the institution.

In the universities, as in the world outside, however, the sense of community has broken down and the old trustful, face-to-face relationship is no longer possible. And if you can no longer by looking embrace the community in which you live, there will be a tendency to resort to abstractions and classifications in your dealings with others. Students, used to abstract concepts in their daily work, now see themselves as a 'class' – and not simply in a particular university but, thanks to the mass media, in a world-wide location. They take on a mass connotation of themselves, interpreting themselves as a 'class' in contradistinction to that other 'class' – ourselves – whom they see as a category of privileged people. Young dons who 'go over to the other side' are not, however, regarded with much respect.

Another, older, strand in the situation is the certification role of the university, now increasingly important because it has become man's principal point of identity in the world. But how many people does our society really need to have educated to an advanced level? What good does a Ph.D.

do except to the person who did the work? It is doubtfully meaningful in many cases; it certainly does not add to the real total of knowledge.

What goes on in junior colleges is also suspect. They mop up young people not needed on the labour market, but many of their students have aspirations far higher than their possibilities of achievement, so in these institutions they are not so much educated as 'cooled out' and gently persuaded into accepting less ambitious courses. Democracy, in giving equal chances to so many, is running a severe risk of being an administrative, manipulative system in which people are given apparently equal opportunities of going through the open door but actually have it slammed very hard in their face or behind their backs as they go though. The junior college record is sometimes of that kind – though it is not alone in being a manipulative agency in our society.

Ben Morris reacted sharply to this point of view. He maintained that the level which a group reaches is related to its opportunities as a group. Differentials between individuals are not as important by themselves as we are apt to think. This ought to be absolutely clear to us if we look at the differences between stone-age men and ourselves: the difference in intelligence between individual stone-age men must have been as great as the difference in intelligence between individuals today. But what any society can do depends very much upon the level of general civilization it has reached. The existence of intellectual differentials is not to be denied at all, but it has to be put into perspective. The level of performance of groups and of populations is related to the degree of education they receive.

This also seems important in relation to the spectre of having too little work for certain sections of the population. In an industrial civilization a good deal of work is still derived from inner compulsions and it is important not to define work in too limited a way. But anyway work is not the only way towards securing a sense of identity. We overestimate the importance of doing and greatly underestimate the importance of being and feeling. The arts must be taken more seriously – both the fine arts and the many kinds of craft. There is a range of talents roughly to be called intellectual which have only a tenuous relationship with feeling, yet it is with this limited range that universities are increasingly identified. There is, however, a whole range of human talents and achievements lying outside the present ambit of higher education that are very important.

Others thought that we ought to be following up more seriously and intensively the topics opened up by this consideration of the ethic of work and the role of feelings. The basic challenge offered by student unrest ought to be grappled with more articulately: and the take-off point could be McHenry's classic assumption that the faculty is essentially the university.

This notion derives from the apprentice-journeyman-master kind of model – and has a high degree of consistency with a guild conception of the academic discipline. Certainly it has an intimate relationship to the notion of professionalization which has affected the academic enterprise ever since the building of Johns Hopkins, particularly since the Second World War. The tempo of social change in the contemporary world, which is quite unprecedented, raises the question of the dominant basis on which the curriculum in the us has been established. There are two aspects: (a) the notion of transmitting a cultural legacy which has to be mastered. The university is a place where a body of knowledge is incorporated, the mastery of which is deemed to be the best preparation for effectively coping with the problems of tomorrow. (b) The professional idea of unravelling or unfolding the inner logic of a discipline – e.g. by studying physics, biology, history. One significant vein in student protest is the challenge to both these ideas. To contend that a cultural heritage is an aid to effective coping with tomorrow no longer seems viable; and the faculty, monopolists of the mystery, are *not* the university. The university has become a place where people attempt to deal, through a process of debate, with the great questions of today in the light of whatever wisdom the race has been able to bring to bear on them. Education might well consist in a growing sophistication in the kind of information, the quality of logic, the types of wisdom, that one can acquire in this quest for the influence one can exert on the rapidly changing society in which one lives. Such a theory not only challenges the basis of curriculum but also the idea that the elders in a society have the right and obligation to instruct the young and the young have an obligation to be instructed.

What we are hearing is a not completely articulate voice saying that a joint quest by the elders and the young represents an ill-formed but none the less perfectly respectable new model of the educational enterprise, under which the faculty will *not* be the university, and where jurisdictional considerations become energized in ways that are not entirely rational in a profession which now prizes chiefly the values of cognitive rationality. On purely social grounds, higher education must be subjected to repeated scanning as conditions change.

CHAPTER 7

Institutions of Higher Education in Canada
Some Recent Developments
Claude Bissell

In Canada, as elsewhere, the last twenty years have been a period of sweeping change in higher education, the quantitative change, although initially over-powering, dwarfed by the subsequent qualitative changes. In some respects, the historical inheritance facilitated the process; in others, it was a complicating, inhibiting factor. At this time, one can report that the system, in both French and English Canada, has demonstrated powers of response and adaptation, and has gained in overall strength. What is the nature of the Canadian inheritance in higher education, and how has it conditioned the events of the last twenty years?

I begin with some positive factors. First of all, the system of higher education has had, in Canadian terms, a long evolution. The establishment of institutions of higher learning coincides with the emergence of the country as a coherent political entity. Laval's roots go back to the original Collège de Québec of 1635, and the first English-speaking institution, King's College, Windsor, was founded in 1789 when Nova Scotia was just beginning to emerge as a recognizable society. As the country spread westward, the founding of a university followed hard upon the creation of each new provincial jurisdiction. Professor Robin Harris, the leading Canadian historian of higher education, records with evident satisfaction the educational achievement of colonial society at all levels.

[In England there] were no publicly supported elementary schools until 1870 and no publicly supported secondary schools until 1902. In 1900 there were only four degree-granting universities in England – Oxford, Cambridge, Durham, London. In contrast, an integrated system of publicly supported elementary and secondary schools was provided for in Ontario by acts of 1846 and 1871 respectively, and in 1867 there were no less than seven degree-granting universities – Toronto, Trinity,

Victoria, Queen's, Ottawa, Albert, and Regiopolis. There were parallel developments between 1840 and 1890 in New Brunswick, Nova Scotia, and within the
context of a much smaller population in Prince Edward Island. In Newfoundland,
which was more directly under English influence than these Canadian provinces, a
comparable system of public education was not developed until the 20th century. In
the West, systems of public education essentially modelled on those already provided for in Eastern Canada were introduced by legislation within months of the
creation of each province. The provincial universities of Manitoba, Saskatchewan,
and Alberta are almost as old as the provinces themselves.[1]

As in the United States, the university foundations were the result of a
combination of piety and public enterprise. In Canada the piety was, if anything, more intense than in the United States, and more durable. Whereas in
the United States the religious associations tended to wither away and to be
supplanted by a stern scientific secularism, in Canada they persisted, although
often in an attenuated and non-doctrinal form. One of the incidental by-
products of the religious association in Canada was the development of the
idea of federation, which was a device for linking the sectarian college with
the non-sectarian university. This is the concept followed at the University of
Toronto and with modifications in several other universities in Ontario and
in the West. This system enabled the religious sects to preserve their
traditions, without denying to their adherents the greater resources of the
state-supported university. In general, the religious colleges concentrated
upon the humanities, and the university on the physical and social sciences.
The result was often a structure more related to metaphysics than to principles of organization, but it provided a basis for a durable college system,
and made it possible for diverse traditions to flourish within one composite
institution. Even when formal religious ties disappeared, there remained a
style, an emphasis, a set of values, that deeply affected students and influenced the scholarship of teachers. Moreover, the religious colleges were
often bolder and more experimental than the university, often less sensitive
to popular pressure. They could be both sanctuary and buffer. In Quebec,
until the 'Quiet Revolution' in this decade, the French-speaking universities
were closely integrated with the Church, and the university was often
thought of as giving moral and philosophical support to the teachings of the
Church. Now the clearest sign of radical change in Quebec is the increasing
secularization of education, and the full acceptance of the idea of the university as a free institution whose primary responsibility is to society.

A second positive factor is the tradition of unvexed liberalism that has

---

[1] Robin Harris, 'English Influence on Canadian Education', *The Canadian Forum*,
XLVI, April 1966, p. 290.

permeated the history of higher education in English Canada. The universities have managed to insulate themselves against political interference. There was a dangerous period in the nineties in Ontario when political interference at the University of Toronto helped to precipitate a student strike. But the record has been generally good despite the virtual disappearance in recent years of the private university, and the assumption by the State of almost complete financial responsibility for higher education. Even this heavy State responsibility has not yet brought any political machinery, such as the public election of trustees or the detailed examination of university budgets by a legislature. It is bringing, however, coordinating, interposing bodies that are variants on the British University Grants Committee. In Ontario, where the system is most advanced, the central body is, I should judge, less intrusive into institutional affairs than the Grants Committee, more closely associated with government policy by reason of a membership drawn partially from government and business.

These have been the principal positive factors that helped to provide a firm base for the rapid developments of the last twenty years. But there have been negative factors as well. Most serious has been the comparative slowness of the Canadian university system to respond to social changes, in particular to demands for widening of the basis of higher education. Canadian universities began with a strong elitist emphasis. The most influential group in the foundation of universities was the United Empire Loyalists who were liberal and democratic by contrast with the family compacts of colonial Canada, but staunchly tory in a North American context. To them a university was essentially a means of maintaining an orderly and progressive society by preparing a group to give guidance and direction to that society. Later on in the century there were infusions of Scottish educational egalitarianism, and lip-service, at least, to the idea that higher education should have a wide, popular basis, and should not be restricted to a small, select social group. But this fell far short of the more ebullient and expansive American democracy. In the sixties, the land grant call to arms was not heard north of the border, chiefly, of course, because Canada at that time was still a group of little self-contained societies in the east, not even daring to dream of its western heritage. The Canadian universities were also unprepared for the expansion in function that came in the United States in the eighties and nineties with the establishment of German-style research graduate schools. Indeed, the Canadian universities were suspicious of this kind of expansion, preferring to believe with Newman that research was essentially alien to the university spirit. The suspicion of research and its co-partner, graduate work, continued until very recent times. Now that graduate work and research are fully accepted as university responsibilities, and have indeed been given first priority at many universities, we are only beginning to reach that second stage of suspicion when research and graduate work are looked upon as relatives who have moved in and taken over the bar and pantry.

The slowness to respond to social factors was accompanied by an indifference to experimentation. English–Canadian universities followed a pattern that admitted of only minor variations from institution to institution. The emphasis was upon education in the liberal arts, with a special tenderness for mathematics, languages, and moral philosophy; by the end of the century the larger universities were beginning to accept professional responsibilities, although Canadian universities have not shown the alacrity in this area that has been displayed by their American contemporaries. No institution emerged as being markedly experimental. No institution emerged with a dominating national importance, as Harvard did in the United States. By the end of the century, Dalhousie, McGill, Queen's, and Toronto were strong institutions that contributed men and ideas to the new institutions in the west. But the Canadian system has not lent itself to the emergence of great peaks of achievement. A cynic might remark that we prefer a general level of mediocrity to any dizzy fluctuation towards eminence.

The French–Canadian university did not have any substantial influence outside of Quebec. The Collège Classique, which formed the undergraduate Faculty of Arts of the universities, was a distinctive body – part advanced high school, part junior college, heavily literary and philosophical in its emphasis, with no relevance to the English–Canadian structure. Moreover, until the third decade of the twentieth century Laval was the only French–Canadian university, and it was thoroughly occupied in meeting provincial needs.

Canadian universities are provincial. The British North America Act insisted upon full provincial responsibility for education, and this doctrine will, in the present atmosphere of regional and minority self-consciousness, be even more strongly emphasized in the future. In varying degrees they depend upon the provincial government for financial support, and with some few exceptions they draw their students from within the provincial boundaries. McGill was the conspicuous exception here, as its English–Canadian base in Montreal was not large and it welcomed students from the United States and from other parts of the Commonwealth. Universities have not been notably successful in working together on a national basis, and in Canada the difficulties for such cooperation are as great as anywhere in the national world.

The universities of Canada, then, entered the age of change with an inheritance that was both strength and weakness. That age – from 1948 to the present – falls into three broad phases. The period from 1948 to 1955 was a period of gradual awakening, when it finally became clear that the extraordinary post-war problems were really the ordinary problems of the future. This was a time of vague stirrings on a provincial and national plane with a good deal of isolated institutional self-analysis. The period from 1955 to 1961 was the period of the quantitative obsession. It was initiated by a report of Dr E. F. Sheffield in 1955 that first indicated, in clear irrefutable outline, the nature of the quantitative problem. In brief, a doubling of student population was assured during the next ten years, with the likelihood of a continuation of the process for some time on an undiminished scale. (As a matter of fact, the prediction was conservative, and the doubling came within a period of seven years. The second doubling occurred within the subsequent six-year period. The total full-time enrolment in 1954–5 was about 68,000. This had doubled by 1961–2 and again by 1967–8. A similar process is expected to take place in the next six years, and by 1977–8 we expect to have more than half a million full-time students.) During this period universities were obsessed with the problem of physical resources; they turned to the federal government, which had begun a per capita subsidy in 1951, for increased support. The need of additional staff stimulated graduate studies; graduate enrolment rose from just over 3,000 in 1951–2 to more than 17,000 in 1965–6 – from 5 per cent of total enrolment to over 8 per cent.

The period from 1961 to the present is the period of self-analysis. The dominating report of the period was prepared by Sir James Duff, formerly Vice-Chancellor of the University of Durham, and Professor Robert Berdahl of San Francisco State College, a typical Canadian blending of British and American, of age and youth. It examined university government in Canada, and prescribed a solution of an interrelated two-tiered system, with substantial faculty participation. The report came out in 1966, too early to reflect the 'student power' movement. But it stimulated continuing analysis by both staff and students of the university structure, and it turned attention away from the quantitative problem. That problem was not ignored; and its dimensions were charted in a report issued by a Commission under the chairmanship of Professor Vincent Bladen of the University of Toronto. But problems of government, and of the quality of university life, became dominant after 1966.

How did the universities respond to the problems raised during each of these periods – to the quantitative, the structural, and the qualitative? What, in particular, was the force of the historical inheritance?

Canadian universities were not initially prepared for a rapid expansion.

Since the turn of the century there had been little variation in the participation rate of attendance at universities, the percentage of young men and women between the ages of 18 and 21, who were in full-time attendance at institutions of higher learning. In 1906 it was between 2 and 3 per cent; by 1920 it had risen to 4 per cent, and it remained at this level until 1940. In 1954–5 the percentage stood at a little under 8, where the comparable figure in the United States was 20. At the beginning of the period of change we had little experience in the problem of meeting sudden expansion. Moreover, the rate of expansion was heaviest in the old central areas, Ontario and Quebec, and in the new, rapidly growing areas like British Columbia, which were least well served in terms of numbers of existing institutions. The Maritime Provinces, where there was little population pressure, had a plethora of small institutions that had resisted union or even the imposition of a loose, federated structure. Quebec, Ontario, and British Columbia had the resources, however, to meet the needs. The ultimate responsibility remained provincial; this was emphasized in 1966 by the decision of the federal government to withdraw from direct payments to the universities and to make available to the provinces tax transfers that would cover 50 per cent of the total operating costs of post-secondary education.

In meeting the quantitative problem, Ontario found the federated inheritance of great assistance. On large campuses like that of the University of Toronto, the college concept was already firmly entrenched, and provided the basis for a structural expansion. The college concept could be used either as a means of expanding the original university, or as a means of creating a new one. Thus York University in Toronto, which will grow to the same size as the University of Toronto, began as a college in the Toronto system and then assumed full university status. A variation on this is the college established some distance from the main campus that remains an integral part of the university, but has its own staff and a freedom to depart from the imperial pattern. A final variation is provided by the college away from the main campus, virtually autonomous but traditionally associated with the parent university, which can quickly transform itself into a university. The University of Waterloo grew out of a college that was associated with the University of Western Ontario, and the University of Guelph grew out of two professional faculties, agriculture and veterinary science, of the University of Toronto. In Manitoba the process of peaceful fission produced the Universities of Brandon and Winnipeg, formerly colleges of the University of Manitoba.

In British Columbia the federal tradition was not strong, and the increase in students called for the establishment of a new university on a generous scale.

In its inception and physical embodiment, Simon Fraser, the new foundation, was the wonder of the university world. A magnificent campus, on top of a mountain, it emerged with the beauty and completeness of a happy dream. But it developed tensions, which a bewildering succession of populist ideas have not resolved. It illustrates the problems of the instant university.

Despite the expansion of higher education in Canada, the gap in participation rates between Canada and the United States remains unchanged. In 1965–6 the participation rate in Canada was 16·5, and in the United States it was 32·3 (45·6 if part-time students are included). In part this reflects the conservatism of Canadians with respect to higher education, and a lower level of economic achievement. But it also reflects a general Canadian reluctance to develop the junior college as a part of the university system. In Ontario the junior college is called the College of Applied Arts and Technology, and is conceived of as parallel to the early years of university and not as an alternative. In short, most of the students attending these colleges are going there for a specific vocational goal and are not intent upon a B.A.

In Quebec, the other area of major population pressure, the problem of rapid expansion has not been solved so readily. As the result of a major report restructuring the whole of education, Quebec established two-year institutions after the eleventh grade as an integral stage in the progress towards the university. These institutions were called Collèges d'Enseignement Général et Professionnel, and merged the final stages of the education formerly offered in the Collèges Classiques with various vocational institutions. It was anticipated that only about 30 per cent of the students entering these Collèges would aspire to go on to university. As it turned out, almost 70 per cent had such aspirations, at a time, moreover, when university expansion was slow. In the province of Quebec there are six universities, compared to Ontario's sixteen, and three serve the English-speaking minority. Only one new university has been established since the beginning of the period of change – the University of Sherbrooke. The government proposes to proceed with the founding of a multi-campus University of Quebec which will be French-speaking, and which will have its first campus in Montreal; but, in the meantime, the crisis of numbers will remain.

Despite the expansion of the last twenty years, there is serious disquiet in Canada on economic grounds alone. This disquiet was strongly expressed in the second *Annual Review* of the Economic Council of Canada entitled 'Toward Sustained and Balanced Economic Growth', which appeared in 1965. In general, the report pointed out that although we were moving closer to the United States in the percentage of our work force possessing primary education, we were falling behind in the percentage of those who had a high school or university education. The report went on to draw the conclusion that the absence of trained manpower was the principal reason for the comparative sluggishness of the Canadian economy.

The rapid growth in size of universities helped to draw attention to the inadequacies of structure and government of Canadian universities. They were, in many respects, prepared to look at themselves critically. They had stability as a result of the honourable position they had enjoyed in society from the very beginning; a capacity for self-analysis as a result of their traditional emphasis on the liberal arts; and a rigorous sense of academic autonomy, which expressed itself in the English manner through an academic senate where the voice of the faculty member was dominant. English–Canadian universities have adopted the American tradition of the lay board of governors as the legal embodiment of the university. As in the United States, the dominating voice in the board of governors was the voice of Business, although it was somewhat less powerful than its American counterpart and entered upon the scene a good deal later. As in the United States, it could be argued that the business board of governors represented a liberal advance over ecclesiastical or political domination.

But the stability of Canadian universities is based upon a readiness to respect fixed roles for each of the estates. Students are at the universities to learn, the staff to teach and occasionally to do research, and the administrators and governors to keep the universities safe, solvent, and of good repute. Over all this was an over-arching distinction: that the academic world was a little unreal, and that the outside world was real and, therefore, the source of direction. Such a system demanded quiescence and an indisposition to question. As soon as questions were raised, the university was suddenly vibrating with tensions, tensions between the estates within and between the university and the outside world. The Duff–Berdahl Report was an attempt to provide a resolution for these tensions; the academic and lay bodies were no longer to be sharply separated, but were to be bound together by a degree of common membership and common concern. But the Report came too early to comprehend the full import of student and staff awakening, and it underestimated the extent to which they had denied the old order. The Duff–Berdahl Report had attempted to reduce or to soften many of the tensions, whereas the mood of the academic community was to eliminate them.

What are the reasons in both English and French Canada for the questioning of the traditional form of university government, a questioning that is more widespread and more radical than it is in the United States? Here are some likely reasons. The first is of a negative nature. It is doubtful whether the lay board of governors in Canada has been as aggressive in the defence and in the development of the university as the board in the United States. Board members looked upon themselves as public trustees whose principal responsibility was to make sure that public money was frugally spent. From time to time they gave leadership in the raising of private funds, but the record here, and in the area of private benefactions, has lacked both American bravado and achievement. As a consequence, the academic saw the lay board, not as leader and protector, but as check and censor. A second and positive reason is that the academic, since the Second World War, has become increasingly conscious of how crucial he is in the working-out and implementation of vast government schemes of national welfare. This is a phenomenon which is, of course, common in the United States, but it is perhaps even more significant in Canada, where intellectual life outside the universities does not flourish, and the academic tends to dominate both the cloister and the market-place. He thus developed a lively sense of his own self-importance and his own right to determine his own destiny, all of which were expressed with varying degrees of eloquence and vigour in a collection of essays, entitled *A Place of Liberty*, published in 1964. A third reason is more speculative. In Canada the radical, socialist tradition has been effectively institutionalized in a party, the New Democratic Party, which has held power in one province, has been the official opposition in at least two others, and entertains the not unreasonable hope of taking over the government of Canada. The New Democratic Party, which is the successor to the Co-operative Commonwealth Federation, has abandoned many of its doctrinaire ideas on economic nationalization. But it emphasizes the necessity of strong democratic control of our major institutions, and it sees in the universities a surviving example of colonial paternalism. The NDP has drawn ideas and considerable support from the universities, and it sees in a reformed university a powerful ally in its struggle for political power.

The movement towards a more unified, democratically based, and academically oriented university government will have a profound effect on the quality of academic life. Canadian higher education, in both English-speaking and French-speaking Canada, has been a blend of the utilitarian and the academic, of the office and the ivory tower. University education was useful, especially in specialized professional divisions, for preparing men and women for important positions in society. This simple utilitarianism co-existed, however, with a belief in the value of learning for its own sake. The humanities have never lacked for defenders in Canada. At the University of Toronto, Philosophy and Classics constitute two of the largest departments, surpassed in numbers only by Medieval Studies. The coalescence of the business and the academic ethic may seem joltingly paradoxical; but one can find a common basis for the two concepts in an elitist attitude towards higher education which prevailed during the nineteenth century and still flourishes. According to this point of view, higher education should be the concern of a specially qualified minority theoretically drawn from all classes, but in actuality largely restricted to the middle and upper-middle classes. From this elite will come those who will dominate business and the professions by reason of their intellectual superiority and superior training.

This prevailing ethos has encouraged a severely traditional academic curriculum. Canada produced no experimental colleges, and, indeed, few genuinely experimental curricula. When, just after the Second World War, American universities were turning out broad studies of general education and exploring the ways by which higher education could minister to moral and aesthetic man, Canadian universities confined themselves to rearranging what they had always taught. The business of the university was teaching and research; the refinement of sensibilities and of moral choice belonged to a personal world and to private societies and clubs. This attitude is now being sharply challenged by student leaders, who look upon it as part of the business ethos, and demand that the university shall respond to personal problems and desires, eliminate or reduce the difference between teacher and taught, and abandon any serious effort at evaluation. But the dominating voice would still be in favour of the university as a place of intellectual discipline, where there is a clear distinction between teacher and taught, and evaluations of achievement are regularly made. The adoption of student activist ideas would lead, it is believed, to a nervous mediocrity, a hectic pursuit of vague ideas that might rapidly turn into anti-intellectualism.

This attitude has many solid virtues. Its real corrective, it seems to me, is to be found not so much in curricular experimentation, as in the intensification of the life outside the classroom. Here Canadian universities have had a thin tradition: undergraduate journalism has been callow and reedy and, recently, laboriously sensational, and no artistic or intellectual renaissance, to my knowledge, has taken place on a Canadian university campus.

The emphasis on the utilitarian and academic has not encouraged the Canadian universities to recognize their social role, apart from responsibility for the preparation of professionals. The Western universities inherited some of the ethos of the American land-grant institutions, and, especially through their faculties of agriculture, brought knowledge to the people. In the Maritimes, St Francis Xavier University gave remarkable leadership to Maritime fishermen in the development of the cooperative movement. But these were largely uncontroversial service roles; and the universities believed that the best way to encourage critical assessments of society was to remain officially aloof. This is the attitude that has come under sharp attack by the student and faculty Left: it is an attitude, they contend, that pretends to a lofty disinterestedness but in reality provides a buttress for the establishment. That establishment is the corporate industrial state, which is further seen as a dark accomplice of American imperialism.

Leftist critics have reason to see the universities as supporters of the establishment, but the establishment has not been big business, but rather the intellectual bureaucracy. The universities have, in varying degrees, been close to the Liberal Party, which, since the end of the Second World War, has largely dominated the Canadian scene. The party has been concerned with preserving Canada as a national entity, and everything has been subservient to that goal. The leaders of the party have diligently practised the arts of compromise and conciliation; they have sought to contain emotion in a vessel of reason; in short, they have practised the academic virtues. Indeed, all the liberal prime ministers have been academics drawn into politics. Mackenzie King might have followed an academic career at Toronto and Harvard; St Laurent lectured in law at Laval; Pearson taught history at the University of Toronto before he joined External Affairs; and Trudeau, a graduate of Montreal, Harvard, and the Sorbonne, taught at his first alma mater. But the most academic liberal of all was Vincent Massey, who was a failure in politics, but went on to a brilliant career in the public service, culminating as Canada's first native Governor-General. Massey began his career as a university teacher, and during his last years cherished most of all the post of Visitor at the college he had established and endowed at the University of Toronto. His greatest contribution to Canadian life was his chairmanship of the Royal Commission on National Development in Arts, Letters, and Sciences (1949–51). The report of the Commission was essentially an attempt to discover and strengthen the basis of Canadian cultural life, now that the influence of the United Kingdom was receding and that of the United States rapidly increasing. The report saw the universities as the great prop of Canadian cultural life, and it did much to recall the universities to a consciousness of national goals. Pearson was, in many respects, a disciple of Massey, and his establishment of the Royal Commission on Bilingualism and Biculturalism will result in an extension of the Massey Report, and a further emphasis on the universities' role in binding the country together.

A year ago when I was writing the introduction to a collection of essays and speeches, I concluded with an attempt to express this relationship between higher education and national feeling, perhaps with a touch of centennial exuberance:

Canadian history has been a search for a focal point for national life, a concept that would give it a role clearly visible within and recognizable without. As early as Lord Durham's *Report*, it was the idea of Canada as the laboratory of the Empire, evolving ideal political patterns that could be transferred elsewhere. Then as Empire and Commonwealth receded, it was the idea of the sage and sober middle power, a respected umpire in the clash of principalities. But in a world of duopoly, each giant obsessed by his own strength, there is no role for the middle power. Always present, emerging clearly at times of national exuberance, has been the vision of Canada as inexhaustible source of material riches, a vision often illuminated by the technicolor glory of the northern lights. But such a vision has never been entirely satisfying, and moreover, there has always been the uncomfortable suggestion that full realization lies in a constantly receding future. Equally pervasive and continuous has been the vision of the union of the two nations, the final creation of a splendid synthesis. Here surely was the Canadian focal point. And, despite our disappointments and failures, this is the surest intuition. But instead of a union, true blue with a few exotic gallic streaks, we must think of another process, more subtle and demanding: the building of bridges of understanding, the cooperative approach to specific projects, the creation of an *entente* so intricate and tough that no crisis can destroy it. Expo was an example of this, a fusing of talents and ideas of the two cultures in such a way as to produce a new creation, something that can be imitated but never reproduced. Expo was an exercise in higher education. It points the way to where our resources should be concentrated and our achievements sought. I can think of no surer way of strengthening our national life, of bringing together French and English and extending our influence abroad, than by the systematic support of our universities, and by the creation, both in English-speaking and French-speaking Canada, of several internationally recognized centres of scholarship. In this way the strength of the university will both reflect and enhance the strength of the nation.[2]

This kind of heady nationalism will not, however, provide a basis for the new life of the universities. The movement for the reform of the university will insist upon other qualities. The new spirit will not be satisfied with the blending of the utilitarian and the academic, conducive as this often was to the free play of the mind. I think the chief result of the breakdown in the separation between estates, and the increasing assertiveness of student and faculty, will be the development of a more diverse and more exciting environment for the university – whether this is seen as anti-university, anti-environment, or simply as healthy reaction to the academic establishment. Higher education in Canada has suffered from complacency, from a not unwarranted sense of efficiency and modest accomplishment. It has avoided most of the ostentatious debilities that have crept into the lower

[1] Claude T. Bissell, *The Strength of the University*, Toronto, 1968, pp. 16–17.

ranges of American higher education, although it has rarely come even close to challenging the highest reaches of American higher education. It has gained a reputation for producing students with well-developed intellectual muscles and a talent for the higher gymnastics. In short, the finest flowering of Canadian higher education has usually been the professor. One of our major exports to the United States has been academic staff. Within Canada the professor, whether he owns to a Canadian degree or not, quickly becomes part of the official establishment. This means that the intellectual life of Canada has been dominated by the clerisy, by the ideologists, rather than by the utopians. They reinforce the potential conservatism of the universities and encourage them to follow traditional ways. This course has now been arrested by the changes that are taking place in Canadian universities, changes that may temporarily throw the universities into confusion and give them a bewildering feeling of having broken sharply with their past, but which will eventually recreate both the universities and the society of which they are a part.

INTERCHAPTER

I

Response to Claude Bissell — PAUL A. MILLER

Academic men are being forcefully asked to become more self-conscious about the universities and colleges in which they carry on their work. There are four areas of pressure: in the relationship between teachers and taught; in the systems of intramural relationships in the government of institutions of higher education; in the connection between universities themselves and between them and other sectors of the educational structure; and in the linkage of these structures with the larger social order.

(i) With reference to the first, which in this Seminar we have scored as an interest in the educative process, the concern tends to be with teaching and learning at the expense of inquiry and service to the larger community. Increased professionalism had caused both faculty and administrators to withdraw into separate blocks, leaving students stranded between them. The instrumental imperatives of university life are today dominant over the integrative imperatives; and this separation is increased in America by the division between the *sources* of funds for the teaching, research, and service functions of the universities. In the American university, teaching is a local or private sponsorship, research is federal, and service is federal or not at all. It is unlikely that one could calculate the financial and perhaps emotional cost, in the United States, of reducing teaching loads for all faculty by one-half or more and financing the difference with quite specified grants. One might rationalize the move as a 'reduction in teaching load' but one would not know if it would really result in an 'increase in research load'.

(ii) The systems of intramural relationships in the government of institutions of higher education. There is a strong tendency to create new structures in order to accommodate the growing research function. Especially in the face of the discrete streams of support which have characterized recent development in the United States, there has been a remarkable encrustation of special institutes, centres, and programmes which may help to overcome the unadaptability of the older intramural arrangements, but which frequently, in the end, compete with one another in claims upon the central resources. Such special features seem to have increased the entrepreneurial and managerial tasks of faculty and administration alike, and created an amorphous yet proliferating perimeter to the university, great portions of which have remained outside the processes of academic government and equally outside the capability of academic planning. Nonetheless, the drain of talent, time, and energy if not financial resources required to keep these special structures going – from within the university and from within the agencies which support them – has something to tell us about discontinuity in the teaching–learning process, about the confusion of views held by the university and various publics, the *ad hoc* reward systems which inflate academic mobility, and the unease of those who are in them and of those who remain apart.

(iii) The connection between universities themselves and between them and the other sectors of the educational structure. It has already been pointed out that one sector may be very ignorant about others. As the educational base broadens and opportunity becomes more general, each sector would seem to possess inherently less flexibility to live alone. Accordingly, no institution or group of institutions can for long remain aloof from the total educational context. Its relationships must be expressed in horizontal ties with sister institutions and vertical ones with lower schools.

In the United States, where extreme decentralization of the lower schools is the rule, the university system has taken little notice of them, at least until very recently. With 50 per cent, and soon a still greater proportion, of the young people moving on to some form of post-secondary schooling, the universities are receiving students who might have been better candidates for higher learning if some larger foresight had been used in teacher education and re-education, improved assessment techniques, and the like. In addition, there is the great tragedy in the urban centres of the United States today of the black child of fourteen, who has fled from the inadequacy of the lower school but is in no position to anticipate anything more. There are also the junior or community colleges, of which one a week is now being formed, with one out of every two American students destined to begin his college or university experience in such an institution. Yet one can find no national policy to cope with this massive development, and only flimsy policies in most of the states. The result is a marginality in these institutions, when they try to escape from being part of the system of lower schools and find no ready interest in them from higher education. A similar political tension comes from the 'regional universities', rapid outgrowths of the transition of the teachers' college to the state college, but now becoming, in some ways, the Land-Grant Universities of our time. Such problems are all consequences of a vast collectivity of schools, colleges, and universities which is still immature in its ways of being self-conscious about intersecting interests and is a sort of halfway solution.

(iv) The social role of the universities. Can the universities be a major and unifying centre of influence, as Dr Bissell hopes, or a model for society as a whole, as Dr Sanford hopes? Jacques Barzun has criticized them for not responding to the appeals from cities for help. But at present, in the US, they have little power to use their own experience as agents of social change. The Land-Grant Universities, far from merely inserting technology into a farming pattern, were in fact a revolution in social as well as technological organization, and went far in integrating teaching with research and with students' interests.

Institutions, universities, and institutions of higher education must become more self-critical, asking themselves what improvements in old instruments are required, what new ones are needed, if a growing proportion of educated people is to emerge in society as an understanding constituency. Meanwhile we should be more careful of over dramatizing either the central position or the up-to-dateness of the university in modern society. One needs only to ponder medical centres surrounded by a sea of ill health, or the campus gates opening upon the most desperate of human ghettos, to find one's enthusiasm tempered; we need to be chary of overselling our product.

II

How far is Canada a nation and how far a collection of separate provinces? 'Every part of Canada is separatist', according to one Canadian present. Certainly the provinces still have a good deal of political power. Yet some of the freedom of Canadian universities may be due rather to apathy on the part of state governments than to appreciation of what they are doing or understanding of what they are for.

But though the political power of the provinces is great, there are many factors making for national unity, one of them the sheer power of the 'clerisy' – those who lead Canadian economic, scientific, and cultural thought. Their ideas are really pretty homogeneous and they are drawn from all the provinces. The pressures of twentieth-century technology and civilization common to them all make for unity, and quicker transport between the diverse parts of this far-stretched country is also a help. The time is past, anyway, when Canadian universities either want to be or can be insulated from matters of public concern. But though this is so, it does not follow that boards of university trustees drawn from business or politics necessarily represent a liberal advance over the ecclesiastical domination that once was so marked.

It is not with the older generation, 'many of whom', we were told, 'love mediocrity', but with the younger that the future lies. Canadian society, despite some of the administrators, will not decay but be rebuilt. There is, however, we were assured, among some of the students in Canadian universities 'a boiling ferment of cultural life'. It may well be true in Canada, as in the USA, that students of science and technology – especially perhaps those in the West – feel that they are engaged, in common with their professors, in making a meaningful contribution to the life and prosperity of society as it is and as they know it. They are highly motivated. There is a tremendous sense in many of them that Canada is about to 'go places': they see the need for change and social progress but they are not revolutionaries and have little wish to attack their teachers. Rather – like many of their opposite numbers in the States – they and their seniors are a community of people, able to talk to one another through their common interests and to make with them a common attack on the technical problems which confront their country.

It is the students of the humanities and the social sciences who are much more concerned about the perpetuation of a culture that seems to them basically not to make sense. In Canada, however, some students who might elsewhere have been protesters in a militant fashion against the *status quo* are exuberantly looking for new forms of expression that will not be antisocial. They are keen these days – particularly perhaps in Quebec and Ontario – not to be parochial. In Toronto, for example, there are colonies of students (makers of films, poetry, pictures, debaters of ideas) forming what was described as a 'perimeter around the academic world'. There is indeed an increasing number of creative outlets for Canadian students of the arts after graduation. Canada is in the midst of a renaissance and many students of the arts live in a different cultural world from their seniors.

But is it not a pity that such idealism and imagination cannot be harnessed more effectively within the university itself? Could not there be, for example, several new-type Centers for Urban Studies in Canadian universities which did not repeat the faults of those in some universities in the US? There urban studies are often approached from a pathological angle. One starts by asking 'What is wrong with our cities?' This is an unfortunate way of approaching the matter: there is immense scope for reconsidering the possibilities of an urban civilization, not only architecturally and from the viewpoint of the planner of physical amenities, but also from those of the educationalist, the artist, the sociologist, the psychologist, the philosopher. Could not students be hitched to the wagon? Several people, however, put in a warning against too much euphoria here: urban problems are desperately real challenges, whose solution requires specific technical and economic knowledge. 'If university students try to go into the cities by themselves, thinking they can cope with such problems, they will be bitterly disillusioned.' One must moreover distinguish problems that have to do with values and social objectives from the severely technical problems of how these objectives are to be attained in practicable ways, though the problems must certainly not be approached as if they were technical ones alone.

Comment was made upon the immense pull in these days of 'the communications complex' to many students, of both the sciences and the humanities. Broadcasting, journalism, and advertising they see as providing an immense opportunity for creative activity involving the skilled use of modern technology and providing also an access to power. The McLuhan cult – whether one goes with it or not – has captured the imagination of many young people and is at present releasing – perhaps even creating – vitality, especially in Canada, where McLuhan himself is such a prominent figure. Discussion about why so many young people should be attracted to work in this field led on to a consideration of what in present society is the relative attractiveness of the idea of technical development itself and the pull of the 'communications complex'. On the one hand progress and the development of a new civilization seem to be attainable only through application of technical skills of one sort or another – through, for example, engineering, chemistry, computer science, economic expertise. On the other hand the new civilization can hardly come to birth if enthusiasm for technology is all or is an end in itself. 'Can we', asked someone, 'hope to find in Canada an increasing fusion of the role of the creative artist with that of the creative engineer?'

At this point, Northrop Frye warned us all that a good deal of the intellectual and imaginative ferment among Canadian university students is extracurricular and that if we plan a curriculum so that it caters for everything, many imaginative and creative activities will die. A lot of the sizzle may be taken out of 'the sizzling youth culture'. A conservative, conventional curriculum is a great incentive to the expenditure of intellectual energy outside it; as Shoben remarked, 'the arts are flowers which will wither if pressed too closely to the bosom of the Establishment.' It was agreed that vested interests within institutions of higher education do undoubtedly keep out new ideas and currents of thought, and that this is one of the things which students are protesting against. Arts and social science students react vehemently against an intellectual closed-mindedness which allows only certain issues to be tackled in the academy and keeps out some of the new feeling and thinking which comes 'closest to the bone of our social life'. One of the attractions indeed of the communications industry, through the many media it uses, is that it enables so much affectivity to be expressed. It gives a sense to those in charge – even if it is a false and self-deceiving sense – that they are in real touch and real community with other people.

Such points as these led on to further discussion of the reaction of students against the impersonality of modern society and its implications for institutions of higher education. Students themselves, not merely in Canada, but in the USA and Britain, are concerned that what is most worth doing should be done in the university context. But how much time should be spent in 'personal fulfilment' and how much in objective study and in working to master relevant knowledge and useful skills? In the academic view this was closely related to the question: what is waste? The typical university professor has a rather puritanical attitude to the subject of waste; he believes not merely in making proper use of a country's resources but that the brain-power of its young people should resolutely be cultivated. He is apt to condemn as wasteful both of time and talents quite a number of things 'that really light up our students' and seem to them abundantly worth doing. We must take more seriously the challenge which comes from the young to our built-in assumptions about what is wasteful and what is worthwhile.

Marjorie Reeves recalled that she had been talking to some of her students one day about stewardship in the sense of their obligation to husband resources (i.e. talents) and to undergo disciplined training in order to be able to use their expertise later in the service of the community. They countered by questioning whether such objective studies really gave them any power to grapple with problems. What did she mean by power, anyway? The hippies had a strong sense of the meaning of power and a definite recipe for dealing with today's ills. What she wanted to do was to pinpoint the need for us to have real conversation, real encounter, with our students on the question of what was worthwhile and what was wasteful. We might find that a number of our preconceived ideas had to be revised and greater weight given to the need for students to experience situations and problems as well as to learn about them.

The comment was made that while some students rejected Puritanism in such matters as work, careers, etc., in favour of personal development, many of the best rejected the ego; they had a sense of close community with one another and were suspicious of the old-style grammar-school concept of 'public service' or 'community service'. To which the retort was that the missing link is not at the level of immediate commitment or communication but at the level of what they think that they should be doing in the course they are taking at the university – in their 'discipline', in the *formal* part of their course.

From which the Seminar turned its attention to discussing the relation between having a feeling of worthwhileness and having a disciplined mind. In the past and still today, universities tend to insist upon a high degree of conceptualization in the subjects studied. They are intellectual establishments and by and large reject from their curriculum subjects that are incapable of conceptualization. The arts get short shrift. The kind of relaxation indispensable as a preliminary to aesthetic creation is suspect or misunderstood by members of faculty, who insist upon the strenuous use of the mind in their students without much regard to giving any encouragement to imagination – which in fact is very nearly the same thing as the vitality of the mind and spirit itself. They use the word 'problem' frequently, in itself a significant symptom of the conceptualized thinking that is common among them. They dislike the unexamined, and especially the unexaminable. They hate mysteries and want definition, analysis, clarity. It is to some extent this attitude of mind and overconcentration upon the conscious that the hippies are revolting against. Perhaps, as Douglas Bush[1] had reminded an assemblage of professors of English, 'we should put much less effort into the indiscriminate advancement of knowledge' and attend more relevantly to the education of our students.

[1] Douglas Bush, *Engaged and Disengaged*, Cambridge, Mass., 1968, p. 250.

CHAPTER 8

University Initiative in Response to Change[1]

F. Champion Ward

I

In *Democracy in America*, Alexis de Tocqueville invited the interest of his patrician French readers in the outlandish world of Jacksonian America by reminding them, grimly but gamely, that there, but for the passage of time, goes Europe. The tide of social equality might rise slowly, but it would never ebb and in the end it would sweep all fixed social forms before it. The process was as irreversible as growing old.

Surely, the world now confirms de Tocqueville's prophecy, even in those parts which started late and still have far to go. All societies appear to be set on the same egalitarian course, including those whose present political leadership would prefer to reverse it. Even when 'reactionary' regimes come to power, they find that they must make concessions to equality if they hope to retain power. Hence, we see non-democratic governments in the Third World subscribe to the principles of universal schooling and widespread land-holding as faithfully as most of the new democracies.

I engage in this second-hand social punditry because it discloses the ground for my hope that what I have to say about higher education in the United States will be relevant for Canadian and British education. If de Tocqueville was right in holding that today's problem in the United States is tomorrow's problem everywhere, it may not be unforgivably parochial to concentrate this paper on the local scene in higher education. This will be done with due regard for the following qualifications:

1. While the broad principle of social equality is at work everywhere, it encounters in each nation a unique legacy of institutions, practices, and resources. These latter will affect the form, the rate, and perhaps the upper limit of the realization of equality in each nation.

[1] Part of this paper has appeared under the title 'The Fabric of Universities' in the 1968 *Annual Report* of the Ford Foundation.

2. It is not too late to shape and re-shape educational systems under the pressure of expanding social demands. That, presumably, is why we are here.

In higher education, the prospect before us all is summarized in a phrase which has acquired an astonishing currency in recent years. That phrase is 'universal higher education'. Far from being dismissed as an obvious contradiction in terms, 'universal higher education' is taken by many educational planners to describe an inevitable future which is just around the corner. In 1964, a conference under this title was held in Puerto Rico, and I think it is worth reciting some of the predictions that were made at that time concerning the implications of universal higher education for the United States.

In a sense, the term is a misnomer, for 'universal', 'higher', and 'education' are all exaggerations. For those planners, 'universal' meant 51 per cent or more of the age-group; 'higher' meant after but not necessarily above secondary school; and 'education' included forms of training and personal growth not frequently denoted by that term. Nevertheless, the prospect they held out is formidable. Between 1970 and 1975, from 50 to 70 per cent of the age-group are expected to be enrolled for post-secondary education, an increment of one to two-and-a-quarter million new students. To attain only the lower figure by 1970, a hundred new colleges of 10,000 students each will require to be opened each year, and to attain the higher figure of 70 per cent enrolment by 1974, the number of new colleges would rise to 200 per year. To staff this expanded system, some 235,000 new college teachers will be needed. The 1970 cost of all this is estimated at 13–15 billions of dollars on recurrent account and close to two billions on capital account.

One evidence that we are all egalitarians now is the surprisingly small number of Cassandras and Canutes to be found among those who expect to wrestle with this expansion of higher education. Few hope to turn the tide back and few even deplore its waxing. In Britain, the Robbins Committee, you will recall, was explicit on its grounds for not viewing expansion as a threat to standards:

> . . . Fears that expansion would lead to a lowering of the average ability of students in higher education have proved unfounded. Recent increases in numbers have not been accompanied by an increase in wastage and the measured ability of students appears to be as high as it ever was.[1]

More recently, in 1968, the Universities Grants Committee has reported a decline in the proportion of students who leave British universities without a degree.

[1] *Higher Education*, Report of the Committee appointed by the Prime Minister under the Chairmanship of Lord Robbins, 1961–3 (London, 1963, p. 53).

Similarly, on the United States side, the recent sharp expansion of the system of higher education has so far not debased it. Strong institutions have, on the whole, become better, and the weak no worse. The present large student bodies do at least as well as their predecessors. As Robert Pace points out, quantity and quality have risen together during the recent past. 'The reasons', he says, 'are quite simple. A generation ago only half of the brightest high school graduates (those who would rank in the top 15 per cent of the general population in measured intelligence) went to college. Today, more than two-thirds of those students are going to college. In another generation we can be confident that almost all of those in this top segment of intellectual talent will go to college. . . . In the expansion that has occurred so far there has been lots of room at the top. . . .'[1]

So far. But it is not at all safe to assume that standards and student numbers will enjoy this happy and improbable union indefinitely. Indeed, three clouds on the horizon have already attained the size of a man's hand.

One of these is simply the prospect that more and more students of modest capacity will expect to be received in higher education and to be 'successful' there, i.e. to emerge with a negotiable qualification. The second prospect is that future student bodies will include a larger number of students from lower-income and 'disadvantaged' groups who combine some competence with poor preparation, both at school and at home. I do not refer to the small minority of brilliant but indigent prospects who now enjoy the solicitous attention of admissions offices and scholarship committees. Plato would approve our present policy towards them. But Plato was not a democrat, and the conscience of modern democrats has been stirred by the continued concentration of opportunities for 'average' students upon students of middle- and upper-class origin. If this dike breaks, the universities may find that, without adaptations not readily made or easy to foresee, many average students from the 'underclass' will find the established requirements and norms of university life and academic work both difficult and uncongenial. They will be joined in discontent by the large minority of affluent heretics who are now disturbing the universities everywhere. Although these dissidents are of the calibre for which the present academic standards were designed, they show a new and startling irreverence towards those norms and their present exemplars and guardians.

I will discuss at later points the problems and opportunities presented by these changes in the numbers, calibre, and attitudes of students.

---

[1] *Universal Higher Education*, edited by Earl J. McGrath, New York, 1966, pp. 160–1. Used with permission of the McGraw-Hill Book Company.

The assimilation of new and more varied student bodies will have both general and specific effects on the size and shape of the future financing of higher education. Unfortunately, it is not safe to assume that the support of education will derive simply from the growth of national economies. As Jencks and Riesman point out in *The Academic Revolution*, since 1950 the expenditure of colleges per student has risen faster than per capita gross national product, and they add that 'if we extrapolated current trends sufficiently far into the future, the entire gross national product would be devoted to higher education . . . hence the much discussed "crisis in college finance".'[1]

Several factors may be expected to exacerbate this crisis in the next few years:

1. The income of professors and the 'productivity' of professors are not positively related. Indeed, the trend has been towards reduced productivity, in the budgetary sense of students taught per instructor.

2. The ratio of postgraduate to undergraduate students is rising in Canada, the United Kingdom, and the United States, and postgraduate education is estimated to be more expensive, by a factor curiously vague but clearly substantial.

3. If a large number of low-income students enter higher education, their subventions will be substantially higher for those systems which normally rely upon a mixture of fees charged to students and student aid.

In short, higher education, in the United States now and in other developed societies soon or eventually, can look forward to admitting and attempting to educate very large numbers of students, embracing a wide range of competence, preparation, and class origins, and requiring from governments and private sources very substantial amounts of financial aid and respectful understanding.

Will aid and understanding be forthcoming? Yes, of course, at some rate and in some degree. But there are signs that suggest that support to higher education may depend increasingly on the quality of its response to forces impinging upon it from planning and fiscal agencies of governments, on the one hand, and from the new breed of student, on the other. These two influences are distinct and, indeed, in part discrepant in their possible effects on higher education. They are also viewed with foreboding by many educators as threats to the autonomy and good order of the universities. In both cases, however, the *questions* about higher education which budgeteers and students

[1] Christopher Jencks and David Riesman, *The Academic Revolution*, Garden City, N.Y., 1968, p. 111.

are asking or may be expected to ask of the universities may be good and valuable, even if their authors' own answers to these questions would not be. Let us consider the cross-examination, in part actual, in part anticipated, to which the expansion of costs and enlargement of student bodies is likely to subject higher education in the United States during the next few years. Let us then look at the state of preparation of the universities to respond to such challenges.

In the case of the planners and budgeteers, the occasion for cross-examining the universities will be the increased portion of the tax revenues of the nation which will be laid claim to by higher education. We may look forward to questions about the higher learning which will be designed to disclose its degree of efficiency as a system of means and ends. Questions like the following have been or are likely to be asked:

1. The educational system appears to be conducted at three levels – school, college, and university. Do these levels have distinct ends and, if so, can these purposes be operationally defined in terms of the competences and knowledge students are expected to acquire, the preparation of staff for each level, and the incentives and awards offered for effective contributions?

2. If most students are now going to extend their education beyond secondary school, how should this new prospect affect the content and length of schooling?

3. If the abilities, incentives, and learning styles of students vary widely, why are most of them taught in the same way over the same period of time?

4. Will increased numbers enter higher education out of intellectual hunger, or because more and more employment has been predicated upon a bachelor's or more advanced degree? If the latter, can educators devise measures of aptitude, interest, and acquired competence which would nerve employers to engage individuals as individuals, without fixed prerequisites embodied in a degree?

5. If most professors do not, in fact, produce research and if the identities of most of those who can are known, why are the 'teaching load' and the 'career line' so nearly the same for most professors?

6. If most college students do not, in fact, become scholars or scientists, why entrust them to research departments for most of their college course?

7. Why confine lectures to enrolled classes or 'sections' of thirty-odd students? Why not have fewer and larger lectures, open to any member of a university, as in Britain?

8 Are there legitimate economies to be found in the thorough-going use

of new media as substitutes for faculty instruction in connection with expository and rote teaching and learning tasks? Have these tasks been dissected with such economies in view?

9. Why is so little known about the actual results secured by various educational programmes and why do results, when they are known, effect so little change?

10. Who acts and speaks for higher education in response to such questions as these?

We may assume that these and other questions concerning the efficiency of higher education will be asked increasingly as straitened budgets cause the universities to turn to the national and state governments for more financial aid.[1]

The questions of students are of a different order. But first one must say which students one is talking about. In spite of the temptation to generalize about them, students remain very different from one another. This is true even of that large minority called 'dissident students'. Some of the latter are so bent on social revolution that they oppose all sanctuaries and all local repairs to existing institutions. Each part of a decaying society, they hold, should illustrate the rottenness of the whole. At least until the Vietnam war is ended, this group will continue to present the universities with problems of sheer security which can no longer be resolved within what is left of the tradition of civility, community, and informal administration. In this confrontation, the stakes for the nation's intellectual life and social progress are very high, for until force can be made to yield to persuasion, there will be a grave danger that university affairs, including the conduct of individual students, will come under an improper measure of control by the political representatives of an alienated public.

A second group of dissidents seeks to improve the universities and colleges, not to demolish them, but many members of this group are so impatient for perfection that no finite amount of reform is likely to be enough for them. They are outraged by the combination of imperfection and persistence which, like their parents, existing institutions present. And they are too ardent to accept, or even entertain, the sad truth of Spinoza's dictum that 'All things excellent are as difficult as they are rare'. Responsive universities can hope to reduce this group, but not to zero. They should assume that a vigilant and reproachful remnant will survive every actual reform, to inveigh

[1] Two recent examples in the United States: (1) *The Federal Financing of Higher Education*, report of the Association of American Universities (April 1968); (2) *New York State and Private Higher Education*, Report of the Select Committee on the Future of Private and Independent Higher Education in New York State (January 1968).

against the renewal of complacency which its adoption has induced and to contrast its superficiality with what must still be done.

There remain many students who are critical of their university or college but are not too visionary to be met halfway. They may be half-baked, but in what they have to say about the programmes and teaching which they often encounter, they are at least half right. In fact, most of the words which these students employ in saying what their education ought to be come straight from the lexicon of educational uplift with which all college catalogues begin and convocation talks conclude. In the mouths of responsible dissidents, even the demand for 'student power' reflects disappointment in the failure of educators to match deed to word, rather than a romantic desire to seize the universities.

These students are asking questions of higher education which are directed to the relation between established disciplines and courses of study and age-old questions of individual fulfilment and commitment, on the one hand, and the world's tensions and demands on the other. They do not wish their minds to be processed or certified, or their morals to be regulated. (Some of them seem not even to want to be taught.) They are irreverent towards established routines and unquestioned goals, and they see in form the natural enemy of sincerity. They want the university to be both liberal and relevant, pure but not detached, involved in the world but not subserving worldly ends.

This drive by the new breed of students to bring the world's pains and passions into the university, to demand 'relevance' as a condition of their attention, to resist prescribed means to extrinsic ends, to help shape the external relations of their universities, and to participate in the processes by which they are to be educated, has been profoundly unsettling to higher education and, indeed, to the general public.

II

Yet there is no basic need to fear the questions of either budgeteers or students, if the universities can first find the coherence and clarity to provide the answers. Because coherence and clarity are not present in adequate amounts at present, the remainder of this paper will be concerned with the possible correction of this deficiency. For whatever else may be said about the present crisis in higher education, it has strained the institutional fabric of American universities and colleges. I believe that strengthening that fabric is now the first order of business if higher education is to make its aims clear and quicken its responses under stress and that there is, in fact, slack to be taken up and new weaving to be done before the universities and colleges can be either despaired of or successfully defended.

The present crisis has made it clear that unquestioned routines and unthinking loyalties no longer ensure the integrity and rational order of academic communities. Students take nothing for granted; faculty members are distracted from institutional concerns; and administrators, trustees, and alumni find themselves calling for unity and civility as fragmentation and disruption increase.

Let us examine the present state of the constituent 'publics' of a university and consider some ways in which each may be reinforced and connected to the others so as to add to the institution's tensile strength. And let us begin where the headlines begin, with students.

STUDENTS

Provisions for enlarging student participation in university governance tend to take one of two forms: attempts to segregate and hand over to students those matters of 'sole' concern to them, and attempts to enable students to share with other constituencies of the university in a wide range of responsibilities. Tidy as the former solution may be, a university's cohesion may be expected to gain more from the latter. To date, universities which have begun to share academic responsibilities with students appear to have encountered some success and no recorded disasters. The level of committee discussion is said to have sunk no lower with students present; students have found some tasks onerous or trivial and others sobering; and some promising ideas have been saved from indefinite deferment or adopted sooner than they might otherwise have been. If experience of educational reform, engaging both educators and students, can be pressed to yield its full lessons during the next few years, the strengths and limitations of 'student power' as an influence in university communities can be made clear. The present 'dialogue of the deaf' on this subject shows how important it is that the universities get beyond the state of affairs now obtaining in many places, where conventional programmes compete blindly with gipsy encampments (called 'free universities') in the surrounding hills. In the end, the yeast and the lump belong together.

PROFESSORS

As students file a new claim to power, some faculties are finding that their own long-held powers have lapsed through disuse. The need to meet extraordinary and fundamental challenges found some of our most eminent institutions without central faculty bodies of manageable size, established procedures for meeting, or open lines of communication to administrators, schools and departments, and students. Torpid and unwieldy senates and distracted professors are not the stuff of which institutional clarity and responsiveness are made, and administrators seeking in time of crisis to share responsibility with faculties (a partnership not always cultivated in time of peace) have found that they could not be sure of a quorum or even of the support of those professors in attendance.

A first corrective is clearly of this structural kind. Faculties should elect deliberative bodies which meet regularly and which have frequent and substantive contact with the administrators of the university in connection with its general policies and educational programme.

But will professors perform or neglect such duties? We are told that they now neglect them, preferring the undisturbed pursuit of personal advancement. Concern for the overall progress and programme of the university is left to administrators, in uneasy association with a few faculty wheelhorses whom the departments depute to protect their interests at unavoidable committee meetings.

This problem is complex and deeply rooted in the academic culture. Yet there are signs that it is going to be attacked by some universities not yet convinced that it cannot be solved. On the theory that strong 'institutional men' or 'educational statesmen' can be developed by deliberate means, Stanford University proposes to place a number of its best young scholars and scientists in a special status as 'University Fellows' for terms of three years to work with academic administrators, faculty groups and others on problems having to do with Stanford's whole programme or aspects thereof that are not reducible to departmental or individual concerns. This is not a device to lure honest professors into 'administration' (half of the University Fellows' time will be available for their own work); rather, it rests on the plausible notion that if faculties are to exercise their *general* powers over university programmes, faculty members should actually deliberate about them from a perspective not restricted to their discipline or department. This may require an altered career line for at least some professors.

Another way in which individual faculty members of high competence might extend their powers as statesmen, teachers, and researchers would be through the wider use of initial appointments of six or seven years' duration. Such a period would be long ehough, so that the professor would not be forced to choose among these faculty roles but could make room in his professional life for serious teaching, contributions to institutional policy, and the completion of a solid book or complex piece of research. An extension of this means of institutional enlistment of faculty members would involve looking upon the whole of a tenured faculty member's career as embracing all these kinds of contributions and perhaps a period of national or international service as well.

Whatever the merits of these devices, they at least suggest that universities need not yet accept faculty itinerancy and indifference to institutional concerns as faults already beyond repair.

ADMINISTRATORS

Much has been written recently about the multiple burdens now borne by university and college presidents. It has been less often noted that presidents now have considerably more help in academic administration than in the past. Academic vice-presidents, provosts, and deans of faculties have multiplied as delegates of the president in matters of education and research. At a time of centrifugal tendencies, this development can have a considerable countervailing influence, if the internal structure of universities can be made more responsive to that influence. One means to that end is the provision of discretionary funds, functioning as a kind of internal foundation, to enable inventive students, faculty statesmen, and academic administrators to finance at least the exploratory phases of educational improvements. 'Venture capital' of this kind has been provided recently at Yale University, at the University of California at Berkeley, at the University of Puerto Rico, and at Stanford in connection with the programme of University Fellows, as a means of strengthening institutional initiative. Whether such devices will begin to restore the balance between internal and external concerns remains to be seen, but the interest of these universities in such a restoration is itself promising in view of the many predictions of final disintegration now to be heard in the land.

Administrators worried about the indifference of professors to institutional concerns might consider another means of enlistment. Professors and faculties with institutionally advertised expertise in such subjects as architecture, law, urban sociology, economics, and management are too rarely consulted by their own university in connection with its administrative decisions. It is therefore hardly surprising that those decisions are often deplored by members of the faculty who might have taken part in them and who, had they done so, might even have reached the same conclusions.

GRADUATES

In general, United States graduates are now related to their colleges through appeals for support, invitations to reunions, and cheering news of campus happenings and achievements. Even in the stronger colleges and universities, alumni activities as now organized often fail either to exploit or to help fulfil the specialized interests and capabilities of alumni as these develop following graduation. Quite apart from the need to reach graduates for the usual fund-raising purposes, increased interplay between alumni and current students and faculty on the basis of shared intellectual and social interests could toughen institutional fibre in two ways. By reducing mutual ignorance, it would lessen the chances of alienation between alumni and the current campus. By engaging faculty, students, and capable alumni in joint activities having intellectual or educational substance and social value, the institution's current faculty and student body would be reminded of the long-term results of their educational efforts. And they might, through such exchanges with able and inquiring alumni, make valuable changes in current programmes.

In the case of most institutions, such an effort would require better direction and more information and planning than most alumni offices and associations are now able to provide.

TRUSTEES

Boards of private universities and colleges have until recently modelled themselves on Aristotle's deity: moving others, they have not been moved. Now there are stirrings which suggest that this may cease to be true. The occasion for change appears to be the 'generation gap', which has made for a certain uneasiness about the average age and tenure of trustees. In truth, the procedures of trustee selection tend to elevate the age of those chosen, whether by co-option or alumni election. It usually takes some time to become wealthy, eminent, or prudent, and to be judged so by those who are already credited with these attributes. Also, it is difficult for recent graduates to become known widely enough to be selected. Yet it seems clear that recent graduates must be added to boards of trustees if the latter are to understand the words they hear from students and younger faculty, or even wish to hear them. Some boards are pondering ways to infect themselves with the virus of youth without subscribing to the full metaphysic of 'participatory democracy'.

Potentially more important, if not yet topical, is the question whether the financial and fiduciary roles of boards of trustees and their roles in respect of academic development should be distinguished more sharply than at present, or even separated. It is tempting to speculate on the possible value to a university if *all* its constituent publics were to be represented on an All-University Educational Council charged with reviewing and advising upon the evolution of the university's whole programme, not distributively, as in the case of visiting committees, but in the light of the university's history and central purpose, its chosen relationship to its environment, and its resources. Such a body should include graduates who have themselves entered academic and professional life elsewhere, other graduates whose occupations enable them to discuss the university's programme in relation to developments in the nation and the world, representative faculty members, students, and trustees. It would be presided over by the president of the university. It would exercise a kind of 'advise and consent' function which tends to be perfunctory or arbitrary when performed as one part of its task by the usual board of trustees, or when limited aspects of institutional problems are dealt with in separation from each other. The deliberations of such a council could arm its university with a body of educational principles and institutional policies which would not have to be conjured up or smoked out in time of crisis because they would already enjoy the understanding, if not the unanimous support, of all of the university's publics.

Would the achievement of greater coherence and clarity by individual universities make them more alike as institutions? In the case of the United States, I am inclined to think not. It seems more likely that clarification of its purposes by each university would mean a greater stress on its individuality and 'style' as an institution. In turn, this would mean that each university would respond in its own way to the queries and demands of budgeteers and students. I believe that this untidy process is better fitted to the prospect of universal higher education than it may at first appear to be. For this prospect will require of the universities as a whole a capacity for differential response which no centralized, homogeneous system of higher education is likely to display. What is to be hoped for is that each institution will know its own mind and define its own role clearly enough to insure that its supporters and its critics direct their aid and shape their criticisms to its chosen purposes and not to theirs.

There remains the chronically difficult problem of concerting action and thought by the diverse members of such a heterogeneous 'system'. Some questions which budget planners ask of higher education are not to be answered severally by individual universities. The kinds of problem which the Carnegie Commission on the Future of Higher Education is weighing are important to all universities and fully soluble by none. An adequate attack on such system-wide problems will require continued and, I fear, intensified research into the processes of higher education and assimilation of its results, joint deliberation on such occasions as the present one, and extended interchange with the public and its representatives. I believe that the very urgency and scale of the present and prospective demands upon higher education will mobilize the attention, effort, and degree of cooperation necessary to meet those demands. But the quality of the universities' response will depend above all on the capacity of each of them to decide what it can best do and be and to secure aid and understanding on the basis of that self-definition.

I

Response to Champion Ward – JOHN DEUTSCH

What can be done about all this, in the context in which we have to operate? Dr Ward touched on many of the fundamental questions; I want to take some of his propositions and examine them further.

In the last fifteen years, universities have been asked to do more than any other social institution, and it is not surprising that their efforts should have included some failures as well as some successes. Factors with which they have to contend include quantitative factors – not only the vast and rapid expansion of numbers of students, but the explosion in scientific knowledge and its technical applications which has had so great an influence on modern life, and the great increase in the amount and the speed of communication between people and places. In particular speed of communication has added to the impact of what goes on.

It is not always noticed that the generation gap is a quantitative one as well as one of age difference. At present the age-group 30 to 45, from which professors and teachers in universities come, is very small. But the birth-rate in the immediate post-war years and the years which followed that was high, so that there are relatively many more people of the age from which students can be drawn. Intellectual and administrative resources for university use are scarce at a time when a vast expansion of knowledge is going on and resources for research in many countries are greater than ever before. Increasingly, questions of public policy lead to a demand for technical knowledge; this is true, for example, of defence and economic policy. And all these things make demands on universities. Such success as has occurred in meeting these demands has not been achieved without stress; this is one of the factors which has affected students. They know there is little time to get what is wrong or missing or distorted properly sorted out. Not without reason they think that the whole set-up in higher education has serious defects.

Some pretty large jobs still remain to be done, some of them indeed hardly having been tackled so far at all. Universities are certainly not as yet serving a wide enough section of the population. They are still predominantly middle-

and upper-class institutions, taking in, in Canada, only 7 per cent of the lowest income group. This therefore must indicate a vast waste of the potential of intellectual resource in any total community. All countries, however, have begun to use or to consider using, a more open-door approach in admissions to higher education; and this tendency must grow in democratic systems, even though it may and must lead to budgetary problems. Subsidies will have to be provided for students from the lowest income groups as a matter of democratic principle. Institutions of higher education are absorbing more and more money in their running costs and their expansion costs. In Canada the rise has been of the order of 20 to 25 per cent a year. It may at present seem a relatively small part of the total budget, but because it is increasing it has a serious impact. Universities, moreover, are competing strongly with other agencies seeking public money – for example, for programmes of urban renewal, for the alleviation of poverty, for health services. Foreign aid is also in demand and there will have to be a more serious scrutiny before demands upon resources, even for university purposes, can be met. No doubt better productivity and efficiency will be asked for both by the public and by politicians.

In such a situation the effects upon university financing can be quite serious. Universities are not inherently popular institutions and anyway they are 'dogged by an elitist image'. If they are to obtain the funds they will need, they will have to put forward a creditable and convincing case for it. Most governments are in difficulties regarding the extent of their international borrowing power; clearly there are limits above which university expenditure cannot go.

Yet universities are under pressure from two sides. There are great pressures from the public that they should not restrict registration of students unduly. There are pressures on the other hand for economy. The publicity given to student discontent obviously does not help: universities pay singly and as an entire group for it. Politicians do not understand the ways of the student mind or sympathize with their methods of protest.

There are several quarters from which demands for changes in university government and systems of government come, though students may at the moment be most vociferous in making such demands. Various readjustments are taking place, but very little is communicated to the public, or even members of university staffs, about who makes the decisions and how they are made. Some of the changes should no doubt have been made at an earlier stage and deliberately instead of, as now, under pressure. Further changes are necessary and, indeed, overdue.

The faculty itself is taking more part in decision-making these days, but it is not itself a cohesive body. It hardly knows itself as a unity, and in large universities many members of the faculty do not know each other, each other's views, or the work which is being done in other departments. Moreover, the faculty in these days is growing very rapidly. Many members are are often young and in Canada drawn from outside the country. The brain drain has shifted: Canada is importing many teachers in higher education as well as exporting some. In these circumstances it remains very difficult to get cohesion, yet more and more important decisions are likely to be given to faculties to make. Specialization and the interests of particular disciplines will continue to militate against faculty cohesion. There are more and more claims on the time of members of faculty and many committee meetings can lead to almost intolerable delays in getting things done. We do need to take a realistic look at the development of the university and the development of its resources and wealth as a whole.

All this probably means that we must innovate administratively. More time must be made available to members of faculty and others who need to spend it in decision-making. This means that we must organize better and more efficiently so as to save the time we need so much. More effective use must be made of students in committee work, but as yet we hardly know how to use them to the greatest effect. Students themselves are usefully exercised with questions of securing the right people among them for participation in committee work. It is easy for committees to get bogged down in the conduct of business by ill-defined rules of behaviour or the determination of some students or members of faculty to carry on a continuous dialogue. The problem of ensuring continuity in student representation is not easy of solution. Moreover, what one year's students want, the next year's may not. Student participation is likely to remain with us, but forms of participating are at present developing faster than we can solve the problems they create.

With regard to the university's relation to the world outside, it needs wide understanding from many diverse groups – its own alumni, its trustees, the general public, industry, etc., to say nothing of members of its own faculty. We need to think up new methods for securing such understanding and this may well involve the idea of a university-wide council as an advisory body, made up of alumni, trustees, and members of faculty.

II

How can institutions of higher education make better use of the resources of interest and concern upon which they might draw – both in society outside and among their own members younger and older? At present the universities are dogged by the 'elitist image' and have too few friends in the community at large with a real understanding of their problems. Their own faculty so often goes on the principle that what's good for the department is good for the university. And far too little attempt is made really to involve younger lecturers, or students, in thought about the welfare of the institution as a whole.

The two matters with which the discussion was chiefly concerned were how university policy is determined and the part which people outside the main body of professors might play in shaping it; and how departmental power and ambition are to be reconciled with the purposes of the university.

The first point taken up was Ward's reference to the possibility of an All-University council. John Deutsch cited the example of the Council of Queen's University at Kingston in Ontario which, by its constitution and structure, contributes effectively to the health and wisdom of university policy. The Council is made up of the Board of Trustees plus the Senate, with an equal number of persons elected by the Alumni. There are some thirty-five people on the Board of Trustees – which includes benefactors and people co-opted for their suitability to act as Trustees. There are about forty-eight people on the Senate which includes representatives of the faculties, the students and the administration of the university. This means that some eighty people serve on the Council from the Board of Trustees and the Senate together. Nearly another eighty are elected by the Alumni on the nomination of its executive committee which has regard to general groups, disciplines studied, and parts of the country and provinces represented. The Council, which meets once a year, takes opportunities for questioning and cross-examining both Trustees and members of Senate regarding current policies and issues and future prospects.

It was pointed out that the annual meetings of the Court of many British universities give to some extent a similar opportunity, though one must beware of assuming that members of Court are always knowledgeable enough to be able to get to the heart of some questions which may be of key importance.

Comment passed to the way in which members of faculty themselves are or are not encouraged to take an interest in the policy of their university and how that policy is arrived at. There was pretty general agreement that far too little is normally done to encourage younger members of staff to take enough interest or have enough opportunity to influence what is being decided. Often neither students nor younger members of staff serve on the Senate, let alone its more powerful, policy-forming sub-committees. In several British universities which so far have no students on the Senate, there is talk of having student representatives on that body though much less talk as yet of having really junior members of staff on it too.

One participant mentioned one of the new universities in Britain where appointments to the faculty are made on the general basis that a faculty member should be interested in two at least of three main areas: research, teaching, and general involvement in affairs. At an interview for a first appointment questions are asked to make clear the order of his priorities as between these three main areas. Promotion will be according to the contribution he makes in two of the three. In a number of British universities there is some feeling that too much attention has been given in the past to encouraging publication, and that more people ought to be spending more time in thinking about institutional policy.

One of the younger members of the Seminar said tartly that in many British universities people other than professors are rarely consulted about the curriculum or its content and so 'just give up as members of the institution and collect stamps instead'. Where they are consulted, they will willingly participate and would do very much more thinking voluntarily if they received any encouragement. They do not suffer from the notion that committee meetings are tedious but if they are asked to do less, of course they do less. On the other hand, some felt that it was very easy to encourage too many people to take part in running a university – thus wasting their own time as scholars as well very possibly as wasting other people's. 'Most people who have the right to go to committee meetings mercifully don't go.'

At this juncture, an American member remarked upon the system by which a department appoints as its lecturers and professors those who are keen upon their subject but tend to have the goals of the institution as a whole only faintly in mind. Given a heavily departmentalized structure to a university, it might be almost a matter of luck whether any particular department has people who are really thinking about or much concerned with institutional objectives. Someone else reflected that whereas one of the newest British universities has sought to ensure in recruiting new members of staff that they believe in the character and goals of the institution itself, in another the ambition is always to appoint 'the best man in his field irrespective'. It is difficult to say as yet which policy is the more successful, but there is certainly more tension between departments in the latter university than the former.

The sheer power of the departments is demonstrated in many universities when one tries to answer the question 'How can one leave anything out of the curriculum once it has been put in?' Where can one get the necessary power with which to alter anything? How can one persuade any department to disappear or join up with another or to transform itself?

'The challenge,' said a vice-chancellor present, 'is how to allow scope to groups of specialists – who are closely associated with one another and naturally plan together – and at the same time have a planning system for the university as a whole which prevents it from being so fragmented that it cannot effectively take account of changes in knowledge or the organization of knowledge. A university which gets rid of departments has got to find some substitute for them. At the same time its planning processes face great complication. At Sussex, for instance, there is a much more sophisticated sense now of the relationship between the subject groups and the Schools of Study than there was when the university was in its earliest days. The attitude of mind with which new forms of organization are shaped is more important than any blueprint universally applicable to all kinds of institution.'

Shoben thought that some of the encouragement towards interaction between departments might come from students who conceived the scope of an intellectual domain in broader and more flexible ways than some of their seniors. It was generally agreed that many universities still needed to be in closer touch with the world and to go into the attack on some of its complex problems through a consortium of departments rather than with the help of departments individually. Experience shows that this is a great incentive towards interdepartmental understanding and initiative. Incidental reference was made to the style of the campus of the new University of Lancaster in England where the diversity of shops, banks, etc., around the central square are open to use by the general public, who are welcomed at any hour of the day.

A good deal more was said about the organization of new universities on both sides of the Atlantic in ways that prevented a rigid or conventional departmental structure. One American professor urged a frontal attack on the departmental system, certainly in the older universities of America. 'The situation now is pathological,' he said. 'I think it has arisen, as often happens in pathology, because of what happened in the past. If you look through the catalogues of my own university, which go back for almost 200 years – and I think this would also be true of still older institutions like Harvard – you will notice that the departmental structure came into being as a powerful influence at the same time as research was making its impact upon the university. It was his research interest above all else that caused a man to become aware of the fact that now he was a physicist or a classicist. A man became proud of being a professor of chemistry and before long there was further specialization, with professors of organic chemistry being appointed.' But as the years have gone on, the most lively scholarship and the most lively research are often occurring in the places where the subjects overlap; a departmental structure is dated and it is in interdepartmental study centres that much of the fastest progress is being made. Centres for population studies, urban studies, transportation studies, language centres, communications centres, etc. are now on the frontier. And these involve the breaking of departmental barriers.

The fact is that in the latter part of the nineteenth century and the first ten years of this century most departments gave much of their attention to undergraduate education. In many cases, we were assured, much departmental attention is still devoted to this stage of university work; and so undergraduates tend to be taught still along departmental lines – and in blinkered ways, while some at any rate of the most creative work at the postgraduate level was being done interdepartmentally. These studies are not at all adequately reflected in what is passed on to the undergraduate; nor is the life and light they radiate conveyed as it should be at the undergraduate level. 'The fact is that we are trying to solve twentieth-century educational problems by using nineteenth-century methods and nineteenth-century organization with an eighteenth-century set-up behind them.' The history of the development of the contemporary university might have a great deal of light thrown upon it by a proper study of the rise and role of departments.

Paul Miller remarked that there is sometimes astonishingly little relationship between the recommendations made by governmental advisory committees in the us, on which members of university faculties serve, and the departmental organization of universities as it exists. The ideas which the heads of university departments themselves put forward on such committees often seem to involve distinctive formats and types of forward manpower planning which pay scant regard to the traditions and the conservatism of the departments from which they themselves may come.

Yet, as the Seminar generally agreed, departments have remained socially necessary to students. Indeed in an institution of higher education with many commuting students and few colleges or residence halls, the department may increasingly be the student's only home. 'I suppose I have got the gloomy view that universities may disappear but not departments', said Champion Ward; 'but it is a very complicated problem anyway.' One might trace, he went on, some of the disintegrative fragmentation of the university to departments and their rivalries. But on the other hand students get a great heal from their departments other than specialized knowledge. 'It would seem that in Britain, where students are expected in many cases to concentrate chiefly upon a single subject, their department often means – and healthily means – more to them even than in America. If one seeks to break up departments students may be deprived of the most human institution they know in their university. What is the answer?'

Few denied that in many departments, as they at present existed in both universities and colleges, there is a hierarchical structure of authority – with the professor or chairman on top – and less democracy than was desirable. All the same, at least in Britain, it is not true to say that most members of staff are 'just looking around for the next job'. Many of them are really concerned both with their subject and with teaching their students, even though their range of interest and loyalty may be largely confined to the department and not extended to the university as a whole.

Further discussions about interrelations between teaching, research, and administration caused several members to allow that a reduction of teaching hours had in many cases resulted in more publication. But the kinds of publication really needed include not only those recording advances in knowledge and research achievement, but also books of an imaginative kind useful in teaching and learning at the undergraduate stage. There are, admittedly, many hack textbooks produced by university teachers, in part because of the financial gains it is possible to make through such publications. But a really seminal textbook is in a different category, and perhaps authors of such books do not get enough credit for producing them. There needed to be a lot more interest in university teaching and in methods, and more writing that would encourage students to feel the life and enterprise in their subject.

But frequent revision of course offerings and the invention of new courses are, it was said, much more important matters than people in departments realized. How many student-initiated courses, it was asked, have found their way into departmental programmes? A very good course might for various reasons be offered only once. Much more thought needs to be given to keeping courses lively and fresh in both content and pattern.

Attention was now turned to institutions of higher education and their public relationships. The number of people who really know what is going on here will have to increase as tertiary education becomes more and more influential in social and national life. At present presidents and vice-chancellors are looked to as public relations officers, but the strain on the individual can easily reach breaking-point. Nor is it possible for one man to stay adequately in touch with the teaching and research going on throughout his institution as well as cope with all the administrative chores and decisions, while at the same time keeping on intimate terms with problems of national and international welfare which could involve his institution and what it could contribute. No one saw a clear answer to these problems!

In his closing remarks Deutsch emphasized the need above all to 'work to keep things on the human scale'. We are getting our proportions wrong. With regard to student discontent and participation, his view was that our job is to get on with doing what we are convinced is the sensible thing to do, making it possible for students to have their say in matters which are their rational concern, cooperating as intimately as possible with the general body of students who are not extremists. There will always be a certain number of extremist students, but given the conditions of reasonable participation and concern on the part of the faculty, these will not be in a position greatly to disturb the general student body.

Not all the members of the seminar took this position. There was strong feeling in some quarters that the malaise went deeper and might have to involve a change of heart. 'A community cannot be set up by a tin-tack method,' said one participant. It was agreed on all sides that the mere provision of more residence halls, better and bigger student union buildings, more amenities of every kind, more permissive co-education, and a greater variety of options for study, would not do the trick. But of the importance of the human scale and of educating students as persons and really keeping in touch with them: of this no one had any doubt.

CHAPTER 9

Elite and Popular Functions in American Higher Education

Martin Trow

I

If we consider American higher education today with any degree of detachment, we are struck by a paradox. On one hand, the system seems to be in serious trouble and perhaps even in crisis. Almost every major university, and many others as well, has been the scene of student demonstrations, disturbances, and even insurrections. Events at Columbia and Berkeley and San Francisco State become national news; on many other campuses (Northwestern and Boston University, Fordham and New York University, San Jose and Howard), militant blacks and whites and dissident faculty confront their university's authorities with bold demands, threats, strikes, and sit-ins. On the other hand, if looked at from another perspective, and especially from a European perspective, American higher education is successful and thriving, and indeed provides the model for educational reformers in almost every European country. Seen in this way, it surely is a success. American research and scholarship make contributions to every field of learning, and dominate many. In applied science and technology we are the envy of the world: as Servan-Schreiber[1] has observed, the Americans have worked out 'a close association between business, universities, and the government which has never been perfected nor successful in any European country'. Our universities are deeply involved in the life of the society, and contribute much to the efforts to solve its problems, from social medicine to the problems of the inner city. And finally, this sprawling system of some 2,500 colleges and universities enrols about 40 per cent of the age grade, over 50 per cent of all high school graduates, and those proportions are steadily rising. In some

[1] J.-J. Servan-Schreiber, *Le Défi américain*, Paris, 1967.

large states like California, where some 80 per cent of high school graduates go on to some form of higher educcaion, our system of mass higher education begins to be very nearly universal. Whatever one's assessment of those figures and their implications, they must be counted a considerable achievement.

But I do not believe there is much gain in celebrating the triumphs of American higher education just at the moment, especially when scarcely a day goes by without another report of a confrontation and a disruption on a campus. There is perhaps more profit in considering its difficulties. I believe these, of which student unrest is only the most visible, can be better understood in the light of the continuing tension between the popular and the elite functions of American colleges and universities.

American colleges and universities, almost from their beginnings, have performed two different sets of functions. I have called these respectively, 'elite' and 'popular' functions, but perhaps more accurately the distinction is between those for which the university sets its own aims, and those which the university takes on in response to external needs and demands. The line between these is not hard and fast; ultimately, it can be argued, all university activities are in some sense responsive to societal interests. But the distinction is a useful one, perhaps most clearly to Europeans, whose universities until recently have largely confined themselves to their traditional and autonomous functions and have resisted accepting tasks set for them by other parts of the society or the population at large.

At the heart of the traditional university is its commitment to the transmission of the high culture, the possession of which has been thought to make men truly civilized. This was really the only function that Cardinal Newman, and more recently Robert Hutchins, have thought appropriate to the university. Closely related to this, and certainly central to our conception of liberal education, is the shaping of mind and character: the cultivation of aesthetic sensibilities, broader human sympathies, and a capacity for critical and independent judgement. The second autonomous function of the American university is the creation of new knowledge through 'pure' scholarship and basic scientific research. Another elite function, of greater importance for European universities than in this country, though it is by no means absent from our own most prestigious private universities, is the selection, formation, and certification of a social elite: the learned professions, the higher civil service, the politicians, and (though less in Britain than on the Continent), the commercial and industrial leadership, as well as the teachers in the preparatory secondary schools where the children of that elite are educated and prepared for their accession to elite status. These functions involve values and standards which are institutionalized in the universities and elite private colleges, and are maintained by them autonomously and even in resistance to popular demands and sentiments.

The popular functions fall into two general categories. First, there is a commitment on the part of the system as a whole to provide places somewhere for as many students as can be encouraged to continue their education beyond high school. For a very long time, it has been believed in this country that talented youth of humble origins should go to college. But the extension of these expectations to all young men and women, as something between a right and an obligation, dates no further back than the Second World War. In part this notion is a reflection of the erosion of the legitimacy of class cultures, and of the growing feeling in every industrial society, but most markedly in the United States, that it is right and proper for all men to claim possession of the high culture of their own societies. In school and through the mass media, ordinary people are encouraged to send their children to college to share in the high culture, both for its own sake and for its instrumental value in gaining entrance to the old and the emerging elite occupations. Higher education is assuming an increasingly important role in placing people in the occupational structure, and thus in determining their adult class positions and life chances. Social mobility across generations now commonly takes the form of providing one's children with more education than their parents had, and the achievement of near universal secondary education in America by the Second World War provided the platform for the development of mass higher education since then. The tremendous growth of occupations demanding some form of higher education both reflects and further stimulates the increase in college and university enrolments. All this shows itself in yet another way, as a marked rise in the educational standard of living of the whole population. Throughout the class structure, already fully accomplished in the upper-middle but increasingly so in the lower-middle and working classes, higher education comes to be seen as appropriate not just for people of wealth or extraordinary talent or ambition, but as possible and desirable for youngsters of quite ordinary talent and ambition.

In the past the relative accessibility of higher education brought large numbers of students to American colleges who had little interest in learning for its own sake, but who had powerful vocational orientations, and wanted the degree and sometimes the skills which would help them better their position. We are now seeing large numbers from more affluent homes who similarly enter college without much interest in learning, but who also are less interested in vocational preparation – who either have little ambition for a middle-class career, or else take it completely for granted, or, as in many cases, both. Such students pose a special problem – they are rather bored, querulous people, resentful at having to be in college, and quite vulnerable to the various quasi-hippy and radical doctrines floating around. For example, it is fashionable among some to deprecate ambition and hard work, and to resent a curriculum which, they charge, threatens to build them into the business world, fit them for jobs, careers, and so forth in a sick society, and whose counter-ideology to the notion of achievement is 'Look, man, you're just putting us on the treadmill and driving us, and your lives are just running around doing things, why don't we smell the flowers a little more . . .' I can't pursue this subject here, except to say that the ancillary functions of higher education for a mass student body – of entertainment and custodial care – are now beginning to take on rather different forms as the character and characteristics of this mass intake changes.

Changes in the occupational structure and educational values are the driving force behind the explosion of enrolments and the emergence of mass higher education in America. But that development has been facilitated by the absence of a national standard or a national system of higher education. The radical decentralization of decision-making in American higher education, together with the extreme heterogeneity in the quality and character of the institutions that it comprises, make the net effect of their decisions highly responsive to social and economic forces. A given college may choose not to grow, but there are ten others that will. And while competition for places in the most desired colleges becomes ever more intense, it is still true that there is a college somewhere in America for everybody. The commitment to a conception of public service is strong enough in American higher education, both public and private, so that the number of places is basically set by the consumer's demand in the market for education, rather than by production agreements among educational producers, as in most other advanced societies. The effective demand for higher education in the American population is a function of how much people want to attend college (or send their children there) and how expensive a college education is. Educational aspirations are rising, while the growth in numbers of municipal, state, and junior colleges, in part in response to the rise in educational aspirations, contributes to their further rise by bringing inexpensive, non-residential colleges nearer to many who could not afford high tuition fees or the costs of college residence.

If one popular function is the provision of mass higher education to nearly everybody who applies for it, the second is the provision of useful knowledge and service to nearly every group and institution that wants it. The service orientation of American higher education is too well known to need discussion. But the demand on the universities for such service is increasing all the time. This in part reflects the growth of the knowledge-base created by the scientific explosion of the past few decades. Not only is much of this new knowledge of potential applied value to industry, agriculture, the military, the health professions, etc., but also new areas of national life are coming to be seen as users of knowledge created in the university. We may know more about how to increase corn production than how to educate black children in our urban slums, but it is likely that the universities will shortly be as deeply involved in efforts to solve our urban problems as ever they were in agriculture.

II

How has American higher education been able to fulfil both its elite and its popular functions? Put differently, what have been the institutional mechanisms through which the colleges and universities have been able, on one hand, to contribute to both the transmission and creation of knowledge, and, on the other, to serve the variety of other demands the society has made on them?

The chief such mechanism has been the division of labour between and within institutions. A very large number of American colleges are essentially single-function institutions, either elite or popular. Swarthmore College or Haverford or Reed are essentially preparatory colleges for graduate and professional schools. Their faculties for the most part are men who have taken the Ph.D. in distinguished universities, but who prefer a career in a teaching college rather than in a big university. In addition there are the elite private universities – the Ivy League universities, or Rice, or Cal. Tech., or Stanford, for example – which are highly selective in admissions, and which subordinate service to research and the transmission of the high culture.

By contrast, a very large number of American colleges are essentially service institutions. The roughly two hundred teachers' colleges, the many small, weak, denominational colleges, the less ambitious engineering schools, the over seven hundred junior colleges: these are serving primarily vocational ends, preparing youngsters from relatively modest backgrounds for technical, semi-professional, and other white-collar jobs.

There is another group of institutions, most notably the big state universities, which carry on elite and popular functions within the same institution. On the one hand, these institutions, along with the state colleges and

junior colleges, have taken the brunt of the enormous expansion of enrolments in recent decades. They are the centres for community service of every
kind, they train the teachers, the social workers, the probation officers, the
market researchers, and the myriad other new and semi-professions required
by this service-oriented post-industrial society. On the other hand, they are
also centres of scholarship and basic research, and contribute to the advancement of knowledge in every academic subject. Moreover, they offer, in their
undergraduate colleges of letters and science, the full range of academic
subjects, many of which centre on the transmission of the high culture, and
are concerned less with public service than with the cultivation of sensibility
and independence of judgement, a sense of the past, of the uniqueness of the
individual, of the varied forms of human experience and expression – in brief,
all the desired outcomes of liberal education.

Within the university the popular and elite functions are insulated from
one another in various ways – ways that serve to protect the highly vulnerable elite functions of liberal education and basic research and scholarship
from the direct impact of the larger society whose demands for vocational
training, certification, service, and the like are reflected and met in the
popular functions of the university. These insulations take various forms of
a division of labour within the university. There is a division of labour
between departments, as for example between a Department of English or
Classics, and a Department of Education. There is a division of labour in
relatively unselective universities between the undergraduate and graduate
schools, the former given over largely to mass higher education in the service
of social mobility and occupational placement, entertainment, and custodial
care, while the graduate departments in the same institutions are often able
to maintain a climate in which scholarship and scientific research can be
carried out to the highest standards. There is a familiar division of labour
between graduate departments and professional schools. Among the faculty
there is a division of labour, within many departments, between scientists and
consultants, scholars and journalists, teachers and entertainers. More dangerously, there is a division of labour between regular faculty and a variety of
fringe or marginal teachers – teaching assistants, visitors, and lecturers – who
in some schools carry a disproportionate load of the mass teaching. Within
the administration there is a division of labour between the dean of faculty
and graduate dean, and the dean of students. And among the students there
is a marked separation between the 'collegiate' and 'vocational' sub-cultures on
one hand, and academically or intellectually oriented sub-cultures on the other.

Now, despite the strains which have developed around these divisions of
function between and within American colleges and universities, they have

worked surprisingly well, especially in the eyes of observers in European universities who have opposed the encroachment of popular functions on the universities as incompatible with their traditional functions to further knowledge, transmit the high culture, and shape the character of the elite strata. American higher education, as a system, has been able to do those things, and *also* give a post-secondary education, often within the very same institution, to millions of students, while serving every institution of society, every agency of government.

But I believe that these mechanisms of insulation and protection are currently breaking down under the impact of a new wave of pressures to expand the popular functions of American higher education. And I should like to discuss a few of the ways in which the enormous expansion of American higher education, in both its number and its range of activities, is creating very great strains on these insulating mechanisms, and thus threatening the traditional functions of the university. Let me sketch a few of these, and then return to them in rather more detail.

First, the expansion of the university is involving it more directly in controversial issues, and is thus increasing the number and range of significant publics in the larger society, including the political parties, which are attentive to what goes on in the university. This in turn is causing severe problems for boards of trustees and regents, and for the overall governance of the universities and the protection of their autonomy. These problems are reflected back on campus in the growing politicization of both the faculty and the student body (a trend that also has other sources). The intrusion of politics on to the campus has many consequences, among them the threat to the procedures by which these institutions govern themselves. At the same time, the growth of enrolment brings to the campus large numbers of students who do not accept the institution's authority to define the form and content of higher education: some of these are middle-class whites, while an increasing number are militant blacks. The characteristic forms of protest by radical whites and militant blacks are in important respects quite different, but both are at variance with the university's traditional functions.

III

Let me turn first to the changing role of Boards of Trustees or Regents. The role of trustees in American higher education is a peculiar one. They are, by law, the ultimate authority over these corporate bodies: they own the physical resources of the institution, they select its chief administrative officers, they possess the formal authority which is exercised by delegation by the administrative officers and faculty alike. And yet two parallel tendencies have been at work to reduce the actual importance of the trustees in recent decades: on the one hand, more and more power has drained away from the trustees with the growth of major alternative sources of funds for academic programmes over which the trustees have in fact had little or no control; and, on the other, the increasing assertion, on the part of administrators and faculty, that powers that have over time been delegated to them are theirs by right. The growth of the contract grant system has enormously increased the power of the faculty in relation to administration as well as to trustees; and the tight competitive market for academic men, together with institutional ambitions for prestige in the academic league standings, have ensured that trustees rarely exercise control over the funds granted to research professors. Trustees have been relatively ineffective in controlling capital expansion, one remaining bastion of their power, when funds for new buildings come essentially to support new research programmes for which professors and administrators have jointly applied. Moreover, administrators are increasingly turning to outside funds, especially to foundations, to support new academic programmes – to set up experimental colleges, or to bring more minority group students on campus. And again, trustees are really not consulted about these. External sources of funds mark a major diminution of the trustees' power to shape the character or guide the direction of 'their' institution.

In addition, the broad encompassing concept of 'academic freedom' has meant that both administrators and faculty members come to feel that the powers they exercise over instruction, admissions, appointments, the internal allocation of resources, and even, increasingly, the physical design of the campus, all are theirs by right. Some of the forces that have led to the extension and deepening of the concept of academic freedom have had to do with the enormous influence of the most distinguished American universities as models for all the others. Characteristically, it is in the most distinguished universities that the academic community had the widest autonomy, the broadest control over its own conditions of life and work. And many lesser institutions have come to see faculty power and institutional autonomy as a mark of institutional distinction, and to be pursued as part of the strategy of institutional mobility to which so much of the energy and thought of academic men is devoted.[1]

[1] It could perhaps be argued that the power of the faculties in the most distinguished universities flow precisely from their academic distinction, through the familiar academic transmutation of prestige into power. The faculties of weaker institutions see the relation, but endeavour to turn the causal connection on its head: they mean to gain the power and transmute it into prestige, for their institutions directly and themselves indirectly.

Boards of trustees traditionally have looked in two directions: inwardly to the government and direction of their universities; outwardly, to the groups and interests which provide the support, and make claims for services, on the university. On the one hand, as I have suggested, boards have been losing power over their own institutions: many things are done, and funded, so to speak, behind their backs. At the same time (and this applies more to public than to private universities) their constituencies, and their relation to their constituencies, have been changing. Boards have traditionally dealt with very specific 'relevant publics': legislative committees, wealthy donors, alumni organizations. In the leading universities, their job has been to get support from these publics while resisting inappropriate interference. And in this task boards of public universities have not been so different from those of private universities: in most of their relationships they have been dealing with people very much like themselves, known quantities, in many cases graduates of the same state university, men of similar sentiments and values and prejudices. And these relationships could be, for the most part, cosy and private. The University of California until recently could imagine itself to be a private university operating largely on public funds, in a relationship to public authorities not wholly unlike that of the British universities.

Today, the constituencies, the relevant publics, of state universities are much wider, more heterogeneous, and less familiar. In part, the growth of relevant publics has accompanied the simultaneous expansion of the universities, and of their functions. When I arrived at Berkeley eleven years ago, the University of California consisted of two major campuses, three small undergraduate colleges, and a medical school, with a total enrolment of about 40,000, operating on a state budget of a little over one hundred million dollars. Today the university consists of 9 campuses with over 100,000 students and a state budget of over three hundred million dollars, with nearly as much again from outside sources. The student body and faculty are not only bigger, but more heterogeneous, reflecting a variety of interests, many of which touch directly on very sensitive and controversial public issues. The School of Agriculture still does research on more fruitful crops and more effective pest control, but other students and faculty are active in support of the movement to organize migratory farm workers; the School of Education still produces schoolteachers and administrators, but also provides expert advice to school boards embarked on programmes of total integration, while others testify in defence of black militants and invite Black Panthers to give lectures on campus; administrative officers still define and defend academic criteria for admissions, while other administrative officers press for the admission of larger numbers of minority-group students outside the ordinary admissions criteria. And the university is just embarking on a major commitment to the solution of urban problems which inevitably will involve it in the most intense and passionate political controversies.

As a result of the expansion of the university, both in numbers and in the range of activities, more and more people in California have come to take an interest in it, and have come to feel that they have views on the university which ought to be heard. In some uncertain sense, the constituency of the university has become the population of the state. But it is out of just this uncertainty about the nature and composition of the university's 'relevant publics' that the regents' anxieties arise. As the constituency of the trustees has grown, it has become less distinct: it is unclear just who the relevant publics are to which the regents should attend. Moreover, with the disruption of the old 'cosy' relations of the regents to specific limited publics, the regents can no longer know their constituents' minds by consulting with them, or by reading their own. And as the regents lose touch with their constituents, so also they come to be less well known and trusted by their new constituents: they become not people one can phone or one has talked to, but merely a remote part of the apparatus of government – the powerful people who need to be pressured. And some unrepresentative part of the anonymous public begins to write letters complaining about the university, and the regents, for want of a genuine relation to these new publics, begin to read them, and become anxious and worried. For one important difference between specific and differentiated publics and a mass undifferentiated public is that the former reflect specific interests which can be met, or compromised with, or educated, or resisted. A mass public, by contrast, does not have interests so much as fears and angers – what it communicates to the trustees is 'Why can't you clear up that mess at the university – all those demonstrating students and unpatriotic faculty?'

These two tendencies – the trustees' sense of a loss of control over their university, and the emergence of a mass public of uncertain size and composition and temper with whom the trustees have no clear representative or communicating relationship – can undermine a board of trustees' conceptions of who they are and what their role is, and generate in them anger and anxiety. This year the Regents of the University of California have reacted to an event at Berkeley with what appears to have been panic and rage. The event was the creation of an experimental course to which Eldridge Cleaver, a leader of the militant Black Panthers, was invited to give a series of ten (unpaid) lectures. The course had been proposed by some students, gained the participation of four faculty members, and then was reviewed, revised, and approved by the regular faculty committee which had been charged with instituting such experimental courses. It was to have had an enrolment of about 200 out of a total undergraduate enrolment of some 15,000 and a total student enrolment of some 28,000 at Berkeley. One can have varying views about the academic value or wisdom of the course (which can be said about a great many of the thousands of courses offered each year at Berkeley) without seeing it as a serious danger to the university or to the students who would be attending it. Under pressure from the Governor, and from what it took to be 'public opinion', the Regents intervened directly in the instructional programme and passed a series of resolutions prohibiting the course as designed from being offered for credit, and censuring the faculty members who had sponsored it and the faculty committee which had approved it. At the same meeting they also quite gratuitously condemned a production of a play that they had not seen which had been put on by the Drama Department at Berkeley during the summer, and directed that future productions should 'conform to accepted standards of good taste . . .' These directives, besides being violations of the regents' own standing orders, were clearly violations of academic freedom even narrowly conceived. More to the point, they had all the marks of a panic response–impulsive, disproportionate to the occasion, and deeply and unnecessarily provocative of the *internal* constituencies, the students, faculty, and administration, which essentially constitute the institution the board is nominally governing, and which strongly opposed the regential action. The situation was of course exploited by militant groups of students, and their effort to create another Columbia disaster at Berkeley was narrowly averted. But the action created a serious crisis of authority within the university – what might be called a constitutional crisis, centring on who actually controls the curriculum and appointments of staff, which is not yet resolved. If it is not resolved, or if it leads to bitter struggles between the faculty and the regents, or between the university and the state government, which involve punitive actions against the budget or individual campuses, then Berkeley's (and the whole university's) capacity to sustain a climate of intellectual excellence will be gravely threatened: its ability to perform all its functions, but most especially its elite functions as an international centre of learning, will be seriously weakened.

California is in many ways a populist democracy: the Governor and legislature discuss and revise the university's annual operating budget in an atmosphere increasingly directly political and responsive to popular sentiments and indignation; and the whole electorate votes directly on proposed bond issues that are required for capital expansion. The Board of Regents, a majority of whom are appointed to sixteen-year terms, was conceived precisely as a buffer between the university and popular or political pressures, to protect the necessary freedom of the university to explore issues and engage in educational innovations that might not have popular support at any given moment. But, as we are seeing, the board appears unable to perform that function; instead of defending the university to its external publics, it begins to function as a conduit of popular sentiment and pressure on the university. And this, as I have suggested, places the elite functions of the university in grave jeopardy.

But the problems I have been discussing are not confined to public state universities in populist societies. The emergence of a mass undifferentiated and angry public indeed poses a special threat to universities. But the more general pattern in which university expansion creates new and easily neglected bodies of constituents can be illustrated in the events at Columbia University in the recent past. As Walter Metzger has noted, the physical expansion of Columbia, situated right at the edge of Harlem, made of that community a highly relevant and attentive public. Over many years Columbia has been expanding its operations into areas and buildings from which minority-group people have 'necessarily' been evicted. But its board of trustees, and unfortunately also its administration, simply had not begun to see that Harlem was at least as relevant to Columbia's fate as were its alumni, and wealthy donors, and great foundations. And it was the representatives of the black community, within the university as students, who precipitated the crisis that then was exploited by white militants, and greatly exacerbated by undisciplined police action.

The transformation of the constituencies of a university from a relatively small known set of relevant publics to a large undifferentiated mass public may be the inevitable consequence of the expansion of a state university system governed by a single board, and thus perceived as a single entity. Decentralization has been argued in universities on educational grounds – as providing diversity, variety, and an educational context of human scale which allow stronger and closer relationships to develop between teachers and students. I would argue decentralization also on political grounds: that enormous universities and university systems which constantly extend their influence must engender mass audiences. One way to reduce the impact of mass publics on the university is to decrease the size of the authoritative (i.e. autonomous) units within it. A university cannot experiment, which implies the certainty of making errors and the near certainty of offending somebody, if it has to satisfy the lowest common denominator of popular sentiment on every issue. What brings many issues to public attention is that they are decided, or at least approved, at a very high level, and thus are seen to have widespread consequences. Many of the popular functions of the universities in the past – mass education and public service – have indeed been popular in the other sense of the word, and have gained the support of the general public. But, as I have suggested, it seems inescapable that the university will in the future be involved much more frequently in highly controversial issues and actions for which mass support cannot always be gained. Such activities may have a better chance of not becoming the focus for a major crisis (as the Cleaver course did) if decisions about it are not taken at the state-wide level in ways that require politicians and other politically ambitious people to take public stands. Reducing the size of the authoritative units (perhaps even smaller than a single campus) may also help to bring the representatives of the larger society closer to the educational process. And there is very clearly a need to educate them to the nature and requirements of the institutions whose governments they head.

IV

I want now to turn to the question of student activism, which is certainly the most visible form our current troubles take. First, this phenomenon has served as a kind of ink-blot to the world: all kinds of people impute to it meanings which support their own diagnoses of what is wrong with the university. We hear from the unlikeliest sources statements that begin, 'the students are trying to tell us . . .' and end with the interpreter's own notions of what ought to be changed.

My own view is that student activism on American campuses has to be seen as the outcome of a number of different developments and forces which have the appearance of a unity only when we do not look beyond the demonstrations themselves. First, the protests do not arise out of widespread discontent with the curriculum and forms of instruction in American universities. I myself believe there is considerable need for reform of the curriculum and organization of teaching, especially at the undergraduate level. But there is evidence in surveys that the bulk of American undergraduates are not seriously discontented with the education they are receiving, indeed, are far less so than many academic men feel they should be. In my own view, discontent with the forms and content of American higher education is centred in the teaching staff and, to a very large degree, in the humanities and social science departments of the big universities. The radical student uprisings themselves are political acts with educational consequences, rather than educational actions with political overtones. They centre on political issues in the larger society, most importantly the Viet Nam war and the racial revolution, and on the university chiefly by way of increasing the amount and changing the character of its involvement in social issues and conflict. At the heart of confrontations are small but passionate and sometimes well-organized groups of political students – some nihilists, some anarchists, some highly ideological neo-Marxists and Maoists. These groups have discovered how fragile universities are, how easily disrupted; they have also learned how to politicize and mobilize much larger numbers by exploiting clumsy or brutal responses by the institutions they attack. The analysis of these movements is not possible here. But it should be noted that their success in causing major disruptions on a campus is affected not only by their own numbers and will, but also by the amount of hostility present in the faculty towards the administration; the administration's own freedom to deal with internal problems without interference from repressive external forces; the adequacy of the administration's assessment of the situation, that is, its intelligence in the several meanings of that word; and the discipline of the local police force. In addition, it is crucially important whether the administration is able to prevent the exploitation of black protest by the radical white movement. As a rule of thumb, where administrators have been able to prevent that coalition, have the support of their faculty, and work with a disciplined police force, the white radical confrontations are not likely to escalate.

But we have to distinguish sharply between the militant blacks and the radical white political activists. Their rhetoric is often equally abusive, their tactics similarly disruptive, and at times it appears that they are in close alliance against the institution and its policies and procedures. But I believe that they are fundamentally different, in that the genuinely radical white activists want to bring down the society and its institutions, while the blacks for the most part want a larger role and more power within them. The different consequences of this for their respective tactics and behaviour are very great: the white radicals are really not interested in negotiation and reform. Their ends, and not just their means, are disruption, the discrediting of authority, and the politicization and radicalization of as many students as possible through the cycle of confrontation, disruption, police repression, mass indignation, and subsequent radicalization of heretofore moderate or liberal students and faculty. By contrast, militant blacks on American campuses typically demand specific changes in institutional policy or practice, centring upon the recruitment and admission of more black students without constraint by what they see as inherently 'racist' academic standards, the recruitment of more black faculty and administrators, the provision of a programme of black studies, under the control of the blacks themselves, more economic aid for blacks, administered by them, and living and dining arrangements also reflecting their new emphasis on separation and autonomy. These are real, as opposed to rhetorical demands, and are in most cases negotiable. The negotiations may be tough, the demands expensive, in varying ways, the accompanying rhetoric and action frightening, but finally the blacks have the one interest without which genuine negotiations for a redistribution of power and rewards in an institution are not possible – that is, an interest in the survival of the institutions on which the demands are being made. This is an interest that the most radical activists, the self-styled revolutionaries, do not have. For them Berkeley or Columbia are merely part of the hated 'power structure', and convenient places to demonstrate its iniquities and gain recruits. The blacks, for the most part, know this, and are not enthusiastic for the alliances which the white radicals urge on them, and for which the whites are prepared to make any concessions, adopt any posture, support any demand. But in general, black militants have run their own show, not only out of a passion for autonomy and self-direction, but also out of an awareness that, however the white radicals join them in their diatribes against the white racist establishment, their goals and interests are really quite fundamentally different and even opposed. So at Columbia the blacks expelled the whites from Hamilton Hall, and thereafter the two movements were really quite separate, with different means as well as ends, running parallel in the same campus at the same time. On the Berkeley campus this Fall the blacks were not prepared to take violent action over the Cleaver case, especially after the campus administration, which has in a variety of ways demonstrated its basic sympathy with black students and their demands, had made provision to permit the course to be given, with Cleaver lecturing. The blacks were not prepared to take to the streets and seize buildings over the issue of course credit; the white radicals had to exploit the issue without the help of the blacks, and their seizure on successive nights of two campus buildings were ended by police arrests. The arrests were made without bloodshed or brutality – the discipline of police on campus is of course a crucial factor in the success or failure of a 'confrontation' – and the Columbia disaster was not reenacted at Berkeley this Fall.

In general, as I have suggested, militant blacks on campuses have resisted the alliance with white militants and have done their own thing in their own way. One apparent exception to this is the current crisis at San Francisco State. In my own opinion, the alliance there has been forged more by the failures of the local administration and the interventions of the Governor and state administration than by any natural coincidence of interest between blacks and white radicals. Moreover, even there the alliance is uneasy and, I believe, temporary.

But while it is possible to negotiate with blacks on the basis of specific demands, in a way it is not with the radical white groups, it is not yet clear what effects the continuing and growing black student movement will have on our universities, and especially on our public universities. American higher education has been extraordinarily hospitable to new demands from the community and the public at large, and many are now trying to respond to the demands of the black community in the same spirit, spurred, in varying degrees, by a bad conscience, a sense of the genuine importance of educating larger numbers of black students, and a lively apprehension of what may happen if they don't. And there is good reason to believe that the universities, and especially the big state universities, will try to take on this new function as they have so many others. If we look at the black demands themselves, the demand to modify or set aside ordinary admissions standards in order to admit more black applicants is, in my view, reasonable, since the criteria are not very good predictors of academic performance anyway, and probably even poorer for black students. More serious is the legitimacy of applying different criteria on racial grounds; that is likely to be challenged from out-side as well as causing grave misgivings within the university. There would be fewer objections if the special admissions were made on the basis of in-adequate early schooling or poverty than if they were made on the basis of race. Some observers are concerned that separatist colleges or departments of black studies may apply different academic standards to the work of their own students than do other departments. But, there again, the variability among departments in the big universities is already very great, and not especially troublesome. More serious is the question of whether racial or political passions will interfere with the free play of critical inquiry in these new programmes. But they are simply too young yet for any such judgements to be made. Quite separate is the issue of how black students will press future demands on universities. If they turn regularly to coercive demonstrations, which seem to be so effective in the early stages of the movement, the damage to the university from the demonstrations or from repressive back-lash will be very great. Here one can only hope that militant blacks will soon find themselves having as strong an interest in the preservation of a climate that permits serious teaching and learning on campus as does anyone else. But it would be foolish to ignore the possibility that the universities may be the scene of a great deal of militant action by the black students, with potentially very serious effects on the intellectual life of the university itself.

This leads me to the impact of external pressures and student activism on the internal government and climate of universities. There are a number of forces which tend to limit the extent and intensity of disputes within the university, which tend to mute them and press towards compromise and accommodation between differing points of view. One of these is the broad acceptance of the legitimacy of the multiple functions of a university. The practical effect of this conception of the university is to remove from dispute the sharpest and fundamentally irreconcilable issues; disputes then can take the form of arguments about relative emphasis to be given to different views or the relative support allocated to different programmes. And even those disputes are further diluted in situations in which there is secular growth and expansion throughout the university, and where disputes then become merely questions of 'priority' and time.

Disputes are also softened by a general agreement to conduct them within the regular academic and administrative machinery – the system of com-mittees and meetings through which major universities govern themselves. Disputes are still further softened by the institutional (and often also the geographical) insulation of conflicting views. For example, the humanistic scholars are typically centred in a university's college of letters and science, or its equivalent; the service orientations in the professional schools, or in the graduate departments. Historians and engineers may have very different conceptions of the primary functions of the university, but they very rarely have occasion to confront one another in argument.

Conflict between different conceptions of the university is also minimized by making the department, rather than the college or the university, the unit of effective educational decision. The departments, or most of them, are more homogeneous than the faculty as a whole, and they have their own strong mechanisms for compromise and accommodation, not least of which is to minimize the number and importance of issues involving collective decision, allowing what might be called the privatization of intellectual life, a withdrawal to one's own classroom and research. On the graduate level, the university *is*, for all practical purposes, the aggregation of departments and professional schools, their satellite research centres and institutes, and the supporting infrastructure of libraries, labs, buildings, and mostly routine administrative help (though in a university, routines are not all that routine, and may require a considerable level of skill and talent). The departments effectively govern their own appointment and promotion of staff (subject to certain review procedures by extra-departmental committees), admit their own graduate students, and organize their instruction. On the undergraduate level (I am speaking here of the central liberal arts college), there is, of course, the necessity to organize some structure of education that is not confined to a single department. The form this takes at many institutions is a set of distribution requirements – so many units required in fields outside one's major, so many in a major field, the remainder electives. This system, whatever its educational justification, has the very substantial virtue of reducing the amount of academic decision-making that is necessary. This reduces the occasions for conflict involving educational values and philosophies, thus letting men get on with their own work. What we see at work there is a spirit of *laissez-faire*, within broad administrative constraints set by limitations of space, time, staff, and other resources, that mirrors the broader philosophy of the multiversity as a whole.

This pattern may be seen as an institutional response to the problem of combining higher education offered to very large numbers of students of the most diverse character with the highest standards of scholarly and scientific work. But the events of the past few years have revealed basic weaknesses in the system which are in a sense the defects of its virtues. One of these is the lack of a central, widely shared sense of the nature of the institution, and a weakness in its capacity to gain the loyalties and devotion of its participants. This means that the institution operates on a relatively thin margin of error. Closely related to this is its tendency to generate among both students and faculty somewhat diffuse resentments, feelings of frustration and alienation from an institution which provides services and facilities but seems singularly remote from the concerns of individuals, responsive only to pressures and problems that are organized and communicated through the regular channels, and not always even to those. It is this kind of institution marked by weak faculty loyalties, vague resentments, and complex administrative arrangements, which is likely to prove to be highly vulnerable to political attack from without and within.

These attacks have other consequences than the disruptive demonstrations and sit-ins that are most widely publicized. The attacks, whether from a governor or a radical student group, work to politicize a campus, to polarize a faculty, and to force its members to make choices in an atmosphere of passion and partisanship. The differences that crystallize around the issue I have been describing differ from the ordinary issues of academic politics: for one thing, they involve the students more directly; for another, they are more stable, more closely linked to deep-rooted values and conceptions of the nature of the institution. Moreover, at Berkeley, and I suspect elsewhere, they are being institutionalized in the form of faculty parties, which will persist as permanent elements in the governmental process, further contributing to the polarization of the faculty out of which they arise. Perhaps most importantly, these tendencies threaten to disrupt the informal processes of consultation, negotiation, and compromise among and between senior faculty and administrators by which universities are ordinarily governed. And they threaten to break through all the devices for softening conflict that I was describing. In their place are put forward two powerful democratic models from the government of institutions. One is the model of representative democracy, complete with a party system and judicial review. The other is the model of direct democracy in the self-governing small community. Both have been advocated for the university, as well as a combination of the two involving the formalization of the governmental process in addition to the provision of a high degree of participatory democracy. Such a system would require a relatively high and continuous level of faculty involvement in the issues and instruments of university government, as well as a basic decision regarding the extent of citizenship – that is, the role of the students in the decision-making machinery. And indeed, both these issues have been raised in a recent student–faculty report on university governance at Berkeley which calls for a high level of participation by both faculty and students in units of government at every level, from the campus as a whole down to the individual department. Now many arguments can be made against such a proposal – its cumbersomeness, the impermanence of the students (they do not have to live very long with the consequences of their decisions on a campus), their incompetence to decide certain matters, and so forth. But in my own view, more important than any of these is the absolute level of political activity and involvement required of teachers and students under these arrangements. The cosy and rather informal method by which faculty members and administrators govern a campus may have many failings, most clearly visible to those who are not part of such a government. Its chief virtue is that it has allowed students and teachers to get on with their work of teaching and learning. Students and faculty who want radically to transform the universities are at least consistent in wanting to change the form of governance, for some, as at Berkeley, by making the process of government itself a central part and focus of a university education. But liberal education, scholarship, and research are not inherently political activities, even when they take politics as their subject. And they are threatened by a highly politicized environment, both by its partisanship and demand for loyalties and commitments, and also by its distractions, its encroachments on one's time and energies. The reactions of academic men who are not much interested in university governance is usually to withdraw their attention, and let others govern. But this only works if those others, who *are* interested in politics, share the faculty's basic values, and are concerned to create and protect an environment in which the older functions of teaching and research can go on without distraction or intimidation. That is an unlikely outcome of any arrangement that makes its own government a central activity of the university, ensures that all disputes pass through its formal machinery, and brings students and faculty with a passion for politics to the centre of the governing process. But that is the direction of much student and faculty sentiment at the moment, and of reforms on many campuses.

One outcome of the heightened political atmosphere on our campuses may be that we will be seeing some academic men leaving the colleges and universities for research centres and institutes where they are more protected from popular pressures and their echoes in campus politics. If the numbers and quality of those who leave are significant, that would be a very grave threat to the quality and character of the universities as we know and cherish them.

V

My theme has been very broad. The growth of numbers, functions, and political pressures within universities takes many forms, and I have touched on only a few of those which I believe are an especially serious threat to the university's core functions of liberal education, scholarship, and basic research. I have not spoken of the crisis in undergraduate education arising out of the complete collapse of any generally shared conception of what students ought to learn; nor of the role of teaching assistants in the big state universities, who carry a great part of the undergraduate teaching on the cheap, and begin to see themselves as exploited employees and organize in trade unions. Nor have I had time to discuss the changing character of our undergraduates, of the boredom of some and the apparently unquenchable anger of others. Merely to point to these issues is to affirm that I do not judge the state of our universities by the conventional measures of success that I mentioned in my opening remarks. But let me close by saying that I am an admirer of American higher education, which, as a system and in its representative institutions, has managed both to fulfil its commitments to liberal education and the advancement of knowledge, and also to serve a nation and a people in all the ways that it has. The problem now, as it has been for a hundred years, is whether those functions can be performed in the same institution. The problem is acutely one for the great public universities.

If the core functions of the state universities are threatened and then crippled by the great flood of popular pressures and demands being made on them, then those functions, at their highest levels of performance, will be confined to the great private universities, or forced outside the university altogether. And if that happens, something very precious – the presence within institutions of popular democracy of the highest standards of intellectual life – will have been lost in America.

INTERCHAPTER

I

Response to Martin Trow – BEN MORRIS

We all greatly regret the fact that Martin Trow was unable to be with us, to present his paper and to join in the discussion. I particularly regret this, since I do not know him personally and on this occasion find myself wanting to take issue with him on the general perspective developed in his paper.

Martin Trow's paper, excellent as it is, I nevertheless feel to be misleading with respect to the most important issues before us. I think it is a mistake to put student unrest at the centre of our concern – for I view this as a symptom only, although a highly important one. I would make five points:

1. The young are disenchanted and disillusioned with our adult world; the world of work, money, institutional roles, social conformity, all that makes up the 'achievement society'. Moreover, science, which should be exciting and liberating, is seen as the servant of the power blocks, military, industrial, and bureaucratic, which control modern societies and, through their various spheres of influence, the world as a whole. In this we are perhaps beginning to reap the rewards (!) of an education which increasingly emphasizes the importance of learning to think for oneself.

2. There is a widespread awareness among youth generally, and among many underprivileged social groups as well, that things could be different – that societal facts are not of the same kind as 'natural' facts – they can be altered. (The kind of sociological analysis which portrays what is as in effect what must be, I regard as a kind of intellectual treason due to overweighting the, admittedly large, 'deterministic' elements in any social situation.)

3. With its natural impatience, youth asserts that what could be, could and should be *now* – i.e. instant Utopia is within our grasp.

4. A marked reassertion of the value of the impulse life, as over against bare cognition and largely hypocritical moral codes, is a common feature of most youth cultures. One of the results, a relatively guilt-free (though not problem-free) sexuality, inevitably excites adult envy and hence disapproval. I find, as does Richard Hoggart, that in their personal (including sexual) relations young people display more comradeship, compassion, and honesty than can be easily found among their elders. And in its way, if only partly, the

'drug scene' may be interpreted as a reaction against what appears as the abstract world of the scientist, the depersonalizing effects of bureaucratic institutions and purely acquisitive and technological societies.

5. Our advanced societies are so arranged that we withhold and delay the assumption of responsible roles in those twin areas of experience through which men find and express their personal identity, love and work. Everywhere we find young people demanding participation in the making of decisions which closely concern them, and a recognition of their capacity for responsibility, i.e. their potential adulthood. Certain phenomena follow, on a fairly large scale, from open or concealed premarital sex relations (hardly in itself a new phenomenon!), often involving co-habitation, to 'love-ins' in the sphere of sexuality, and from radical political action to 'dropping out' in the social sphere.

I believe that all these factors are common in varying degree throughout the world and that all express themselves in different ways through the particular vicissitudes, problems, and issues of particular educational systems. It is against this background that I would set the problems of higher education today and in so doing reach a different diagnosis from Martin Trow. While I think that the major theme of his paper, 'elite and popular functions', is an illuminating one, through the treatment he gives it, it does, I think, prove misleading about the nature of the basic issues.

'Elitist' functions he regards as the transmission of the high culture, the creation of new knowledge through scholarship and scientific research, and the selection, formation, and certification of a social elite. Popular functions are seen in the first place as the giving of access to the high culture to as many of the young as have the capacity and interest to grasp it, and in the second as the provision of entertainment and custodial care. (This latter admission is surely a most damaging criticism of our current educational effort.) No one will deny that this is a commonly held perspective. I could not deny it its share of *de facto* truth, but I would suggest that it is a superficial perspective and that our current problems arise in large measure precisely because this is how we interpret the issues. I would proceed differently, as follows:

(a) The very distinction between 'elitist' and 'popular' almost of necessity carries hubristic and narcissistic overtones, revealing that it is a sophisticated form of one-upmanship, and implying certain basic valuations which I reject.

(b) There is an important sense in which the high culture does not exist and never has existed except as an abstraction. What exists concretely are persons acting in community to create, sustain, and enrich a common symbolic world. Call this symbolic world the high culture if you wish, but the activities concerned form a large part of what it means to be human. The central job of education is therefore the care of persons, and a major part of this care is their nourishment through the common symbolic world.

(c) Moreover there is no conclusive evidence that entrance to this world is, of necessity, restricted to a privileged few. Historically, education has been *used* by ruling groups to create and maintain privileged sections of humanity in terms of religion, race, class, and sex. If we ask the old question 'Who is to be educated?' we must today I think return the answer 'everyone'. Any other answer is to deny to some individuals and groups the right to attempt to lay hold upon their full humanity. While enormous difficulties arise from it, it is the giving of this answer which is significant. Varieties of talents of course exist, but while individual differences may remain relatively stable after about the age of three years, the differences between the average level of achievement of different human groups would appear to be mainly a function of opportunity and stimulation.[1]

(d) Education is not primarily about the transmission of anything. The illusion that it is results from a superficial analysis of what happens in relatively static societies. In fact education is always a transaction between the generations in which ideas, skills, and values are renewed and are often redefined in the process of renewal.

Proceeding thus suggests the possibility of a radical reconstruction of educational systems which would at one and the same time begin to dispose of these artifacts, 'elitist and popular functions', help to meet the aspirations of the young, and do something to maintain the central values which characterize our humanity. Of course, this is an enormous task. It involves a radical transformation of present-day cultures, with all their ideological, economic, and social characteristics. That is no reason for not beginning to envisage it. Among the educational features of such reconstruction would be the following:

1. A healing of the split between thought and feeling, so clearly revealed in most academic views of the nature of subjects and of education, and revealed too in the tendency of many of the young to opt for feeling and reject intellect. Northrop Frye declared he was 'not intellectual' if that meant he was not concerned with feeling, and he gave us a fine demonstration of what is meant by creative mind in its wholeness.

2. This in turn would require us to redefine the scope of educational activities to include at all levels the world of concrete achievement and skills, and the world of sensuous, indeed sensual, values also. The enemy here is

[1] B. Bloom, *Stability and Change in Human Characteristics*, New York, 1964.

largely the tyranny, through misuse, of language. Language is as essential to the refinement of feeling as it is to the advancement of thought, but it often seems to achieve the latter at the expense of the former, and at the same time in practice to encourage the denial of the importance of other symbolic forms. This applies particularly in higher education to music and the plastic arts.

3. Again, in turn, this means enlarging our concepts of the talents and skills to be nourished to include all those required by a complex society at work and play. Perhaps we require articulate dancers and philosopher-technicians as much as we need the more commonly accepted cadres of artists and scientists.

4. We must develop and stress in practice the idea of mutual adventure and discovery as the basis of the teaching–learning situation. This entails perceiving that education involves a partnership that transcends the inequalities inherent in the teacher–taught relation and that the fully adult predetermined curriculum dealing with predigested experience is anti-educational.

5. We must consider educational reconstruction not merely in terms of institutional forms but also in terms of phases of life and changes of roles. There is no *a priori* reason why an educational system should take the form of a series of linear and end-on programmes beginning around five years or earlier and terminating for the 'elite' in the early twenties, and much earlier for others. It would seem much more realistic to consider the possibilities in terms of a multi-decker educational sandwich occupying a whole life-span. By doing so we would at least avoid two of the fatal traps into which we at present fall. These seem to me to be:

(a) Postponing the achievement of personal identity in terms of love and work to an age much later than that which seems biologically and psychologically appropriate. It is scarcely surprising that such postponements bring a heavy crop of problems with them;

(b) Introducing young people to kinds of experiences and to varieties of symbolic worlds long before they are ready for them. At twenty I would not have responded well to either Northrop Frye or Marjorie Reeves, but I have been immensely stimulated by their contributions to this seminar at the ripe age of fifty-eight! I was sufficiently engaged by Northrop Frye to want to disagree sharply with him over his interpretation and treatment of dialogue. He seemed to have overlooked Buber, to have discounted genuine conversation, and also the genuine interchange and mutual learning which can take place between teacher and student, and to have been unlucky in his experience of free discussion. Perhaps I still misunderstand him, but at twenty

I would simply have been floored. We are all familiar too with those students, often among the most able, who suddenly in midstream, or at graduation point, realize that they are in the wrong subject or discipline. In England particularly, with its early and sharp specialization, we are confronted with students who realize that their first love was only calf-love, or was precipitated by non-intrinsic factors such as the influence of an enthusiastic teacher.

In conclusion, the value of student unrest and the present revolt of youth as I see it, is that it gives us the opportunity to do some radical thinking about the educational enterprise as a whole, of which higher education is the present terminal stage.

II

A whole series of topics came up for discussion following Ben Morris's introduction. Among the more important were: the meaning of the term 'elite'; the sociological viewpoint; the kind of wholeness a university should seek; and the place of 'Education' within an establishment of higher learning.

We were reminded that earlier in the Seminar the elite had been defined as 'those who guide, shape, and articulate the aspirations of a society'. This seemed to most of those present a much more acceptable use of the term than one dividing people up on a class basis, as if people could be categorized so statically. Good students anyway are immensely suspicious in these days of being given, or educated for, a status that labels them. They seek an identity which is less class-oriented. It is the process, not the brand mark, which matters, they think.

Hoggart, in particular, felt strongly that they were right. 'I want to underline', he said, 'the uneasiness one feels nowadays at the use of phrases like "high culture", let alone "elite". I don't personally know a sense in which I recognize their meaning. No one now uses the phrase "high culture" except a communist; and the phrases "high brow", "middle brow", and "low brow" are never likely to come into current usage again. What one has here is a model of cultural transmission which is interesting historically and which most of us may have been given at the university as a viable model, but which has increasingly become impossible.' Another participant declared that the terms 'elite' and 'popular' put the whole idea of university education awry. Undergraduate courses that are good must depend upon the idea of discovery – the discovery shared by teacher and taught as in some sense common human beings at the moment it is being made.

'Anything that is cut off from the life-blood of the community is a dying thing,' said another member. The word 'elitism' is used to characterize a group of people who create a problem both within the university and between the university and society outside. The problem is created because our whole educational process in the university is geared to intellectuality, to conceptualization, to the analytic method. Any training in analysis is a divisive thing – you literally cut things up with a knife – and it can also be divisive in personal relationships. We are in danger of going too far in this, and neglecting the imaginative side and the education of the emotions, by introducing this knife-like analysis. The answer is not to throw away training in analysis and in thought; we shan't get out of the dilemma by giving up our rigorous disciplines and techniques, as this could end up in a lot of woolly thinking. But the dilemma is a basic problem in the university between different types of approach to subjects and different teaching methods, between the so-called elite of the university and the rest of society; and it is a problem of communication, because, once you have mastered techniques of analysis and articulation and the using of ideas and conceptualizing, you are going to be more powerful in a relationship than the person who thinks in other ways, since the latter cannot communicate. The people who dominate are the people who can articulate. We have to overcome this dilemma, not losing our analytical rigour and clarity but seeing it in relation to other forms of perception and understanding.

Invaluable and indispensable though the sociologist's approach may be to the study of human life, one participant maintained, and important though the influence of groups may be upon the behaviour of the men belonging to them, there was a sense in which sociology – like any other science – escapes from facing some of the facts. It is reductionist in tendency, concentrating only upon some fraction of the whole truth. But to concentrate only upon the truths which a science reveals is to avoid the need for attending to the quality of one's experiences, or to their value relative to one another, or to making any judgements which are evaluations of experiences. The sociologist is often justifiably reluctant to step outside or go beyond the framework his science imposes. But this does not mean that any man can be or would wish to be a sociologist only.

It was agreed that the temptation was especially acute for a sociologist to wish to classify society in terms of 'elite' and 'popular' classes of people, but that this had many dangers. Even the division of people in a university into those labelled students and those labelled staff could lead to misunderstandings that could be avoided. 'The idea of putting people labelled students into one building or complex of buildings where they can be identified and reacted to on the basis of a class label is a vicious one – and one which has a good deal in common with the tendency to segregate ethnic groups in ghettos,' said one member of the Seminar. In his view this has a big bearing upon what young people could learn about their institution and themselves: it was significant in telling them by implication how they stood in relation to their seniors. One ought so to arrange community life that people from widely different sections of the university – both students and staff – could sometimes meet one another over the meal table under unforced conditions. Students should be encouraged rather than merely permitted to discuss and contribute to the formation of their own curriculum. As their values changed, their information increased and their powers of conceptualization became more sophisticated, their contribution to the modification of the curriculum would become greater.

At any rate what is certain is that teachers and students share a common humanity. One of the functions of the teacher is to be a resource person, his role in this regard being to surround the student with a variety of stimuli leaving the student to choose and use those which are significant to him.

It was urged that there was evidence for thinking that our whole culture was in a state of major transition. Long ago now there had been the first major period of transition – from a society in which there was relatively little specialization to one which allowed for a high degree of specialization – thus releasing people, some to be physically skilled in particular ways, some to devote a lot more of their time to thought and study. This first transition involved a certain liability for people to lose wholeness, and even lose humanity, in order to be efficient specialists. The second period of major transition which we might now be entering was one which, while taking advantage of many of the benefits of specialization, might lead back to a more adequate involvement in society of the individual as a whole man. Student unrest may be one mark of this second period of transition between a culture which was essentially labour-based, believing in work, progress, and specialization as a means largely to material ends, to one based upon human needs more generously and widely conceived.

Someone remarked that it might be a significant tendency among institutions of higher education today that their excessively specialist function is tending to disappear. Liberal arts colleges are developing professional sides; teachers' colleges becoming far more like liberal arts colleges; technical colleges increasingly developing liberal studies departments.

Asa Briggs agreed that institutions of higher education today are by and large much more successful at handling conceptualized knowledge than non-conceptualized. Enthusiasm in teachers, intellectual excitement, and so on are extraordinarily important, but one cannot without danger expect universities or any other institutions of higher education to give a high place to the non-cognitive in their formalized programme of studies. The recipe for nourishing non-conceptual feeling and thought is that institutions of higher education should be communities of persons with a wide range of activities which are not all formally structured. Universities cannot lay on in too deliberate a way all that a liberal education may require. If they try to do so, they will do nothing properly. But they should encourage, on the side, the playing of games; art exhibitions; concerts; lectures on a great diversity of cultural subjects; even religious services. There were some forms of education, however, which are best served by community enterprises outside the campus entirely. In Paris, students are in the theatre of life. 'It is Paris that is the university, not the Sorbonne', they say, 'we are much more independent than students at the universities of X or Y; we can make our own lives against the background of the Seine and of Paris itself.'

All this might well be the case, came the retort, but the fact is that the bias of much of the modern world, as represented in a high degree by many university studies themselves, is in favour of a detached and external way of looking at everything. This is indicated by (a) the ease with which one can avoid having a philosophy of education, or indeed a hierarchy of values, of one's own and still be an excellent technologist or chemist or philologist: (b) the worldly-wise, half cynical advice given by a university president about the best way of helping a young department to grow: 'Start with research and attract foundation grants; think about what you are going to teach after you've got going.' It is certain that subjects that cannot be researched into will only with difficulty today find a place in a university curriculum. And the harder it becomes to attract funds for university enterprises, the more likely are departments which are supported by foundations to find it difficult to expand, and the more likely will informal activities suffer from financial impoverishment. University teachers need to be not only thinkers, not only research workers, not only transmitters of knowledge, but people with the imagination and vision to cope with the age.

To build up an institution of higher education that will in fact be more than a place of advanced technical training does call for a philosophy of education — which must include some appreciation of the relative human importance of various kinds of learning to one another. The study of education ought not to be the prerogative of a separate department alone – however necessary such a department may be for one purpose or another. Education, said one participant, is in essence 'having a look at what growing up within a culture implies.' This is a wide enough definition to bring within its ambit every subject which a university teaches as well as its informal activities. But how narrow the attitudes of universities tend to be towards many of the subjects they purvey!

In his closing remarks, Ben Morris made it clear that he did not want everyone to have the same philosophy of education, but he did want a much more widespread effort on the part of those teaching in tertiary education to think about their educational presuppositions. In this Seminar we had given an undue proportion of our time to considering universities and tied the idea of the university too tightly to the actual institution. But the contemporary university, even more than its precursors, has a missionary effect; it has powerfully influenced many other types of higher education institution. 'You start up a new technical college and before you know where you are it is teaching English, art, drama, and foreign languages.' When students talk about their students' union they assume absolutely that it should belong to *them*; this idea is very much part of the university principle of freedom – freedom for the individual and group to develop traditions of their own.

With regard to the business of teaching and learning, he went on: 'I don't want to devalue the cognitive at all. But I do not think that learning is ever purely cognitive; it is also affective.' The problem is one of regenerating teaching on a wide scale. Partly this is a problem of size of institution and class or seminar. But enthusiasm and intellectual excitement are indispensable and these are non-cognitive. 'There is an awful lot of dead learning about, which stifles intellectual curiosity. Yet there is also a great deal of potential keenness among students to be taught.'

CHAPTER 10

Higher Education and Personal Life

Changing Attitudes

Richard Hoggart

We have been seeing clearly in the late sixties a major change in the relations between students, universities, and society. This change is the culmination of two slower developments spanning the last two decades. The first was a change in the relationships between universities and society, when our universities became much more institutionally tied to the needs of society. In this phase – though many more students were admitted to universities and in Britain they were given reasonable grants – some of the more important needs of students were relatively neglected. In the second phase, which began in the early sixties, students (and some staff, especially junior staff) have judged the nature of the changes in the universities and have found them on the whole unacceptable. The major authorities within universities and in society are now being asked to justify themselves by the people they are training to serve that society; in particular, they are being asked to justify the gap between public moral assertions about the nature of the university and the reality; and these are fair questions.

The literature on the subject is already voluminous. There is material on the sociological, social-psychological, and individual psychological backgrounds of the more revolutionary students, on the correlation between subjects studied and the propensity to rebel, on the comparative historical development of student activism in different countries, on the links between administrative structures within different universities and student dissidence, and so on. Much of it is useful, but none of it is or can be decisive. The phenomenon is too complex and subtle to be caught within the language of one discipline or in a massive aggregation of different disciplines. It engages our assumptions about society and the individual at levels we are not fully aware of, but which affect our inquiries no matter how 'objective' we try to make them. The subject needs the comprehensive, controlled, subjective insight of a good novelist. In the nature of things, what it gets almost always is either intelligent partial 'objectivity' or intelligent impressionistic guesswork. I am not trained to be 'objective' in the social scientist's sense and I do not claim the insight of a creative writer. But the best contribution I can make lies on the subjective-literary side rather than elsewhere. So I will describe the changes in British university life during the last few decades (in particular, in the relations between students and staff) in a local and personal way. Perhaps it might seem also a parochial and provincial way. But we abstract and generalize enough. It is just as important to try to interpret the feel of our own experiences day by day and as year has succeeded year, to recall as accurately as we can what it felt like to live through these changes. We will never know 'the whole truth'; but this way may recall some aspects of 'the truth' which tend to be neglected. And so they may find an echo in the experience of people thousands of miles away in societies which look, at first, very different indeed.

I attended, as an undergraduate in the middle thirties, one of the larger British provincial universities, Leeds – large for Britain and those days – about one thousand five hundred strong. I had been born and educated in the town. Most of us were provincials, Northerners; from our type of area hardly anyone went to Oxbridge. Not that the university as a whole was full of working-class scholarship boys. The medical students, the engineers, the chemists were mostly middle class. But Northern professional or mercantile middle class, probably many of them educated at a Northern public school which had smoothed but not removed their Yorkshire voices, sent along to the university by their fathers with a good allowance and a sports car to be well trained and go back into the business. This was in the sciences; but in the arts faculty the students were overwhelmingly working class to lower-middle class. Students whose parents were teachers were in our upper social grade. Most of us were the first members of our families ever to go to university.

What did we expect? We expected to have an enjoyable, even an exciting, time in some respects. We had read Evelyn Waugh and though we did not expect to behave like his characters, and didn't particularly want to, we looked forward to some moments of suitably irresponsible student fun. We expected to be helped to 'get on', professionally. Some of us expected to be introduced to the intellectual life. Though some of us had strong political interests, a critique of the university as such and of its role in society didn't usually figure in them. If you belonged, as I did, to the Socialist Club you looked outwards; you did not discuss the university. The list I've given shows that we expected quite a lot from the university; but in a crucial sense we expected less from it – less of social and individual meaning – than students expect today.

What did we find? We found a remarkably ordered and, on the whole, satisfied society. We found a society willing, if we were prepared to make the effort, to introduce us to the intellectual life; and a society pretty well assured about the nature, scope, and relevance of the intellectual life. The number of potential intellectuals among the students was small and so was the number of staff willing to introduce them to the life of the mind. This was not only a provincial characteristic. I believe it applied to Oxbridge too, though to hear some people in Britain talk about the small proportion of 'genuine intellectuals' in universities today, as compared with their time at Oxbridge in the thirties, you would think that eighty per cent or ninety per cent of Oxbridge undergraduates at that time were committed to intellectual life. I simply do not believe it. The evidence suggests that only a small minority were of that kind, and this is not surprising in view of Oxbridge's social role at that period.

The staff at Redbrick universities in the thirties knew that most of us were destined to become school teachers, that only a minute minority would ever work in universities or become intellectual journalists, and that even fewer would become what used to be called 'civilized businessmen' or 'cultivated professionals', that only a very few would be actual contributors to intellectual life or well-heeled supporters of it. But they assumed, vaguely but nicely, that something was gained by a period there, that a glimpse of the intellectual life was never quite pointless.

Socially, the university community had a similar assurance about what it could and should offer. It was, in a phrase I often heard, though usually accidentally, 'rubbing some of the rough edges' off us. It was introducing us to the social style with which British intellectual life was then worn. This was presented as, by implication, a universal intellectual style but was, as one can see now, a very special style, one definable in historical and social terms. It was not the style of Hardy or Lawrence or Burns, or even of the LSE, but the style of Oxbridge from which most of our teachers came (and to which many of them hoped eventually to return), and it was predominantly pro-fessional middle-class and southern in its origins.

Quite a lot of the staff, including the senior members, lived out their assumptions about their social role in ways which it is easy – and sometimes justified – to laugh at, and I have often done that myself. Those of us who are professors today tell ourselves that we are kept far busier than our prede-cessors with routine work, and this is probably true. But they had books to write, and anyway selfish men can always find excuses for filling their day with other things than entertaining students. So they had to make a special effort to entertain us to sherry and other touches of gracious living in their homes, and I've no doubt they often wished they could simply not bother. But they did bother. Their social lights may have been curiously tinted but a surprising number tried to live up to them, and lived up to them well.

In the halls of residence, university senates tended to install as wardens gracious widowed ladies or dignified elderly gentlemen. They carpeted and curtained them at remarkable expense (and to some extent still do). The expensive fittings were partly justified on the ground that the best is cheapest in the long run. But they served a larger purpose. The whole enterprise of hall provision was felt to be an integral part of the civilizing aspect of university education. And it expressed itself in a very English way – slightly comically, like something out of an early issue of *Punch*; but also humanely – it wasn't mean or hard or mechanized. You could, as I did, resent the faint overhanging air of patronage, but you didn't feel like a 'thing', a 'number', just an item in the computer of the multiversity. The tone was taken, without much stopping to think, from a particular socio-cultural group; and it shared the limits of that group's outlook. It also had some of its virtues, the virtues of the liberal-minded, intellectual English middle class – a very special kind of integrity, a patient tolerance, a remarkable directness, and an overriding concern about people.

But we, especially those of us who came from the poorest kind of homes, had to make our own sense out of the profound clash. We were invited, especially if we were bright or in other ways particularly acceptable, to become part of that decent, civilized middle class. Hardly anyone recognized what contradictions psychologically this posed for us. Most of the staff were themselves from professional middle-class backgrounds and those who had worked their way up had usually taken the tone of the group they had joined. They might retain a working-class burr or a relish for salty jokes, but that was a form of role-playing within their new class and so served their membership of it. By default, if not more explicitly, the assumption was that we were growing away from our background and, if not positively rejecting it, at least quietly letting it go, finding it increasingly dull and un-nourishing. In many ways this was true, especially when viewed from their position. But, though we might reject much in our background, we also found a lot in it which pulled us, even though we couldn't say what it was and no one helped us to say. There was a gap between our emotional evidence and our intellectual evidence which could be painful, but which had to be bridged if our emotional and intellectual growth were to continue. The problem couldn't be solved – though some of us tried this way – by digging a deep ditch between our professional and intellectual life and our personal and emotional life. That way you got all sorts of sports – the socially bitter research chemist or the professor who managed to be both sentimental about his humble origins and snobbish about his present elevation.

Overall, we knew that jobs were hard to get, movement limited, opportunities abroad not common (nor often desirable, in the fag-end of the Empire) and that practically all of us taking courses in the faculty of arts would go into the State teaching system. In fact, most arts students had scholarships or grants, e.g. many were supported by their local education authorities (city authorities), sometimes having promised to teach for a stated number of years after graduation. Some local authorities made loans, not grants. I don't think this intimidated many, but it did draw invisible boundaries round possibilities, temper the atmosphere, cause some submerged anxiety and playing safe.

So the universities did reflect the nature of a dominant part of their society, of its trained and 'civilized' middle class; they had remarkably little close knowledge of the body of working-class people outside, or the potentialities of more than that minute proportion of the working classes whom they saw in their classrooms. In this sense, they were sustainers and servicers of a certain view of society. In another sense they stood apart from society. They didn't draw much money from industry and commerce for services directly rendered; they were jealous of their freedom from government intervention, and they had an idiosyncratic, amateur independence of style. Even though most of the funds of the civic universities came from the UGC, you had the feeling that that body was composed of gentlemen, all of whom belonged to the Athenaeum – that the vice-chancellor certainly did and that most provincial professors did too. Most of the universities were pyramidal in their structure of authority and the professoriate was at the top of the pyramid. The professors soon reminded their vice-chancellors if they got uppish that they were only *primus inter pares*. One might not be willing to accept the professors' particular social forms or assumptions, but one could learn a great deal from their independence of public power and authority. They really did see themselves, and act, as people who believed they had special rights and freedoms and capacities. This made a few self-willed and self-indulgent in their professional conduct. But hardly any were public-relations men or government's men.

Jump twenty or thirty years on and most of this has changed. Society itself, the universities, the students, the universities' relations to society, the students' expectations from university – all have changed. Like most countries, Britain has become since the war more technological, more managerial, more professionalized. So her universities have expanded; not as much as in most countries but still a good deal, enough to have shocked some people and made them talk about opening the doors to the unintellectual multitude. As far as I know there is no evidence that university standards have gone down and some things suggest they may have gone up. It is probably harder to get into British universities nowadays than ever before. The pressure from the sixth forms, from people with very good A-level certificates, seems to build up all the time. Of course, the A-level examination may have been made progressively easier, but that doesn't seem likely.

So jobs have become easier to get, even for arts graduates. You don't have to go into schoolteaching now, though many still do. You can think of management training in industry or of interesting new openings in a range of institutions of higher education, or of the mass media or of a year or so abroad, in North America or one of the newly independent countries; again, many do. On a close look, some of these openings prove to be less numerous or less attractive than they seemed on the Appointments Board notices. But still, undergraduates have less of a feeling that they are going straight down a single line, blinkered.

The feeling of inhabiting a firmly three-tiered pyramidal society has been weakened, but we are less sure of exactly who is speaking to whom and from within what relationships. The sense that there was a smallish group who did know the relations and due tones, who had authority and style, a tight, confident, prescribing group (of which the university world was a small offshoot with some saving variations) – this sense has all but gone. Or should have. Naturally, there are some people who haven't noticed and act as though nothing has changed. In such a situation you can walk on the water for a time, and it then does seem as though nothing *has* changed. There are people like this in politics, in the higher levels of administration and in senior common rooms. But that tells something about the tenacity of personality, not about changes in British society.

The universities have more and more become servicing agencies for this increasingly complex and centralized society. They have geared themselves to, more and more taken money for, its purposes; they have trained the experts it needs for the middle ranges of its work upwards. Their professors have become 'department heads' and their vice-chancellors managing directors of multimillion-pound institutions, under pressure to talk about 'plant' and 'cost' efficiency, rather than about 'The Idea of a University'. One of the odder paradoxes is that some large provincial universities have managed to become cellularly bureaucratic while still retaining their old pyramidal structures of power – a remarkable physical phenomenon. No wonder it has become fashionable to say that the secondary beneficiaries of the students' demand for participation will be the non-professorial staff.

But here comes in the biggest paradox of all. I have argued that the universities have more and more become, on the one hand, servicing agencies of large-scale centralizing forces in society. On the other hand, the British universities, to a degree that we have not on the whole recognized, have also been over the last dozen years the proving-grounds for immense changes of attitudes among young people generally. The causes of these changes are not to be found in the universities; they lie outside in society and they have a long history. But they are coming to full expression now, in universities; it is the students' role to cause the wave which has built up within society finally to break. They are more intelligent and emotionally articulate than most; they are at the moment free of continuing professional, financial, and domestic responsibilities. More than anyone else they are able to stand, as it were, apart from society and ask what it's all in aid of. They are acting out a phase in what could be one of the most important secular changes in attitudes of the last two or three hundred years. We could be seeing the beginning of the end of the Protestant Ethic in its two main forms of expression: in its attitudes to competitive work and to the sexual life. Both are coming under very powerful challenge.

It may seem strange that all this has been going on in universities while at the same time they have continued publicly to claim a pastoral function. But universities have become the arenas for this change in a fit of absence of mind, almost unconsciously. By and large, they haven't really known what was happening, what contradictory forces were at work within themselves. One result has been that, in most places, they have steadily relaxed their *in loco parentis* rules to an extent that by now would startle conventional opinion in the country if it were widely known. At provincial universities only about five years ago there would be a shocked response if it were discovered that (say) the campus hairdresser was selling contraceptive sheaths; at such places today the Pill is likely to be available, if not exactly on demand then certainly without stringent conditions. Over the last few years, in most universities, there has been a steady loosening of the rules in halls of residence, of the conditions on which students may go into flats, and so on. Most members of staff know that a great many students live together.

Or one may get a hint of these changes through the difference in students' attitudes when they discuss with a member of staff a problem which involves sexual behaviour. As, for example, when an unmarried girl asks for two or three weeks off so as to have a baby. Up to seven or eight years ago such a girl was likely to be at least slightly embarrassed. Latterly, this doesn't seem so. A girl may be upset about the mess she has got into or composed because she has sorted out the difficulties. But she does not feel, in my recent experience, that she is telling you something in which you are morally concerned. In case anyone has misunderstood me, I am not saying that students today are promiscuous. I am suggesting that in their attitudes towards sex – in so far as one can tell from the sort of meetings a university teacher is likely to have – they seem to have made two important changes: they do not give the moral weight we were taught to give to the idea of premarital virginity or, if that is broached, of confining sexual relations to one member of the opposite sex, the one you eventually marry; second, and this follows from the first, they do not think we have a role as moral mentors in matters such as these.

It would be wrong to put the main stress on changes in attitudes towards sexual life. More important and trickier to describe is what looks like a change in attitudes towards ambition and competitiveness. Many intelligent students today are deeply suspicious of internecine strife, of 'getting on'. They have decided to be unpushing. I have known them decide to settle for a Second Class degree rather than a First, not so as to 'have a good time' in the old way but, as they argued, so as to stay with their group – because that is more 'real' than the kind of ladder-climbing isolation the degree structure invites. The stress is on the small-scale, particular, personal, non-materialistic. Or think of the student case against examinations: it is not at bottom a reformist case – that examination methods need to be improved. It is a revolutionary case – that they must be done away with. This is part of the wider rejection of quantitive competitiveness, the insistence on the importance of communality and on the superior reality of the personal and particular. The ideal is of a world much more fluid than ours, much less pyramidal.

How do the students view the universities themselves? Again, there is an apparent paradox. In one sense they expect less than we often assume; in another sense they expect more, more than we ourselves always expect and more than we expected when we were students.

They expect to be able to go to a university if they are bright, almost as a right; and more of them will expect that as time goes on. But they do not want to be introduced to a style of life that goes with the professional training. They want neither the cultivated bourgeois style of before the war, nor the meritocratic life-style which some university departments have spatchcocked together under the new pressures. They may believe in style but not as something passed on from us to them. Style is their own 'thing', not ours.

The search for style is part of the self-defining search of their generation, part of their independence from and as against the world of adults. So here they don't want much from the university.

But they also expect a great deal from the university. They admire the Idea of the University. They want the university to stand for that Idea, for the integrity and courage of the intellectual life. And they are disappointed. They find most of us interested in our 'subject', not in the life of the mind. They find most teaching simply dull rather than a dialogue.

They want the universities to stand in a critical relation to society. With the detached clarity of their time of life they regard society as a mess if not an affront. To them, the overarching realities of the situation – the Cold War and the profit system – make decent human relations almost impossible (again, the stress on the 'real' and personal); and they are not at all amused to be told that this is the impatient idealism of youth. They justifiably feel patronized when that is said to them by people who seem to have hedged their bets all the way as university teachers. They think themselves involved in a politics of mistrust, of deep mistrust.

Yet their basic attitudes are not at all distrustful. Listen to their vocabulary, to the recurrent words, such as 'real', 'real event', 'genuine happening', 'participant', 'significant participation', and so on. They are rejecting the split life implicitly offered to them by the universities for the future: first, that they shall be trained to serve society, quite lucratively; second, that they will then be allowed a limited degree of freedom as individuals, so long as that freedom doesn't lead them to any sort of active larger commitment, to taking action against the overall thrust of society, its drive towards what they see as empty, authoritarian materialism. They are angry because they dream of a university as a moral community and they find that most members of staff, though they may say this themselves on platforms, do not live it out.

Of course, it is easy to find reasons for discounting what the more active students are saying. One can argue, quite rightly, that there are only a few of them and that most students seem to want just to get on quietly with working for their degrees. But this has always been so with any movements for reform. The important thing is that the few may be in touch with, and implicitly speaking for, a great many others. Or one can say, as is often said, that there is some correlation between being a leader in student revolt and having personal psychic difficulties. Perhaps many of the catalysts were prompted by some inner need in themselves. But it's at least as important for us to ask why they were able to become catalysts, what that reveals about the culture. Or some people say that most student rebels come from the arts and social science faculties and go on to suggest that that indicates that students are not expected to work in those faculties and have no proper 'motivation'. It would be rather surprising, in fact, if a large proportion of student leaders did *not* come from the faculties which are concerned with thinking speculatively about society. So any such correlation is fairly obvious as a fact and scandalous as an attempted rebuttal.

To all this the reaction of staff has been very mixed and rather slow. On the largest, single, clear challenge we have had over the last twenty years – expansion – the record is good. The universities have expanded quickly and, on the whole, well. They have done so not simply to serve more effectively a technological society but because a great number of people within universities as well as outside were convinced that we had been mean in the provision of higher education and that there was a human duty to provide far more. So we have admitted several times more university students than there were before the war and have, on the whole, kept up standards well. We have been slow in devising changes in teaching and examination methods to meet this expansion, but all in all the expansion has been carried out humanely. Almost everywhere, university people have fought to keep the close tutorial system, even though it has meant that their own teaching-loads have gone up steadily right through the decade. And we have refused to accept the kind of harsh wastage which can so easily come with rapid expansion, as it came in France and several other countries.

We have been less adequate on the two trickier challenges: on the need to look again at the structure of power and responsibility within the universities themselves; and on the changed relationships of the universities to society. So that when both these challenges have been put, often aggressively, by students we have been in difficulties. It is never pleasant to have thoughts which you should have had years ago prompted for you, least of all by people you are supposed to be leading intellectually. Academics can be as resentful as other people, and where their professional pride is touched are quick to react. Then their combination of high drive, introversion, articulateness, and self-justification goes into action; and it is fierce. In the circumstances, I have been surprised by the number who, after the first jolt, have recovered themselves and been flexible and open. They don't want to be paternalistic, though they may enjoy being fatherly where they can; but they are ready to change the modes if that seems needed and right. They can't, as they say, 'go all the way with the more extreme advocates of change', whether among students or younger members of staff; but they have gone a long way in re-educating themselves. On the other side of the range are members of senates who feel deeply resentful. They are hurt because their paternalism is part of their self-respect; they think the existing system is by and large the best; they are sure they know every student in their departments, and so on and so on; and now they feel rejected. So they look for forms of words which will allow them to express their sense of outrage without actually using what they recognize are the tainted words of paternalism today. For instance, they often use false analogies to justify their mild authoritarianism. A common one, in response to the student demand for participation, is to say that no one in his senses would let a first-year medical student attempt a heart transplant; he has to learn and be under authority for a time. But a first-year medical student ought to be involved in some sort of dialogue, at the right points, about the social assumptions behind the medical training he is being given.

Another response by those who are hurt is to fall back on a pure, detached, narrowly academic definition of the purpose of a university, as in these extracts:

The university staff are appointed to research and to teach certain disciplines and for no other purpose . . .

A university should not be loosely compared to a democracy. Its purpose is to establish that some citizens are more gifted and intelligent than others, and to give them extra opportunities (to continue with research, to take up posts in higher education, to accept the best openings in industry) . . .

Examinations are the best possible way of grading students in any highly competitive area of society. . . .[1]

All of which has a fine confidence but hardly seems to have risen to the height of this great argument. In fact, it is another form of the professionalized, un-Socratic conception of the university as a production belt for computerized intelligences.

This kind of thing shows the gap at its most dramatic. The active students see themselves as standing for a platonic conception of the university, engaged with bringing a fresh stream of thought to bear on its society. To them it seems that, with a few exceptions, the staff take up one of two positions, neither acceptable. Either they believe that the universities are generally educative, cultural and intellectual bodies, but interpret this as the presentation of a style of life which seems to the students increasingly out of touch. Or the staff say that to think that universities have any such 'civilizing' function is to be wholly mistaken. To them universities are the institutions in which are trained the higher intelligences of a society, for its service. They can say this in a variety of tones. Some of them say it in a tone of weary, unexpectant cynicism; they know that's the way the world wags and always will wag. Others are rather more unpleasant, since they seem never

[1] 'Comment', *Critical Survey*, Summer 1968, pp. 190–1.

to have worried enough even to feel disillusioned. To them it is a nuisance for anyone, whether staff or students, to talk about the 'civilizing' purposes of a university. One gets on with the job in medicine or engineering or what you will and leaves all such questions to the journalists. The first group – the old-style, civilized bourgeois – are, of course, disappearing, though, as I've said, quite a number are still to be found in arts faculties. The second group – the neutral technocrats – are increasingly powerful, especially in faculties of science and technology. They are hard-nosed reductionists. This was bound to be so; it is in the nature of the situation. But it is a dangerous situation and one that cannot be settled by neat tactical arrangements. It requires us not just to look at the universities but to look at society far more than we have been used to doing, and then at the relations which have grown up between the two; and then to make the most searching value-judgements we can.

We have each to make sense of the picture as best we can and to decide where we stand. So I will now try to sum up my own position.

I think a lot *is* wrong with our universities and that we have been too slow to think about anything other than practical answers to pressing problems, such as expansion. The structure of power within universities, syllabuses, the methods of teaching, and the systems of examination, all need serious critical examination. They received it in the planning of some of the new universities; but in some of the older universities this kind of scrutiny only began (where it *has* begun) as a result of student pressure.

I think, too, that a lot is wrong with our society, that in becoming central-ized and technologized it is in danger of losing its own sense of individual human beings, of creating feelings of alienation (and that it has done this in many instances); and that, in particular, it is making us less able to feel that we can be meaningfully committed to relationships outside our face-to-face acquaintances; and that the media of mass communication on the whole re-inforce this sense of being no more than voyeurs at the interesting but non-significant succession of events. Tragedy and comedy become aesthetic objects mediated through technology and of roughly the same weight – or weightlessness, since they are not connected to any decision by us.

But I also think that there are many things which are valuable within British universities and British society, and that these things are cavalierly slid over by most student radicals. Whatever the international links and parallels, we shall go wrong if we do not start with the peculiar virtues (as well as vices) of the British situation; and this is not in the slightest degree chauvinistic, but a recognition of what it is fashionable to call 'existential' reality.

British universities are in some ways creatures of the State, of the society which pays for them. But not altogether. They are not in the position of

German universities before the war, or Russian universities now; they do not have the kind of problems with local authorities or trustees which some American universities have. To say, as Mr David Triesman of Essex says: 'Universities are linked to a set of productivity norms which, in order to be met, need a system as authoritarian as any other factory'[2] – to say this is to over-extend a sound point, to abstract it from the cultural setting which qualifies it and gives it meaning, and to express it in a rhetoric just as unreal, abstract, and technologized as the world it sets out to attack. British universities are not wholly or simply subservient to State or government, or to local businessmen. They have a lot of freedom and on the whole it is *real* freedom, freedom to say and do a great deal. Of course, if an academic is persistently awkward, some other people are likely to try to silence him and their methods are not always fair. But this is human nature and has to be fought, and fought openly. It is still a long way from organized witch-hunts. There is room for free controversy and more than lip-service is paid to integrity in speaking out. Naturally, those who exercise this right of critical controversy do not attract big private grants for their departments. But what do we expect?

One can say much the same about the atmosphere within the universities. There are a great many rigidities and snobberies; and since snobbery has many disguises, its forms are often not recognized even by the most snobbish members of staff themselves. But there are also a great many decencies. The same professor who resists any suggestion of even partially opening the senior common room to students (usually on the ground that it is the equivalent of his 'club' on the campus) or who stands up for the principle of double discipline for students caught breaking the law (on the ground that the university as a whole is a sort of 'club'), that same professor may spend a large part of his weekend trying to sort out fairly and humanely a problem to do with one particular student in his department. On the whole, staff are not remote from students, nothing like as remote as they are in most other countries; in most departments in most British universities, every student is known quite well by at least one member of staff, and often by more than one. You need only attend a final examiners' meeting, especially when borderline students are being discussed, to have this brought home.

This mongrel mixture of attitudes within the universities reflects a similar mixture in society at large. The extreme student radicals argue that society is thoroughly corrupted and at bottom authoritarian. The amiable part-yielding which it (like the universities) seems capable of is worse than frank opposition because, in the end, it gets you nowhere but meanwhile blunts

[1] Scanner–I, *New Left Review*, No. 50, 1968, pp. 59–71.

your cutting edge. So-called free speech is only a five-per-cent permitted deviation, permitted only so long as it doesn't cause anything to change importantly. If it seems to promise to do that, then it is either withdrawn or subverted. The much talked-about patience of the police is only a façade. If anyone really tries to push things to the point at which they challenge the structure, then the mask is dropped and the police become ruthless, exposed as the agents of naked power. On this reading, the circle is complete. There can be no way out through the channels and styles of thought of society today. Rational challenges to the rationalistic, goal-conscious, closely structured societies of the late twentieth century are dead ends, tricks of the system.

So the only remedy is to destroy the system before one begins to think of alternatives. Till then, one is not in any condition, any condition of the spirit, to think of viable alternatives. Possible alternatives will emerge as a result of living within a new, unstructured revolutionary situation. We shall not know what the new society can be like – though we know it will bring new modes of experience, will be goal-less, open, non-hierarchical – unless we let it 'happen'; and therefore it is a form of intellectual mediocrity to talk about 'negotiation' within the present system. This is where student political revolutionaries and unpolitical hippies come together. But it can only be a temporary and partial accommodation, and political revolutionaries recognize this. They have goals. Goals are 'in' for them, but they are not for the hippies. So the politicals expect to have the hippies with them while they are destroying the old structure, but recognize that when they go on to restructure, the hippies will fall away. But there are subdivisions at all points on the spectrum, and there are some, for instance, who want neither new participant structures nor new structuralist 'happening' situations; they want the universities to follow their traditional path in the traditional way – to pursue learning; but they think they can only do this by stripping themselves of all their modern sophisticated comforts and starting again with only the bare essentials of the intellectual life.

The general picture of the universities as the agents of an authoritarian society has some truth and a lot more attraction, a sort of apocalyptic attraction. But it is distorted, over-extended, over-generalized. The allowing of a limited degree of 'free speech' can be used to neutralize real dissent, it is true, and this society like any other highly-centralized, commercial democracy has a thousand and one ways of ignoring or rendering useless anyone who makes use of his freedom of speech so as to say something unpalatable. But the process of what the revolutionary critics call 'containment' is simply not as successful as they make out. And the areas where free speech is particularly practised – that is, some parts of some universities – are not simply 'harmless islands inside capitalist society'. Free speech is more than a successful trick and a good deal more than a 'mystified absolute' (as Mr Triesman calls it).[1] It is an indulgent oversimplification to call it all a 'cynical fraud'. We have not got far, and it has taken a very long time – human nature being what it is – to get this far; but we are at the point still where one can speak and people can listen, and sometimes do listen. A great many forces are ranged to discourage us from speaking and even stronger forces try to divert us amusingly so that we do not listen. I have particular experience of this from observing the reception of a report on broadcasting in Britain, which pleased none of the powers-that-be – but I do not think it was altogether wasted. The situation is more complicated and motives more mixed than the out-and-out radicals suggest. Airholes do exist and are not simply ways of piping-off permitted and neutralized deviations. One can speak and oppose this society as radically as one wants; and there are some men with consciences to listen and be moved and, even if very slowly and in small ways, to try to get things altered. We do not risk five years in Siberia or serious violence from the authorities for speaking or for listening.

The police can be brutal in Britain and if they have been told to prevent entry to a street, on the grounds that there is some danger to public order, and find themselves being taunted and pushed around, they are likely to hit back. This ought to be too obvious to need saying. But it has to be said, so as to distinguish them and the forces controlling them from charges of organized, deliberate, and premeditated police brutality, from accusations that we exist in a 'Police State'. Only people who refused to learn how the police act in other countries could use that sort of image.

It is true that there are bullies and authoritarians in power in local politics, in national politics, and in big business (and in universities too, for that matter). But I do not believe that what it is now usual to call, contemptuously, 'consensus politics' is just a game; and I think the alternatives are worse. There is some tolerance, there are some decent humane reactions, some cracks through which conscience can act. These things may seem small, but they are immensely important. It has taken centuries to build up the very notions that they should be allowed to exist, to create structures within which they can have room to operate, to let them pass into the bloodstream of British life and, to some extent, affect it. At its worst, some things are badly wrong with British society. At its best, it still believes in the overriding importance of the human scale. Much may be pushing us towards an impersonal and inhumane centralized life; but we are not there yet and might be able to reverse the

[1] ibid.

trend if we recognize what moral capital we have in the bank. It has taken me a long time to see this because I have had, and still have to some extent, my own quarrel with a great many aspects of British society. The result is that, though I hope to be an uncompromising critic of that society, I do not want to be – I don't think I can afford the luxury of being – an apocalyptic critic.

My own approach to change within the universities themselves follows from all this. We have to learn to talk to each other better than we have done before and not in such a canalized way; and it has to be talk meant to inform action. But learning to talk like this is not easy; there is enormous mistrust on both sides. One side finds it difficult not to patronize, however slightly, or be remote; the other side tends to hector and accuse of bad faith. Then you hear the stiff language of the Establishment facing the emotional rhetoric of the rebellious, and since both are thin-skinned the situation soon escalates. I think the students are right to say that in many places much in what we call an educational training is not sufficiently educative; and that they are right to ask for much more participation in many aspects of university life. I think they are right to say that in many universities the structure of authority is out of date (though the students are not the only group who are relatively deprived here). I believe the best place to start the kind of dialogue they want is in staff–student departmental committees, where there are precise, personal educational issues to argue out. For example: are subject bounds and syllabuses too rigid? Have we got the right balance between lectures, seminars, and tutorials (and are all of these effectively carried out? – many of us have not seen our colleagues at work or been seen by them, and could well have hardened in all sorts of elementary mistakes). What should be the pattern of assessment?

I am not assuming that we would all agree on all points at the end. Nor do I think that a majority show of hands, whether from students or from staff and students, or from staff alone, is necessarily the best way of making decisions about the way a department should go. I am not quite sure what some students mean when they call for 'complete democratic control of content'; but I suspect I would not agree with what they mean. I think some activists have insisted so much on the importance of face-to-face teaching situations (much needed) that they have become contemptuous of research. It would need a very long discussion to convince me that universities should scrap all kinds of evaluation. Some kinds of assessment certainly do test certain kinds of quality, such as differences in intellectual grasp or imaginative insight or application or fairly straightforward ability to organize. Whatever sort of society we have, these qualities will be needed. We need to free the possession of them and their further training from irrelevant and divisive status-marks.

Even if we work in this way, some students may insist on direct action. It can pay and it has paid. Possibly the wave of reform in British universities only got under way after the students became really a nuisance. It is easy to say that it would have occurred anyway, but I think it would have happened very much more slowly. But so far we have had little really violent and destructive disorder. It may come from some who will either have refused to join in discussions or, having joined in, will inch up their demands each time the preceding demands are met so as to force a 'direct confrontation'. For them university reform is not a primary target. The primary target is society. but the university is a useful 'proving-ground':

> What we should do, if the situation were to arise again, would be to behave as provocatively as necessary and to effectively sanction the University to the extent that they *need* to use force, probably the police. Complete occupation of offices rather than corridors will achieve this. It is at this stage, that the administrations commit their ultimate folly, and it is at this stage that the staff and less political students will feel encouraged to enter a situation already politically structured. . . .
>
> One, we will lose; but the loss of 'socialism on one campus' is inevitable and should stimulate support in all the others during the really hard struggle. Two, we will have won, because we will force the Administrations to openly show their relation to the capitalist machine, and the institutions' implicit aim of producing a new generation of managers to rule the working class.[1]

This is a new voice on British university campuses, the voice of the fully political student. It is obvious that they are able to engineer situations in which they will have to be opposed. One can do one's best not to give them grounds for claiming that they have been victimized, and one can be ready for some shut-downs of indefinite length. If they insist on going further and taking action which might harm other individuals, then we may have to call in the police. This won't at all prove that behind the elegant façade of universities there lies naked power ready to be used; it will merely prove that, if the frankest exchanges have not avoided direct destruction, then people and property have to be defended until worthwhile talk aimed at real reform can start again.

But this approach to internal reform must go along with an effort to re-define the universities' relations to society. The students, remember, are saying that a university which trains men in highly skilled disciplines should also make them critically aware of how those disciplines are used, what values they are made to serve in society at large. They are acting from the belief that

[1] ibid.

universities should not be simply or primarily the passers-on of acceptable styles among the controllers and sub-controllers of society, but places where those values are continually questioned. They are asking for a special kind of commitment and engagement. It is easy to accuse them of being ridden with the wrong kind of social concern, to argue – as in one sense it is right to argue – that a university *should* be a kind of ivory tower into which we go to learn *before* engaging with society, in which we learn to think disinterestedly, to get a perspective in time, to entertain other imaginative and intellectual experiences than those of the immediate, the expedient, the time-bound, the pragmatic, the contemporary.

That is fine in so far as it rebukes the call for the cruder kind of socially committed courses which a few of the revolutionary students have made; and in so far as it rejects the claim that a university should be specifically 'a pressure group on major social issues'. The links are not as simply one-to-one as that.

Such qualifications apart, the claim that universities should be 'outside' society is based on a misapprehension. Universities are not and cannot be uncommitted, unengaged. They are socially engaged in a thousand ways and at various levels, some complicated, some simple. They are engaged when they decide to take on this research rather than that. I do not mean simply when they take on a certain kind of research because funds are offered for it from outside. I mean something more in the bone than that; that the nature of the culture suggests some lines and not others, and that only the rarest people will be free from that kind of atmospheric pressure. We are engaged as individual teachers in the very way we regard degrees and career prospects, in our assumptions about where the university, our subject, and our students 'fit' into society. We all have such a picture, no matter how unexamined it may be. We are engaged in the way we live out a certain relationship to the value-judgements of our culture, and this affects our whole personal and professional styles. Hence we are engaged in the way we treat other members of staff and in our manner towards our students as we pass them in the corridors. It is in the air of departments, in their grain, no matter how little some of us may have thought of it. We are all members of this society, in some sort of dialectical relationship to its assumptions; and as university teachers we are professionally involved in institutions which are closely and paradoxically related to that society – institutions which underwrite much of its main thrust and also are arenas for criticizing it. There can be no such thing as 'unengaged' university work and teaching. There is no such thing as an 'unengaged' university teacher; we are all, in a way, promoting styles. This is true of all subjects. It follows that it should be impossible for students in some of the major professional departments – in engineering, medicine, law – to have their training without also being made to articulate and question critically, within their departments' courses themselves, the relationship of those professionalisms to society. I remember one university teacher saying, 'We mustn't spoil them for the world of work'; but we may have to risk just that, so that they will improve that work and that world.

All this has been about the larger relations of universities to society. But, just as real participation between students and staff as members of a common body must start in departments, so the rethinking of relationships between the university and society ought to begin in local action. Most British cities hardly know they have a university. There are some public connections through court and council; there is Rag Day and its mixture of resentment and amusement; there are a few cultural offerings from gown to town. But not much else; and most academic staff live in their favourite enclaves and go round each other's parties. It is a very *in*organic relationship.

I have, for what seemed good reasons, talked chiefly about the active, articulate minority and especially about the politically active minority. But there are many other kinds of student and towards them all we have to decide where our responsibility lies. What about those who are unexpectant and silent disapprovers, apparently? Or those who drop out? Or what about the quiet girls from sheltered homes who are bewildered rather than stimulated by the huge breakers of the new permissive group life? 'I wish I'd been born in Jane Austen's time. I'd have known what the rules were,' one said to me. What sort of meaning can that hoary old phrase 'pastoral care' have today?

Speaking for myself, I would at any time have been uneasy about assuming a pastoral role in the way that used to be defined. It implied two attitudes, neither of which I possess: acceptance of certain fixed social norms and a certain sense of personal completeness. As to the first I am, to put things as briefly as possible, republican, agnostic, and socialist. I don't promote these positions in my teaching. But I have no doubt that, in a deep-seated way, they permeate my style, as do the attitudes of those of my colleagues who are royalist, religious, and right-wing. One has to try to make sure that students are not tempted into imitation by charisma, and that they have as good a chance as possible to keep separate what you are saying from what you are. I do not think they can expect more, or we do more, than that.

The doubt about the second pastoral assumption – 'a certain sense of personal completeness' – is more fundamental. Like most fairly self-critical people anywhere, I expect, I feel most of the time and in most important things quite *un*finished, *un*assured, not like one who can give students an example of 'balance, maturity, wholeness'. Those who are most confident here, confident of their ability to advise, are not usually best fitted to do so, except in minor matters.

I believe my most important act of pastoral duty towards my students is to try to help them to respect the intellect and imagination used with integrity. Can I go further than that? I argued earlier that students today do not want us to be fathers or uncles, to assume that we are *in loco parentis*. The hold of their peer-group is stronger than any pull we have. But some students do get into serious difficulties and then may want someone to talk to. Again, often their own colleagues can help best. But sometimes an older person *can* help. Here a university tutor might be more useful than a parent, just because he has some emotional distance; this can clear his mind and reassure students too, since they are wary of emotional involvements which might damage their independence. But I would not call this kind of thing 'giving advice'. It is more like listening, talking together, thinking aloud and commenting 'in parallel', as it were. It is a strange situation, but that is where I would start if I were trying, having rejected the old definition of 'pastoral care', to describe the sense in which I do still feel that I have a responsibility other than the academic to my students.

INTERCHAPTER

I

Response to Richard Hoggart — EDWARD JOSEPH SHOBEN, JR

From 1636, when Harvard opened its doors, to the middle of the nineteenth century, most students in America did not *go* to college; they were sent. Their parents, not they themselves, entered into an agreement with an institution of higher learning, following the model of what lawyers call a third-party beneficiary contract. Relatively affluent and relatively well up on the scale of social status, they offered to pay a college a suitable fee for looking after their offspring in a proper manner for four years during which it polished him and outfitted him with the skills and graces necessary for the position in society to which his familial circumstances destined him. However, the recipient of these benefits, the youngster – usually of course, a son – had nothing to say, once he had willingly or unwillingly acquiesced in college as a stage in his experience, about the conditions under which they were conferred. In this arrangement, the concept of *in loco parentis* found its roots, and the American version of elitism had its beginnings and its early reinforcements.

Some two hundred years later – after the Civil War and in a time somewhat similar to our own, when democratizing influences were strong and new inventions and new aspirations were energizing our economy – a new pattern was added to this original one. Note that the new pattern did not *replace* the old; it simply joined it and, in due course, became dominant over it. In this new dispensation, helped by the founding of Morrill's new 'colleges of agriculture and the mechanic arts', students entered into their own agreements with institutions of higher education. Their contract was to abide by whatever regulations and requirements the college might within wide latitudes impose; in return, they were to receive, in the form of a degree, a functional hunting licence for a larger share of America's wealth and a more favoured place in her pecking-order. College was a means of social mobility through trained competence, a device for honing the talents that could be gainfully employed in factory and field for larger amounts of money and greater prestige than one's parents had known. In the fusion of elitism with populist impulses, in the shift from third-party to direct personal benefits, and in the immediacy of the relationship between higher education and both industrial need and social position, we can see the dynamics of American life typically at work during this first great burst of technological development.

Today, although most of our undergraduates are in college for vocational reasons and in the interest of improving their social mobility, and although a significant fraction of them is still 'sent' out of elitist motives, a third basis for college-going has, I think, entered the picture. If the benefits of higher education accrue massively – perhaps more massively than ever before – to the individual, they also define a condition essential to the very survival of an overwhelmingly complex, technologized, technical, and managerial society. The United States *must* have a continuous, always increasing flow of cultivated brainpower to insure its sheer existence. College graduates are far less a cultural adornment and even less a resource for leadership than they are a straight-forward necessity if America's elaborate engines of industry and commerce, government and professional services, are to be maintained. In consequence, students are not merely given a more inclusive opportunity; they are wooed, lured, and even bullied into college attendance. Our national policies of long-term, low-interest loans and of increased scholarships, our newly discovered anxiety about college drop-outs (which rarely allows room for the possibility that leaving college may be developmentally facilitative), the efflorescence of public-service advertising about the desirability of college, and the hard line taken by high school guidance counsellors with respect to college attendance and its advantages are all consistent with the hypothesis offered here – that college-going is a societal benefit as well as a personal one, that the student confers advantages as well as receives them, that the youngster in college is serving society as well as enjoying an opportunity it has made available to him.

To the extent that this reading is a meaningful one, it accounts in part for the irrelevance of gratitude in the contemporary student's repertoire of responses and for his tough negotiator's stance. If his involvement in higher education defines societal as well as personal benefits, then he has ample basis for criticizing the conditions under which the benefits are generated and even of raising the question of their ethical and social value, either in some absolute sense or relative to other benefits that could be created in the college's setting or through a different utilization of the college's resources. In short, students have a fair warranty for saying to their institutions, 'The society you represent needs me. Before I accept the opportunities (and the rules) that you offer, I insist that that need be examined for its moral frailties, that you as an agency of learning and human development show that you are something more than simply a pander to the forces of industry and the military, and that I have some space in which to determine on my own terms the conditions under which I will contribute myself to the nation's urgent and greedy demands for educated manpower.'

However abhorrent this view may be to many of us of the donnish calling, if it is at all correct, it predicts a permanent state of campus affairs, a growing and increasingly irresistible critical position among students towards the nature of their educational experience, and an ever more relentless probing of the connections – and of the absence of connections – between our universities and society. This situation is made troublesome by not only its unfamiliarity and our lack of preparation for it, but by the way it interacts with at least two other emerging issues on which Mr Hoggart's paper touches. One has to do with a threat to the ethic of civil liberties, both generally and in its special educational significance; the other pivots on the relationship of the tempo and directions of social change to the credibility of our major policies in higher education.

The ethic of civil liberty represents, it seems to me, the only principle men have invented for protecting themselves against the inherent imperfections of the human condition. It is the only conceptual and moral device the race has hit upon for allowing maximum freedom for human impulses, interests, and ideas to jockey each other in a reasonably peaceful competition for adherents and that both permits and encourages minority attitudes and values to persist in a quest for majority support. If, as George Eliot once observed, 'Justice is not without us as a fact but within us as a great yearning', then the ethic of civil liberties defines the sole route by which that yearning may be realized and objectified without destroying it by the means through which it is sought. The likelihood of more closely approximating a just pattern of human affairs is less when the approach lies through naked power and riot, greater when it moves through free speech, free press, free worship, free assembly, meaningful petition, the right of privacy, due process, and the other forms – not always entirely comfortable – of social relationships that emanate from the ethic of civil liberty.

At the moment, this ethical position is stringently under fire. Ideologically legitimized by Marcuse's notion of repressive tolerance and emotionally vitalized by the underdog's victories of guerrilla fighters in the Third World, a segment of Western youth would scrap our Bills of Rights as outmoded liberal baggage, replacing them with a commitment to the tactics as well as the goals of today's revolution or, one often thinks, with nothing at all. One is entitled to wonder why; and if one wonders openly enough, one is struck, I think, by the frequency with which the ethic of civil liberty has been violated in our major institutions, including the university.

Item: Stimulated by the billboards on the main streets and by the advertisements in the newspapers of their cities and towns, students have often been barred from performing the plays or showing the films that the larger community supports.

Item: Raised on a tradition of freedom of the press, students not atypically find their own journalistic efforts subjected to censorship either blatant or subtle, put under postpublication review that exceeds the restrictions of press law, or curtailed by rules of editorial eligibility that maximize conventional safety.

Item: Given our vaunted concern with the right of privacy, student resentments are noteworthy mainly in their having been so long in the making with respect to the general quality of dormitory housing, to the lack of protection against unwarranted search-and-seizure procedures, to restrictions on the self-determination of whom they may visit and whom they may entertain in their living-quarters, to the regulation of their dress and personal comportment, and to a host of other inroads on their essentially private conduct. It is not that institutional interference here is without a basis in reason and reality; the point is that the interventions are made with neither an explanation nor an effort to enlist students in the safeguarding of the university from external harassment. As a result, it is easy to perceive the university as only too willing to abrogate the right of privacy when its special concerns are at hazard.

Parenthetically, it should be noted that few faculty members have any current, intimate, and sustained awareness of the quality of life in dormitories. Understandably, it is a trifle hard to build an image of an institution that cares when the most visible official personnel are so preoccupied with other matters that they can't expose themselves to the conditions under which the university's largest constituency lives.

Item: In eleven of America's fifty states, the mandatory penalties for convicted users of marijuana are more severe than those for second-degree murder. When this observation is taken together with the picture of post-30 parents and professors inveighing over their third cocktail against the degenerate young who smoke pot, then there is some basis for comprehending the charge of hypocrisy hurled by youth against the established order and for some sympathy towards youth's questioning of the legacy of values that has been bequeathed to them.

Item: The university is portrayed as an arena in which ideas contend subject only to the rules of evidence and logic, thus exemplifying *par excellence* the intellectual side of the ethic of civil liberty. Yet the Velikovsky case[1] represents a startling insistence on orthodoxy from the community of academic scientists. *L'affaire* Bernstein[2] at Yale had about it the sickly smell of man's being outside not the canons of competence but the limits of professional fashion set by his colleagues. The cost of winning the battles of The Year of the Oath[3] at California was extraordinarily high; the academic library is rare that does not have a locked case of books the circulation of which is restricted on moral or political grounds; and the American Association of University Professors, hardly a radical or impetuous organization, consistently has a score or more of academic freedom cases under review and a dozen institutions or more on its censured list. The point here is not to multiply horror stories – although the list presented represents hardly the barest beginning of the academic gothic tales that could be collected – or to neglect the very great deal that is right and admirable in America's institutions of higher learning. My objective is simply to argue that we have done a rather bad job of illustrating in our collegial organizations, policies, and actions the moral principle on which the life of our universities in a very real sense depends. In failing to attend more scrupulously to the ethic of civil liberties in our own institutional behaviour, we have left ample room for cynicism and for other values – values which I regard as much more primitive – to gain footholds in our student bodies and, to a somewhat lesser extent, in our faculties. In implying that the time for a re-examination of our ethical posture is somewhat overdue, I am not promising that the reforms called for will markedly reduce student unrest; I am only suggesting that they

[1] In such works as *Worlds in Collision* and *Ages in Chaos*, Immanuel Velikovsky has been a dramatic illustration of Thomas Kuhn's observation in *The Structure of Scientific Revolutions* that 'Normal science . . . often suppresses fundamental novelties because they are necessarily subversive of its basic commitments.' For treatments of this important case in the politics of scholarship and intellectual freedom, see Eric Larrabee's 'Scientists in Collision: Was Velikovsky Right?' in *Harper's Magazine* for August 1963, and the entire issue of the *American Behavioral Scientist* (vol. 7, no. 1) for September 1963.

[2] A professor of philosophy at Yale, Bernstein was interested in metaphysics in a department heavily dominated by philosophical analysts who regarded metaphysical questions as 'nonsense'. Denied promotion on the ground of insufficient scholarly productivity, his case became a brief *cause célèbre* that was never publicly resolved because he chose not to make statements to the press and because he left Yale for a post elsewhere. Accounts in the newspapers and by Yale faculty members indicate that during the period under review by his departmental colleagues, Bernstein had published rather widely and that his professional output was less at issue that his intellectual idiosyncrasy and his being out of the current intellectual vogue.

[3] For accounts of this convulsively agonizing battle between the University of California's faculty and staff and its Regents, see George Steward's *The Year of the Oath* (New York, 1950) and David P. Gardner's treatment, longer in its perspective, *The California Oath Controversy* (Berkeley, 1967).

will strengthen and make more palpable the integrity of the university, just as I am arguing that the kinds of learning, especially the kinds of normative learning, that we facilitate are as much a matter of our institutional style and the models we present as they are a consequence of what we formally teach.

Finally, I should like to turn very briefly – much too briefly – to the ways in which the rate and shape of social change bear on the relationship of the university to society and on the character of the university community.

One symbol of our age is the complete encapsulation of the history of aviation in the lifetime of a man just ready for retirement. From those first hesitant moments aloft at Kitty Hawk, to the jets that sweep us across oceans and continents at speeds with which our stomachs and sleep-centres cannot keep pace, to the unmanned spacecraft that fly close to Mars, and to the vehicles that actually land astronauts and equipment on the moon – that whole development has required only 68 years. In that same period we have invented the computer, very nearly broken the genetic code, turned television into a commonplace, and by bouncing signals off satellites, made people in Sydney and San Francisco simultaneous eyewitnesses to events in Paris. We have created electronic devices like the cardiac pacemaker and surgical techniques for the transplanation of organs from one human being to another, thus, as Arthur Clarke has reminded us, making more than a dream the notion of the android, the being half-human and half-machine who can not only occupy but become a spaceship, a submarine, or a communications network. Perhaps the sharpest, most ominously stinging irony of all lies in the fact that the most creative achievement of man, the unlocking of the atom and the release of its treasure trove of power, has produced a genocidal weapon as almost its only monument. What remains beyond the bomb is the nuclear submarine, virtually entirely an engine of war, and some scattered and not highly developed applications of atomic energy to domestic power situations.

It is no good to pass off these changes or the suddenness with which they have occurred by referring to the opening of *A Tale of Two Cities.* The question is less one of whether ours is the best of times or the worst of times than one of whether ours is a time for which any guiding historical precedents are available. One suspects that the answer, relative to our need at least, lies heavily if not entirely with the negative. For one thing, there are the problems of scale. The statement that a thermonuclear bomb detonated half way between Baltimore and Washington would destroy both cities defies imagination. In less than ten years, we must expect four billion souls to be roaming our planet, representing a doubling of the earth's population in forty years and presenting a potential for misery, ignorance, disease, and hostility quite without meaningful forerunners in the race's experience. We have fouled our natural nest so that both Lake Erie and Lake Baikal may be irreversibly atrophic, so that air pollution defines a major health hazard in virtually all of the world's great cities, and so that wilderness and recreation areas have shrunk in many places to a point where the balance of nature can no longer maintain itself. Barry Commoner is not the only one to sum up our situation by arguing that the environment is under stress to the point of collapse and that 'this planet is approaching a crisis which may destroy its suitability as a place for human society'.

But there is also a peculiar callousness in many aspects of our contemporary culture. In the United States, it is not only the questions of imperialism and international arrogance that make the war in Viet Nam an agony; it is the apparent imperviousness of those in power to the reality of violent death. It is as if casualties are merely counters in some terrible game the significance of which is lost on the players. A good day is one in which 'our' sum of stopped lives and maimings is smaller than 'theirs'. This erosion of personal identity as a factor in social policy is reflected in our too-little-and-too-late efforts to create some harmony and to reintroduce some decency into our pattern of race relations, and it appears again in the lack of preparedness with which we face a cybernetic future in which America may have to absorb a quarter of a *billion* unemployed people as an inherent part of the new order of things. When we remember what work has meant to one's self-esteem and how central it has been to social mobility, we can suspect grave troubles in making the transition from a society in which the values of work have been paramount to one in which the ethic of work must be kept alive quite selectively.

What all this means, of course, is that old creeds, old norms, and old precedents are violently scrambled together. The test of what is the best that has been thought and said in the world is not survival in the libraries and endorsement by academic men, but the extent to which a body of literature or a set of pronouncements seem to shed light on the desperate confusions we have been discussing. Students are not the only ones pressing for this kind of highly personalized, even idiosyncratic, evaluation of the content of their education. What is essentially common in these demands is the idea of relevance, a notion that can neither be dismissed by authority nor argued away by limning its fuzziness. Relevance simply refers to those concepts or to those embodiments of shared experience which result in a heightened sense of selfhood or a degree of insight into how the trends of the modern world can somehow be turned in more humane directions. When relevance is lacking, then training may be taking place, but whatever may be happening, it does not merit the name of education.

In short, the challenge of our time to the universities is that of finding alternative models to the old liberal design of mastering a heritage or the relatively new professional design of unfolding the inner logic of the various disciplines. The former is untenable, so its attackers would put it, because our cultural legacy is, above all else, what is being acted out before our eyes in the crises we have touched upon so inadequately here. The latter won't do because it would turn each person into a professional scholar rather than a person, into an observer of doom and tragedy rather than a participant in building a better world. If the ancient mission of reinforcing and extending the examined life has any merit, then it is highly probable that the universities must take more seriously the component of *experience* in the formula of 'experience deeply reflected upon'. Today's students are not likely to find an idea, the shape of a historical period, a literary document, or a formulation in social psychology to be of much worth unless they can try its fit against some element in direct experience from their lives. In consequence, it seems almost certain that opportunities for experience off campus must be provided in wholesale lots and made an integral part of the education of young people. In flexible ways, this kind of probing of the real world can then be made the object of reflection with libraries and faculties turned into resources for the investing of experience with meaning and for making it comprehensible by transcending it through the illumination of thoughtful and insightful men from other times and other places. If this vision, seen only through a glass darkly, indicates a greater emphasis on persons than on programmes, a degree of diversity that matches the diversity of our burgeoning student bodies, and an end to the faculty-kept order that most of us and our academic forebears have enjoyed for over a century, then I can only say so be it. If it is not entirely to my taste, it commands my preferences far more than the crippling of the most humane and freest institution the West has yet created.

Obviously, this kind of orientation outward on the part of our universities must be balanced by some inward changes. It can be argued at some length that the notion of an academic community is little more than a shibboleth. There may well be societies of faculty members, but the idea of students and professors as defining a genuine community of shared interests and values rarely has more than a little substance. The values of the professoriate – what Talcott Parsons has called the values of 'cognitive rationality' – are fundamentally cool, removed, impersonal, and essentialist; those of activist students, who clearly speak for a much larger group than their own number, are, on the other hand, warm, involved, personalized, and existentialist. Until some more encompassing and comprehensive system of discourse and conduct has been evolved to include both sets of styles, it seems probable that conflict will both too frequently and too massively be our lot to permit education to serve effectively either the individuals who come to our campuses or the society which supports them.

A beginning here may lie in breaking down the old distinction between student and faculty member – tutor, professor, or whatever – and to start creating a community of students. Such a community would be marked centrally by a common quest, a search for the ideas and values (for the appropriate reflections on experience), that would permit a man to think more productively about his own personhood and to engage himself more constructively with the affairs of his social world. As such a community, the university would function, regardless of its other business, as a forum, and progress in it would be defined by the development of greater sophistication in the criteria of significance one brings to the debates in which one engages, by growth in logical skills, and by an enlarging command over the information germane to the issues one holds under consideration. The inward counterpart of the forum would be the processes of critical thought and the fusion of thought with emotionally coloured judgement into the convictions on the basis of which a man acts and takes risks. In its outward forms, the forum would provide a laboratory for the seeking of humane styles in which differences can be accommodated within a framework of liking and respect with the limits firmly defined and in some meaningful sense justified as to when belief and commitment legitimately render impossible a relationship of friendship or decent toleration. And this question, too, would specify an aspect of experience on which reflection can be brought to bear within a communal structure.

Given my own faith in diversity and an incapability to find in pluralism any sensible implication of villainy, I can hold no brief for these sentiments other than the strong one that they can be ignored only at the peril of the university as all of us have known it. In many ways, Mr Hoggart, in a quiet fashion that I can only envy, has sensitively indicated some of the directions in which this move can be begun, and for this reason, along with a number of others, I am grateful for both him and his paper.

II

'Students want us to be people,' said Morris, opening the discussion, 'neither welfare officers nor the kind of parents who aren't people, or at least don't behave towards their children as if they were.' All agreed that we make a mistake if we think that students are rejecting the older members of the group; their need for belonging to the human race is too great for that. An attitude of pastoral protectiveness on the part of members of faculty is in reality very different from a full acceptance of the principle that we are members one of another. It can even be a proclamation of difference of status. It is not enough for students merely to care about other students and faculty about other faculty–though, starting from that, a more general concern may conceivably arise on the part of each for the whole university. Anything like an aristocratic stance is incompatible with real caring, which must have as its basis an acceptance of a common and equal humanity possessed by seniors and juniors. Any form of patronage is rightly resented. A concept of pastoral care can easily be translated into a set of restrictions upon civil liberties.

Students may demand, without realizing quite what they are asking, some privileges not easily justified or compatible with democracy and some kinds of nourishment from their education which it is particularly hard to supply given the technical and research orientation which members of university, and even college, faculties have. There are some privileges which students accept as rights almost without noticing that they have them. One is their relative freedom in ordering their expenditure of their own time. Another, at any rate for British students, is in the matter of the student health service. In fact in Britain today, we were assured, students get about five times as much medical care, in terms of cost, than workers of their own age-group in factories – and this in years when money is short and the economy under strain.

As regards the personal nourishment which higher education may supply, much of this must necessarily come 'on the side'. Education at this level must be concerned with structured knowledge. Not all the aspirations and expectations of students can be satisfied by what it can offer. But it can continue to supply, even if only to a minority, contributions of several kinds to their personal lives: (i) an introduction to the process of learning, in addition to what is being taught. There is a certain privacy about such learning: the process can be hindered by too much publicity and the wrong type of examinations; (ii) an opportunity for making contact with people who matter as key authorities – scholars, research workers, and teachers – who can have influence long after one has forgotten what they told one; (iii) chances of learning from a peer-group who have much to give. But it is a mistake to think that a period of higher education in itself is the final contributor to personal development. Students adjust quickly to the outside world, both during and after their university years, far more rapidly than faculty will – or can. They will go out from college to work in industry, school, or office and many will no doubt bring to those organizations a new supply of the vitality, ideas, and criticism they need. But their new environment will in turn provide for them the current of fresh experiences which they need to keep their personal and social lives healthy.

One of the needs of universities and colleges themselves, of course, is to be in closer touch than they often are with this outside world. Some of the separation is artificial, some of it academic in a bad sense.

What must constantly be borne in mind is that communication between teachers and taught in universities is a much more subtle affair than anything that can be defined in terms of subjects or conveyed through words. 'Words are not the only form of communication and the reason why they have become supreme is an interesting question.' The techniques of verbal analysis and mathematical analysis are rigorous and must be mastered. But they are insufficient instruments with which to deal with the whole of experience. The unconscious mind has a life of its own: to understand the truth about the development of personal life both in university years and beyond one needs to recognize the significance of motivations and drives that may come little into consciousness.

To take two examples: one of the problems of higher education is student perplexity in the choice of courses. It is more than possible that the choices of subjects they make are sometimes related at unconscious levels with their struggles against parents. Mistaken choices may be made which it may never fully be possible to escape from; for it is difficult to change a major subject in midstream, especially in the British tradition. Yet changes take place in the personalities of the young as they develop which are not all under their own control by any means. There is a lot of unexplored territory here and there is much in it to explore.

The other example is the need of human beings to maintain the life of impulse and feeling. Freud declared that the indispensables for achieving and keeping personal identity are being able to love and being able to work. Those may not be the only ones – but the selection of these two shows profound insight. The wish of the young to preserve the life of impulse and affection is a healthy one, however dangerous it may sometimes seem to staid members of the public and of the faculty. Their rejection of the Puritan ethic may not be anything to worry about. After all, we have not so far, even with its help, proved capable of solving the problems of the world - food supply, population, conquest. We may need to approach our problems in a different temper and with different presuppositions. Many today are concerned about love and promoting love; and this is good. But there is a real problem too about finding work, in an age like ours, that is fully acceptable to conscience. So much of what we call success is achievement merely in military or materialist terms. A new approach is needed that may help our materialist deficiency; there is much to encourage us all in the attitudes and new determination of the young to be free from undue dominance by the old.

Whether or not the Seminar agreed with this diagnosis, no one disputed that an immense fermentation is going on in the outlook of the young. Students, in particular, are 'anti-complacent'. But the difficulties of changing the conventions, some quite superficial, and the in-built assumptions of a mature society are not to be underestimated. 'A candyfloss society under one political leader', said Ninian Smart, 'is apt to continue to be a candyfloss society under his successor with only the colour of the candyfloss altered.' But university people – both faculty and students – could do much more to bring about desirable directions of change than they normally did. It is a weakness that there should be so many artificial distinctions between 'the university world' and the world outside. The intellectual resources commanded by universities are far from fully used – for they are in these days places with a greater proportion of a community's top brains serving in them than at any previous time. They have a correspondingly greater responsibility than in the past for exporting ideas instead of hanging on to them themselves.

In his remarks at the end of the session, Shoben said, 'I am much heartened by the concern of this group with ways of knowing other than those which have become enshrined in the academy of our time. Paul Weiss's book *Man's Freedom*, for example, has been marvellously ignored. Academic institutions have a great capacity for swallowing up offerings that are out of fashion and rendering them essentially impotent by a kind of massively indifferent acceptance.' Nobody fights and the novel contribution can easily get lost. If the great issue of the ethic of civil liberties is to be kept alive we shall have to provide within its guidelines for commitment. We are not in our universities thinking anything like enough about this kind of concept or working towards this kind of style.

Illustrative of our failure to use our enormous mental resources in right ways is the tragic irony that the main outcome of that most amazing of recent intellectual achievements – the solving of the mystery of nuclear fission and fusion processes – is a genocidal weapon. The deeply worrying question is whether man is busily constructing a world in which he literally cannot live; that the creations of his intelligence are beyond his capacities to manage as a very imperfect organism conatively and affectively. Yet it is of the conative and affective spheres that university people largely wash their hands.

CHAPTER 11

Insight and Foresight in Higher Education

W. R. Niblett

At the junction of a railroad when the lines diverge, the trains taking either line will not at first be going in very different directions; but before long, as the lines curve away from one another, they will be heading for cities far apart over the horizon. The change of direction may be made unnoticeably and without a jar, but the consequences in due course will be marked. It may be that in all our countries we have already made irreversible choices where our universities and colleges should go, about the kinds of places they should be in future, and the scope of the education it is right for them to give. But I do not think so. It is only recently in fact that we have begun to realize the importance of studying the decisions they make and to see how far-reaching the human and the social significance is of this choice or that – about the assumptions within the courses offered of what is relevant; about the relationships or non-relationships of some institutions of higher education with others; about attitudes to students and to student involvement; about co-operation with the world outside. One of the motivations for such studies is our growing realization that changes of orientation and of organization are imperative. To make them rightly requires insight as well as foresight. This seminar, with its forays, probings, and suggestions, is a sign of the times. All this week we have been concerned essentially with the question: how can tertiary education be made more relevant in future both to the needs of persons and the needs of society?

Among the most obvious continuing functions of higher education – as from medieval times – is that it should certify and authorize the suitable young to serve the community as professionals. If society demands graduates for its use, the natural (and the profitable) thing is to produce them. But what is 'use'? Most people today prefer to concentrate on short-term and instrumental goals and, generally speaking, they want universities to do the same.

Is this, however, enough? Utilitarianism is a word with a Victorian flavour, but the economists who speak so crisply of productivity, of cost relations, of input and output, are our contemporary utilitarians. We should take warning from Bryan Wilson's hint: 'It may be uneconomic to socialize men fully if you are only going to employ them for particular functions.' It is quite possible through the education one gives to take people without their knowing it a long way down the road towards what C. S. Lewis called, with devastating simplicity, the abolition of man.

But academics do not, by and large, usually think of their universities primarily as places of education, rather as places of research and scholarship where the boundaries of knowledge are pushed back. Many are single-mindedly concerned with exploring and deepening the territory of their subject and find it natural therefore to want to extend the empire of their subject department. They can pursue both these objectives with remarkable tenacity and increasing incidental mastery of the complex skills required. It is true that their devotion to their subject may be stained on the edges by self-interest: by thoughts of fame or reputation, for example, or innocent victories over Globb and Pusch, their competitors in corresponding departments of other universities. They may recognize happily the freedom which the disposal of grants from foundations gives them as compared with dependence upon funds from their university's own budget. But at the same time they do pursue knowledge with clear-sighted obedience to the evidence yielded by rigorous experiment or by imaginatively compiled and meticulously administered questionnaires, and – whether they are scientists or humanists – they analyse the results with a passionate intelligence. They are often successful; success breeds confidence and anyway argument is useless against success. All this, however, will not always or necessarily fructify or humanize their teaching, except, it may be, the teaching of graduate students in small categories. Indeed the whole orientation of their professional lives, and sometimes their personal ones, can cause at times a certain alienation from humanity. They are devoted to the perfecting of exquisite instruments for use with precision – and woe to the inept, the ignorant, or the blunderer who ventures a criticism. The surgeon – no longer associated with barbers or other impious folk – who operates with such perfection of timing to transplant organs into a human body must sometimes find it not merely annoying, but also rather irrelevant, that the patient should die. Indirect evidence for this is perhaps to be seen in the putting out of statements, almost every time, that it was not the heart or liver transplant itself which was the cause of death: the operation was technically a hundred per cent successful. Unfortunately some other organ developed a defect, an irony of fate such skill did not deserve. But the attitude of, say, the anthropologist or sociologist to human beings can be – if less obviously – much the same. He is concerned to defend the integrity and power of his scholarship against all accusers. But it still may be a two-dimensional integrity, as it were, insufficiently reckoning with the realm of values or the nature of human knowledge – which has depth as well as length and breadth. In their attacks upon the ignorant and the stupid, scholars and critics assume that by their bloodletting they can help purge the body politic of untruth, show up the pretensions of the ignorant and so bring more health to us all. This is the point of their clever and exact incisions. Their object is to cleanse: but what if *en route* they kill the patients: men's capacity really to believe very much in things, or in their fellows, or themselves? To deprive men of this is very near to killing their spirit and *raison d'être* – a phrase using the word reason more generously and profoundly than normally comprehended in the term rationality.

Any place of higher education, as we have seen, must without doubt today be a pluralist institution: inevitably it will have within it numerous parts, most of them dealing with particular areas of knowledge and particular ways of knowing. There is fruitfulness in such diversity, the chance of challenges that will compel fresh consideration of conflicting evidence and incompatible theories. From the opposition and interplay of minds, if they can come close enough to hear each other, new understanding can arise. But if this is to happen, a university must be more than a collection of contiguous departments: and it will only happen if within the plurality there is a deeper unity. The existence of pluralism does not in itself compel self-examination so as to find if any unity underlies it. 'There is no academic community now, only a set of professionalized groups,' remarked one of our number. A multiversity is a triumph of the *laissez-faire*, representing in essence an abandonment of all effort to make sense of the world.

Can, indeed, a structured and unified society result from a collectivity of individuals who have been educated in blinkered departments? We are almost everywhere engaged in saving money on the general education of students and regard it as less important than we used to do to spend much money on providing amenities for them extra-departmentally. The departmentalism even of one of the newest university campuses to be built in England was evidenced by one of its architects who told me how delighted he was by the interest and explicitness of the heads of departments about the design of the buildings to house them. But when it came to the overall provision of amenities and their siting, few instructions were obtainable, except about limits of expense. It was largely left to him and to his team of planners and architects to decide upon the principles to be followed. When they came up with their answer, few arguments were raised against what they proposed.

Incidentally, remarkably little thinking seems to have been done in Britain about what *kind* of education a polytechnic should give or what *kind* of institution it should be. What the limits are of its range of responsibility or of amenities appears so far to have been judged almost entirely in terms of cost and cost comparison. But this is only one of the most conspicuous examples of failure on the part of all of us who are in higher education to see the importance of bringing up into as full a consciousness as we can what we are aiming to do. In a permissive and fluently changing society, we need to hook up and examine our objectives much more rigorously than was necessary in an age which knew, or thought it knew, where it was going.

It has been suggested this week that the recipe for general education during the years of tertiary education is 'an intensification of life outside the lecture room'. Again we should ask: is this going to be enough? And how far can such an intensification be brought about by universities and colleges themselves – with senior and junior members both playing their parts? The fact is that universities are only intermittently concerned about the general education, whether inside or outside the lecture room, which they are giving their students.

And inside the curriculum itself, *who* is deciding what should be taught? Who is deciding how it should be taught and by what sorts of people? If institutions of higher education are to be chiefly centres to provide the technology and technologists for meeting short-term social needs or even chiefly places which add to knowledge irrespective of the human cost, the future is simply not safe in their hands. And men in time will rightly turn against them. The wider the social and intellectual range of their students the more important it is for them to be creatively humanizing as well as effective in training mental skills. The more people there are who study at the tertiary level, the more imperative it becomes that our understanding of the scope of higher education should be wide.

In an essay contributed to a symposium called *The New University* published in Britain in 1968, Adam Curle of Harvard pointed out, rightly, that our problem was to devise an educational system at all levels which would not only admit to the existence of many types of excellence but which would also identify and encourage the other qualities which lead to high achievement. It is not enough that universities should train the mind as an intellectual instrument only: teaching it how to get hold of factual material, how to analyse data and situations, how to think with resolution and logic. Indispensable though such mental acquisitions are to civilization, they will not in themselves provide a flow of people who are cooperative, or sensitive, or tolerant, or able to contribute with originality to the arts, politics, religion – or even business. It is easy to find ourselves, without in the least meaning to do so, destroying talent which might have been creative, people who might have been musicians, or teachers, or even creative administrators, in order to produce too many, fairly safe, graduates and postgraduate students. In the past, after all, in the USA, Canada, and Britain it is people who have not been through the university mill who have so often taken the risks and been the leaders. In future the Jacques Cartiers, the Andrew Jacksons, and the Bernard Shaws will all go to universities.

But to return to our question. Who is deciding what should be taught? The traditional curriculum in higher education has consisted in a body of knowledge to be passed on and in disciplines to be mediated on the decision of scholars and members of an academic hierarchy who were masters of the mysteries. Some of the student protest is directed, fairly or unfairly, against just this inheritance of right – the whole assumption, stemming from medieval times, that the elders really represent all that is fit in our civilization to be passed on. Our culture must, they demand, be poured through funnels with wider mouths and wider necks. It is not right that higher education should be so class-biased, so much identified with the industrial–military–capitalist ethos; that it should be so exclusively conceptual in its intellectuality, should take the aesthetic and moral modes with such little seriousness; that it should neglect the contemporary situation socially and internationally as it does; that it should be so merely impersonal in its apprehension of significances.

Be this a biased analysis or not it remains true, as Eric Ashby[1] has demonstrated with great clarity, that as the university works today the content of what shall be taught rests almost entirely with the teachers themselves – influenced no doubt by social demand but only influenced by that in so far as they are themselves sensitive to it. It is not trustees or councils, presidents or vice-chancellors, even senates, so much as faculties and departments which have power over the curriculum. And even many arts professors 'instead of contributing to a university what the Victorians understood by a liberal education . . . are doing with grammar and documents what scientists and technologists can already do with formulae and instruments'. 'The danger is not that universities will fail to respond adequately to the short term demands of an age of technology; it is just the opposite

[1] e.g. in *African Universities and Western Tradition.*

danger: that in responding so readily and so efficiently they will run the risk of self-disintegration through too facile an adaptation to tomorrow's world.'[1]

But it is not only what should be taught that is important; how it should be taught, and with what objectives, and with what assumptions about the nature of man, are also of great consequence. It is common enough for a university to want to capture the best scholar in the market to head his department, irrespective of whether he is interested in students or in teaching or will be a good judge of those who might make up for his deficiencies in these respects. Our convenient principle that 'research fertilizes teaching', though it has much truth in it, is often too simple a rationalization, a compensation for lack of a broad enough or subtle enough theory of education. In any educative process the medium matters as well as what is mediated: the human medium more than technical media. What will get over is dependent upon the keenness, but also upon the presuppositions and the hierarchy of values, of those who teach it.

Among the signs of hope is the recent revival of concern for better quality teaching within higher education. In Britain the Hale Report of 1964,[2] despite its lack of subtlety, highlighted the problem and some, perhaps, of the remedies. Champion Ward asked pointedly in his paper why, if the abilities, incentives, and learning styles of students vary widely, most of them are still taught in the same way over the same period of time. It may be that if we can learn how to educate the relatively unintellectual students we may discover more about how to educate the cleverer ones already with us with whose unintellectuality we have not sufficiently reckoned. We tend anyway, as things are, to give all our students much the same material at much the same age, whereas we know that at earlier stages of education different people need different things at a given time. We need to take a lot more interest and to deploy much more skill in the educative process. But at least we have begun to be worried about such questions. We are also beginning to be concerned at the lack of personal involvement in their teaching with which many university teachers are content. The problem is more than one of discovering new methods of teaching: it is how to communicate not simply knowledge but ourselves as knowing.

Much depends upon whether we can communicate our own enthusiasm and purposiveness in ways that energize individual and rational reflection. Teaching is rarely simply a conveyance of facts or skills. Education indeed is not just a transmission of anything, but rather, in Ben Morris's words, 'a

---

[1] *Technology and the Academics* (paperback edition 1963), pp. 87–8.
[2] *University Teaching Methods* (H.M.S.O.).

transaction between the generations in which ideas, skills, and values are renewed and often redefined in the process of renewal.'

The truth is that teachers in higher education cannot avoid – though they often would like to do so – initiating others into various aspects of civilization. Whether they are aware of the fact or not they are passing on values and value-judgements whatever the subject they teach and whether their students are very, or not very, able. A university is an academic community but it is also willy-nilly an educative community too.

The enlargement and comprehensiveness of institutions of higher education has meant, as Martin Trow made clear, that today they contain many who have little commitment to academic enterprises and traditional university concepts. This must be increasingly the case, for the forces in Western society making for equality of opportunity are powerful indeed. Is the right long-term policy to extend the pecking-order – so that the most intelligent and the most likely to become leaders are in fact educated in a small distinguished fraction of the total number of universities a country has? In the USA the name of the university which is put after the degree a candidate gets matters greatly. It may matter still more in future. In Britain, though Oxford and Cambridge undoubtedly have, at any rate up to now, been socially selective in potent ways, the academic standard of degrees awarded by universities throughout the country, including Oxford and Cambridge, has been by and large not excessively dissimilar. This may not be true, however, for much longer. The value of an M.A. degree, for example, is becoming very different in different universities where it is to be worked for, as distinct from awarded free of extra academic charge as in Oxford and Cambridge or the Scottish universities. The more universities there are, and the wider the intellectual range of student admitted to university courses, the more difficult inevitably it will be to secure that standards throughout the system are the same.

This Seminar has never been more than a short distance from the volcanic eruption of student power. That fiery challenge has indeed snatched, living, from us not merely several of our would-be participants but has forked out one or two who actually started the week here with us. However dangerous student protest may be, and however easily students can get diverted in the objective of their attacks, it is clear enough that one of the main causes for their disquiet is the rather anonymous, depersonalized, higher education mediated to them, with subjects in unrelated compartments and too many courses out of touch with life and with their needs as late-twentieth-century people. Universities tend to overlook how close the interrelation is between intellectual and personal development. Without a personal evolution some kinds of intellectual development become impossible. But becoming human is not a matter even of becoming what one already is. Beethoven said somewhere that as he created his music he created more of himself – becoming differently though more really Beethoven in the process. At a time when external controls have rigorously to be obeyed in so many areas of life, if men are to survive in a technically advanced civilization, it is easy for the individual to drift along – training himself for a job which will bring him, it may be, an adequate income and a fair degree of mental or physical activity, but little else. Drift itself, however, is a kind of depersonalization, a subservience of the individual to passing fashion. In present circumstances tertiary education not infrequently fails to arrest drift. Anarchism is a violent protest, deliberately thoughtless, against it – but desperately religious too, a blind proclamation of personality.

Among the most valuable gifts which universities and other institutions of higher education can ever offer are conditions which give freedom to their students to develop identities of their own, more inclusive and differentiated than those permitted by custom or fashion for public expression in their society. This will involve an acknowledgement by universities of parts of human experience which usually go unrecognized and a finding by students of excitement in events which normally yield few experiences or none. Often, for example, travel is regarded by ordinary people simply as a means of getting somewhere; physical environment as surroundings (though the artist finds much more in it); early childhood experiences as to be forgotten; the inevitability of death as to be ignored. Men are rather good today at organizing their world so that they do not have to experience it. But experiencing is an indispensable. The life of the instincts does not yield ready-made values – but it is impossible to value at all without the impulse life: experiencing and thinking are both needed. Can the individual be allowed to retain the freedom of impulse from time to time to break the bonds of conventional perception of these things and 'escape into himself'? Without such retreats he will be impoverished and superficialized.

Even if higher education abundantly succeeds in producing well-informed and well-socialized people, they may still be profoundly dissatisfied, finding that life has little real meaning and that they personally have little identity. The traditional collegiate university pattern did permit, at its best, quite a number of chances for meaningful contact with other people without having to tie oneself to a single cause and even if the other people were making in many different directions. The collegiate ideal, at any rate in England, has lost its attraction: it is too expensive, too tainted with paternalism, too dependent upon a society dominated by its upper classes, too much organized as if only one sex at a time existed. It is indeed in and through friendship with the other sex that contemporary young people find one of the routes to meaning and depth in life – an unprofessionalism and a kind of socialization that are liberating.

At the present time the department and the laboratory must be looked to as among the substitutes for colleges. It is there, after all, that one meets one's fellow-students and makes most of the contacts that are possible with members of the faculty. Far more students are in a real sense members of a department than are in any active way members of the union; they may of course visit the union almost daily and especially one or other of its cafeterias, but even there it may well be with students from their own department that they will chiefly sit or talk. Increasingly in Britain students in the larger departments of some universities and technical colleges are organizing general social activities on a departmental basis – dances and meetings of clubs other than the subject-specialist societies which formerly were almost the only ones organized departmentally. In part this development is due to the greater size of the bigger departments than was the case when the universities or colleges themselves consisted of 2,000–2,500 students instead of 7,000–9,000. The chemistry or the English department of a civic university may be catering for 1,000–1,500 students of whom 500 or more may find it the chief focus of their loyalty within the whole university. It very much remains to be proved, however, whether life within the department can provide all the freedom necessary in our time for the growth of identity.

We are not saying, of course, that universities and colleges are the only educative medium which affects their members while they are there. Far from it, indeed. There are limits to the power even of the best institution to educate its students, permeated as they will be by influences coming from their homes and society.

So far we have been speaking chiefly of the influence of institutions of higher education upon their students. But to concentrate upon the personal development of students is no guarantee that social relevance will be secured. Nor should we assume that right social purpose is only the sum of the best intentions of the individuals who live in a society.

The cut-offness of the university from society was illustrated, perhaps not altogether fairly, by one participant in the Seminar by a reference to American university medical schools 'surrounded by cesspools of ill health' and campuses 'opening on to slums'. Clearly, colleges and universities are not, and should not be, political agencies; their contribution to the health of society could be greater, however, if they became more aware that the purity of a discipline need not necessarily be sullied if it is set to work, perhaps in company with others, upon social problems, at least at the postgraduate stage. The Seminar rightly saw as significant the foundation in recent years of numerous interdisciplinary Centres in graduate schools: centres, for example, of Urban Studies, Population Studies, Transport Studies, Communication Studies, Language Centres, Centres for the Study of Contemporary Culture, Centres for Cognitive Studies, Centres for Latin American Studies, Far Eastern Studies and so on. Such centres can help to offset excessive departmentalism and also be an excellent way of exploring new territories with the help of a variety of disciplines. But though some of them bring together town planners, architects, engineers, geographers, historians, anthropologists, linguists, and medical experts, it is very rare for philosophers to be associated with their work. This is even less likely when the interdisciplinary units are established by a government outside universities altogether.

Most units of this kind in universities are at present functioning at the postgraduate level, but there is an increasing tendency for undergraduate courses to involve combined studies in several fields – the idea of schools of study at new British universities (e.g. Sussex, East Anglia, Essex) is spreading. Some of the encouragement to integrate a diversity of disciplines at the undergraduate level comes from the increasing tendency to make a first degree an important part of a professional qualification or a professional qualification in itself. A very early example of this in university history was of course medicine, with surgery added later; but now there are degrees in engineering; in business studies; in architecture; in town planning; in education combined with subjects-to-teach. But we still take fright if some unconventional combination of subjects appears called for to equip a professional to function in the world. How often, for instance, are ethical studies included in the medical curriculum or administrative studies made part of courses for ministers of the church?

The very existence of graduate interdisciplinary centres, however, is likely to have an increasing influence in making university courses at many levels more relevant to social needs. There would seem to be potentialities too in the establishment of centres which involve departments and faculty members in two or more differing types of institution of higher education; and this might be an admirable kind of bridge building. The British example of University Institutes of Education which bring universities themselves into intimate and organic relationship with all the colleges for teacher-training within their region is an imaginative one, much more successful in practice than is always allowed, but capable of immense development given good will and more support by the universities themselves.

The need for higher education to be more socially relevant highlights the importance of its public relationships. At no time have universities been in more need of friends than they are today. Their relations with schools, on the one hand, and with the world of work, on the other, need to be more intimate in understanding. Even their relationships with other institutions of higher education need to be closer, with less competitiveness and duplication of scarce facilities. In Britain and America snobbishness takes different forms and is called by different names: but it still exists. Yet we dare not add to the pressure on presidents and vice-chancellors: the public responsibilities of heads of departments will almost certainly have to increase; but more of their present load could sometimes be carried by some of their less senior colleagues.

There remain conflicts and doubts in many universities, in view of the contradictory demands of society upon them, about their own purpose and their own unity. President Bissell mentioned the frequent Canadian assumption, until comparatively recent times, that the academic world was a little unreal and that the outside world was real, and, therefore, the source of direction. But if the outside world has lost its sense of direction? If there is no one to tell the universities what their priorities ought to be? There is nothing like incompatible demands to make a choice imperative, but before the choosing is done, battles in the conscience may have to be fought which are both sobering and extraordinarily maturing. To take a decision at the right depth may, however, demand a degree of self-examination which is as yet rare. It may demand the reorganization of universities so that they are less like collectivities and more like communities; but, if this is the recipe, how to apply it in a long-established university can defeat the wisest administrator. At a Santa Cruz or a Trent it may be possible; it is a different matter at, shall we say, a Tokyo or a Paris or even a Birmingham or a Chicago. The Robbins Report of 1963 said curiously little about the objectives of contemporary higher education or the reorganization of university administration so that priorities of goal could be thought about and reviewed. In the next decade we shall be driven to a more continuous examination of what we are up to. There is value in Champion Ward's suggestion for many universities of an 'All-University Educational Council, charged with reviewing and advising upon the evolution of the university's whole programme . . . in the light of its history and central purpose, its chosen relationship to its environment and its resources.'

But it is not only the physical and geographical environment in which a university is placed that matters. The ideational environment matters enormously and here institutions of higher education have very much a duty to be contributors as well as recipients. It will, however, quite inevitably be greatly affected by social facts, including the economic climate and climates of opinion. The British Vice-Chancellors' Committee, as Asa Briggs reminded us, said in 1947 that 'it must satisfy itself that every field of study which in the national interest ought to be cultivated . . . is in fact being cultivated in the university system'. But this implies at every sensitive point the ability to understand what is in the national interest and the levels of national interest, which it is by no means sufficient to define in economic or utilitarian terms alone. Such a standing back to examine the reasons for our practices in relation to the needs of society and of our students as persons might give us firmer ground on which to place our feet when we are called on to convince our tax-payer masters that we have a sense of responsibility – that we are even, if not quite obviously safe, yet entirely sane. And it need do nothing to prevent us from convincing the young that we are unhandicapped by blind adherence to the status quo.

Again and again in determining their priorities, universities are of course influenced by their pre-suppositions, largely unconscious, about the nature of man. Perhaps a more adequate concept of the range of the abilities of the human mind is called for than is common at the present time among trustees, professors, or students. Most tertiary education is better at encouraging men to manipulate than to create. We keep our students pretty much 'nose to the grindstone'; our programme causes them to concentrate on their grade point average, their assignments, their coming examinations. Yet there will never be enough foresight without insight. Both logical thinking, which emphasizes succession and sequence in an argument, and existentialist thinking, which emphasizes the need for feeling and thought simultaneously or in rapid alternation, are necessary. It is an error, as Coleridge said, to try 'to shape convictions and deduce knowledge from them by the exclusive observation of outward and sensible things as the only realities' instead of attending 'to the simple truth that as the forms in all organized existence so must all true and living knowledge proceed from within'.[1] But our concept of the nature of rationality may not allow for the degree of insight we need to exercise. Full conceptualization helps some kinds of rationality but not others: even an unbridled lucidity can sometimes be, subtly, an enemy. It is perfectly possible to be tough-minded and soft-headed at the same time. Clarity of mind is sometimes bought at a cost of closing oneself up: but the thinking that is or most worth needs openness to experience. Education of course, as we have been reminded, depends heavily upon the culture of the society in which it is given – a culture produced and sustained by shared experiences, often expressed through symbols. It is impossible to learn anything without also

[1] *The Friend* II, 10.

learning, organically as it were, the presuppositions necessary to understand it. Nor does consciousness that we have made certain assumptions enable us to dispense with them. Indeed we must often make assumptions simply to go on living.

Any human sharing of presuppositions implies the potentiality of relationship between those who make them in common. This is one of the bonds between seniors and juniors in a university, which needs people to be members of it not only as students, teachers and research workers but also as men and women, if it is to be adequately a university. Many students have to be believed in not only as intellectuals but as people if they are to be able to develop. The belief or disbelief of a teacher in his students is capable of enhancing on the one hand, or dissolving on the other, their confidence in themselves, their stature in their own eyes. University teachers need to be human beings, much alive, if they are to be able to communicate more than a narrow range of their learning. An insect or an animal which is alive is not a collection of parts which work mechanically together. But while the foresight necessary to an ant is small and not conscious, that needed by a man is the greater the more civilized he becomes. There is no survival or evolution in a right direction for a man as we know him without the necessary quality and kinds of foresight. But one must understand one's own nature and one's own needs in order to have the kinds and quality of foresight necessary for their fulfilment as circumstances change. A wrong or inadequate self-concept means a wrong calculation both of the outward and inward kinds of environment necessary for continued development.

Seeing the simplicities of a situation through the complexities is no easy task. The necessity of the good life is a matter not only of individual but of social need: but the two are in a cogwheel relationship. It is only the developed individual, as Nevitt Sanford pointed out, who can adapt himself creatively and productively to the world of work. The individual is intimately dependent upon his family, his teachers, his workmates, his society, for the amount of trust in himself he develops and which of the potentialities in himself he trusts. But society in turn is dependent upon the quality, toughness and sense of purpose which individuals who make it up manifest and feel that they are allowed to manifest.

Freedom is most real when it opens the way to perceiving more often what one really wants instead of – because, it may be, of the pressure of group conformity – what at a more superficial level one thought one wanted. There is really no substitute for the experience of being a person and this involves sensing, imagination, sympathizing as well as reasoning. Granted that the central function of a higher education may be to teach one to reason, it can be purchased at too great a price. The kinds of freedom most needed are those which will open up further vistas of freedom. But freedom is never an end in itself: finding more of it will only bring satisfaction if it enables students or members of faculty to identify more of their roots. Without roots there can be no growing; without some depth, little height.

If universities are content to be service institutions or are preoccupied with research or exact scholarship as ends in themselves, they will fail to influence society or social development as it is imperative they should do. They will come to occupy chiefly a technical role, one which supplies services to help policies forward which they will have done precious little themselves to form. They will be uninvolved in a way that disables them from knowing or discovering enough of the truth about themselves, man or society. There is a connection between becoming involved and bearing fruit: as Ortega pointed out in a percipient passage of *Man at Crisis*, the question 'What must I do now?' is at bottom much the same question as 'What must I be?' But men need to find support in their society for the kind of persons they become or feel that it is worth becoming.

Yet Winston Churchill's wartime question remains: is nothing to be done till everything can be done? We have to start from where we are – our tutorial group, our lecture audience, our student riot, our department, our senate – and from what we are. 'I am in favour of intellectual education,' said a bright young university professor to me the other day, 'because I am not confident enough of my moral and personal position to be in favour of anything else.' Many have to start from a position like that in these days: but there is promise in their consciousness of doing so and their act of will in facing such a fact in the presence of others. The essential is to see that there is a connection first between ourselves as persons – with a concept and knowledge of a subject, a belief in the value of teaching it – and the human development of our students as individuals; and a connection too between their development and the direction in which our society can go. With the help of such insights we can begin to operate from a different level of responsibility and with clearer foresight.

Appendix

MEMBERS OF THE SEMINAR

Professor Asa Briggs, Vice-Chancellor, University of Sussex

Dr Mary I. Bunting, President, Radcliffe College, Mass.

Dr James Cheek, President, Shaw University, North Carolina

Dr Junius A. Davis, Director, Educational Testing Service (Southeastern Office), USA

Dr John J. Deutsch, Principal and Vice-Chancellor, Queen's University at Kingston, Ontario

Professor Northrop Frye, University Professor in the University of Toronto

Dr Kenneth Hare, President, University of British Columbia

Professor Richard Hoggart, Director, Centre for Contemporary Cultural Studies, University of Birmingham

Dr Everett Hopkins, Director, Regional Educational Laboratory for the Carolinas and Virginia

Dr Robert W. Jackson, Director, Ontario Institute for Studies in Education

Dr James Jarrett, Associate Dean, School of Education, University of California at Berkeley

Dr Warren B. Martin, Center for Research and Development in Higher Education, University of California at Berkeley

Dr Dean E. McHenry, Chancellor, University of California at Santa Cruz

Professor Paul A. Miller, Department of Education, University of North Carolina at Charlotte

Professor Ben Morris, School of Education, University of Bristol

Professor Arnold Nash, Carolina Population Center, Chapel Hill

Professor W. R. Niblett, Department of Higher Education, University of London Institute of Education

Dr Marjorie Reeves, Fellow of St Anne's College, Oxford

Dr Nevitt Sanford, Scientific Director, The Wright Institute, Berkeley, California.

257

Professor E. F. Sheffield, Department of Higher Education, University of Toronto

Dr E. J. Shoben, Director, Center for Higher Education, State University of New York at Buffalo

Professor Ninian Smart, Department of Religious Studies, University of Lancaster

Dr F. Champion Ward, Vice-President, The Ford Foundation

Dr Bryan Wilson, Fellow of All Souls College, Oxford

Unable to attend

Dr Claude T. Bissell, President, University of Toronto

Rev. Dr Roger Guindon, Rector, University of Ottawa

Dr Harold Howe II, US Commissioner of Education, Department of Health, Education, and Welfare

Dr Martin Meyerson, President, State University of New York at Buffalo

Professor Martin Trow, Department of Sociology, University of California at Berkeley

Select Bibliography

ARMYTAGE, W. H. G. *Civic Universities*, London, 1955

ASHBY, SIR ERIC *Technology and the Academics*, London, 1963 – *Universities British, Indian, African*, London, 1966

BARKER, ERNEST 'Universities in Great Britain', in W. M. Kotschnig and E. Prys (eds.): *Universities in a Changing World*, 1932

BISSELL, CLAUDE *The Strength of the University*, Toronto, 1968

BUSH, DOUGLAS *Engaged and Disengaged*, Cambridge, Mass., 1968

CURTIS, M. *Oxford and Cambridge in Transition 1558–1642*, Oxford, 1959

DAICHES, DAVID *The Idea of a New University*, London, 1964

DAVIE, G. E. *The Democratic Intellect. Scotland and her Universities in the Nineteenth Century*, Edinburgh, 1961

FLEXNER, ABRAHAM *Universities American, English, German*, New York, 1930

FRYE, NORTHROP *The Educated Imagination*, Bloomington, Indiana, 1964

GOODMAN, PAUL *Growing Up Absurd*, New York, 1956

GRANT-ROBERTSON, SIR CHARLES *The British Universities*, London, 1930

HARRIS, ROBIN S. *Changing Patterns of Higher Education in Canada*, Toronto, 1966 – *Supplement 1965 to a Bibliography of Higher Education in Canada*, Toronto, 1965

HARRIS, ROBIN S. and TREMBLAY, ARTHUR *A Bibliography of Higher Education in Canada*, Toronto, 1960

HETHERINGTON, SIR HECTOR 'The British University System 1914–1954' (P. J. Anderson Memorial Lecture), Aberdeen, 1954

HUTCHINS, ROBERT M. *The Higher Learning in America* (1936), New Haven, 1965

HUXLEY, ALDOUS *Ends and Means*, London, 1937

JASPERS, KARL *The Idea of the University*, London, 1960

JENCKS, C. and RIESMAN, D. *The Academic Revolution*, New York, 1968

JOHNSON, H. 'The Economics of Student Protest', *New Society*, 7 Nov. 1968

KENISTON, KENNETH *The Uncommitted*, New York, 1960

KENNAN, G. *Democracy and the Student Left*, Boston, 1968

KERR, CLARK *The Uses of the University*, Cambridge, Mass., 1963

LAWLOR, JOHN (ed.) *The New University*, London, 1968

LEAVIS, F. R. *Education and the University*, London, 1943

LEFF, G. *Paris and Oxford Universities in the Thirteenth and Fourteenth Centuries*, New York, 1968

LIVINGSTONE, SIR RICHARD 'Some Thoughts on University Education' (Fifth Annual Lecture of the National Book League), Cambridge, 1948

MARTIN, DAVID (ed.) *Anarchy and Culture*, London, 1969

MARWICK, A. *The Deluge*, London, 1967

MCGRATH, EARL J. (ed.) *Universal Higher Education*, New York, 1966

MOBERLY, SIR WALTER *The Crisis in the University*, London, 1949

MOUNTFORD, SIR JAMES *British Universities*, London, 1966

NIBLETT, W. R. (ed.) *The Expanding University*, London, 1962 'Recent Developments in Higher Education in Britain', *Ontario Journal for Educational Research*, 1967

ORTEGA Y GASSET *Man and Crisis*, New York, 1958

REPORTS

United States

The Harvard Committee *General Education in a Free Society*, Cambridge, Mass., 1946

Berkeley Academic Senate, Select Committee on Education *Education at Berkeley*, Berkeley, 1966

Association of American Universities *The Federal Financing of Higher Education*, Washington, 1968

Study Commission on University Governance *The Culture of the University: Governance and Education*, Berkeley, 1968

United Kingdom

University Grants Committee *University Development:* 1935–1947; 1947–1952 (Cmd. 8875); 1952–1957 (Cmnd. 534); 1957–1962 (Cmnd. 2267), HMSO, London–
University Teaching Methods, HMSO, London, 1964 (The Hale Report)

British Association for the Advancement of Science *Post-War University Education*, London, 1944

Committee on Scientific Manpower *Scientific Manpower*, HMSO (Cmd. 6824), London, 1946 (The Barlow Report)

Select Committee on Estimates *The Grant in Aid of Universities and Colleges*, HMSO, London, 1952, H. of C. Papers 163

Committee on Higher Education *Higher Education*, HMSO (Cmnd. 2154), London, 1963 (The Robbins Report)
Department of Education and Science *A Plan for Polytechnics and Other Colleges* (Cmnd. 3006), HMSO, London, 1966
Committee of Vice-Chancellors and Principals of the Universities of the United Kingdom *The Quinquennium 1962–1967*, London, 1968

Canada

The Economic Council of Canada *Towards Sustained and Balanced Economic Growth*, Ottawa, 1965
Duff, Sir James and Berdahl, Robert O. *University Government in Canada*, Toronto, 1966
Sheffield, E. F. 'The Universities of Canada', *The Commonwealth Year Book of Education*, London, 1968, pp. 981–97

ROSS, MURRAY G. *The New University*, Toronto, 1961
ROTHBLATT, S. *The Revolution of the Dons*, London, 1968
SANFORD, NEVITT (ed.) *The American College*, New York, 1962– *Where Colleges Fail*, San Francisco, 1967
SCHACHTEL, ERNEST G. *Metamorphosis*, New York, 1959
SNOW, C. P. *The Two Cultures and the Scientific Revolution* (Rede Lecture), Cambridge, 1959.
SPARROW, J. *Mark Pattison and the Idea of a University*, Cambridge, 1967
DE TOCQUEVILLE, ALEXIS *Democracy in America*, 1835 and 1840 (reprinted, abridged, World's Classics; trans. Reeve)
VEBLEN, THORSTEIN *The Higher Learning in America*, New York, 1918
WEISS, PAUL *Man's Freedom*, New Haven, 1950
WORLD UNIVERSITY SERVICE *The University Today: Its Role and Place in Society*, Geneva, 1960
YEATS, W. B. *Last Poems*, Dublin, 1939

Index